2004

W9-ADS-752

3 0301 00213593 3

A Primer on Business Ethics

A Primer on Business Ethics

Tibor R. Machan and James E. Chesher

LIBRARY
UNIVERSITY OF ST. FRANCIS
JOLIET, ILLINOIS

ROWMAN & LITTLEFIELD PUBLISHERS, INC.
Lanham • Boulder • New York • Oxford

ROWMAN & LITTLEFIELD PUBLISHERS, INC.

Published in the United States of America
by Rowman & Littlefield Publishers, Inc.
A Member of the Rowman & Littlefield Publishing Group
4720 Boston Way, Lanham, Maryland 20706
www.rowmanlittlefield.com

12 Hid's Copse Road
Cumnor Hill, Oxford OX2 9JJ, England

Copyright © 2002 by Rowman & Littlefield Publishers, Inc.

All rights reserved. No part of this publication may be reproduced, stored in a
retrieval system, or transmitted in any form or by any means, electronic, mechanical,
photocopying, recording, or otherwise, without the prior permission of the publisher.

British Library Cataloguing in Publication Information Available

Library of Congress Cataloging-in-Publication Data

Machan, Tibor R.
   A primer on business ethics / Tibor R. Machan, and James E. Chesher.
      p. cm.
   Includes index.
   ISBN 0-7425-1388-2 (cloth : alk. paper)—ISBN 0-7425-1389-0 (pbk. : alk. paper)
   1. Business ethics. I. Chesher, James, 1941– II. Title.

HF5387 .M3 2002
174'.4—dc21

                                                                2002004229

Printed in the United States of America

♾™ The paper used in this publication meets the minimum requirements of
American National Standard for Information Sciences—Permanence of Paper for
Printed Library Materials, ANSI/NISO Z39.48-1992.

174.4
M149p

$75.75

We dedicate this book to the victims of the attack on the World Trade Center, most of whom were professionals in the field of business.

Contents

Acknowledgments

Some of the work in this book is based on previously published essays. We thank the *Public Affairs Quarterly*, *Business and Professional Ethics Journal*, *Global Business and Economics Review*, *Philosophy of Education: An Encyclopedia* (New York: Garland, 1996), *Blackwell Companion to Business Ethics* (Oxford: Basil Blackwell, 1999), and the *Interdisciplinary Environmental Review* for permission to use materials from work that they have previously published. John Hasnas and Michael Blasgen were helpful in selecting both the fictional and factual cases we present for class discussion or assignments in appendix B. We thank them.

We also wish to thank John Raisian and the Hoover Institution for helping us with this project. The editorial and administrative work by David M. Brown and Tina Garcia, respectively, is also very much appreciated. And Freedom Communications, Inc., as well as the Leatherby Center at Chapman University, have been very supportive of this project and we wish to thank David Threshie, Sam Wolgemuth and Lynne Doti for their continued backing of efforts to advance an understanding of human liberty, especially in the realm of political economy.

Preface

The enterprise of business has seldom enjoyed an enviable reputation. Great success in business brings great wealth, but as Jesus tells us, it is "easier for a camel to go through the eye of a needle, than for a rich man to enter into the kingdom of God."[1] More recently, we learn from August Bebel that "the nature of business is swindling."[2] And from Thorsten Veblen that "All business sagacity reduces in the last analysis to a judicious use of sabotage."[3]

That was certainly the message of *Dallas* (1979–1991), the popular American television series about Texas oilmen, featuring the charming but unscrupulous J. R. Ewing. If anything more than bribery and backstabbing are required to get oil out of the ground and distributed to markets, it wouldn't have been learned from watching *Dallas*.

Fast-forwarding to more recent times, we find that the most vehement critics of Microsoft attribute its success to luck and underhandedness, with Bill Gates assuming the role of crafty corporate villain. In the minds of many, the phrases "profit-seeking business executive" and "money-grubbing scum" are synonymous.

This hostility toward the business enterprise has not failed to affect the field of business ethics. Most texts concern not so much the occasional difficulties that arise in business but discuss its very essence, such as making profits, owning shares, employing workers, and trading on the stock market. This makes business itself seem morally problematic, as if when discussing medical ethics the topics include mainly going for checkups or treating the common cold.

When writers do argue that moral conduct can occur within the context of doing business, the possibility is often justified on arcane game-theoretic terms—a framework that treats agents as narrowly rule-bound strategists—rather than in the normal human terms of right and wrong that ordinary persons would understand. Our deepest commonsense understanding of moral values is often virtually banished from such discussions. In the work of Eric Posner, moral commitments amount to mere "behavioral regularities," engaged in purely for strategic reasons.[4] Peter A. Danielson of the Centre for Applied Ethics in Canada considers that it may indeed be possible to imagine "how a firm could become morally constrained even if [!] it began as a straightforward maximizer," as if he were pulling a rabbit out of a hat.[5] Others are not so generous, believing that business ought to be curbed and regulated at every turn, as a matter of course, and that no assumption of innocence is to be granted in this realm.

Business Bashing versus Business Ethics

Why does business ethics so often amount to either business bashing or business taming—as if business per se were a morally suspect activity? Part of the answer is philosophical.

The ancient Greek philosophers considered prudence to be a basic moral virtue. They called it "practical wisdom"; it was characterized by Aristotle as "a reasoned and true state of capacity to act with regard to human goods."[6] Aristotle also tells us that "it is thought to be the mark of a man of practical wisdom to be able to deliberate well about what is good and expedient for himself, not in some particular respect, e.g. about what sorts of thing conduce to health or to strength, but about what sorts of thing conduce to the good life in general."[7]

Since the writings of Immanuel Kant in the eighteenth century, however, the virtue of prudence—the exercise of practical wisdom and providence for the sake of one's own individual welfare—has been seriously demoted. It was converted, initially by Thomas Hobbes in the seventeenth century, from a moral virtue to an innate drive (variously characterized as the profit motive, the drive to promote one's self-interest, the instinct for self-preservation, etc.). Economists, among them Adam Smith, who were inclined to embrace capitalism—the system that made the most room for commerce and business—defended this system on grounds other than its hospitality to the virtue of prudence. Instead, they defended capitalism on the grounds of its hospitality to the innate drive to seek profit—which would in turn, and more significantly, promote social good. Bernard Mandeville coined the prescient phrase "private vice, public benefit" to characterize the curious result. Capitalism was to be the smooth path, with minimum friction, to attaining, via the disreputable pursuit of self-satisfaction, the public good, the general welfare, Pareto optimality, or what have you.

Critics of capitalism, facing up to its supposedly questionable motivations, thus cornered the market on morality. Today, we see the result: If we speak of morality, we tend to think of actions that are altruistic, other-oriented. The principles of commerce or business are mainly dealt with by economists, business school professors, or specialists in market matters, rather than by moral philosophers as such. For business, this has meant that, while it is permissible to strive for profit, government must be charged with regulating (taming?) this activity so that it does not get out of hand. The "money-grubbing scum" would otherwise wreak havoc on the community.

But the activity of business does, after all, seem to directly serve our objectives and advance our lives and well-being; the sundry products and services on the market often help us to live and enjoy life. On its face, business seems to be a good thing, deserving of praise when done well.

So, let us approach the issue of ethics and of business ethics without bias and see what we can learn. After we've arrived at a few fundamental principles, we will consider their relevance for several areas of business, such as advertising and employment, where moral problems face managers, executives, and others involved in the procession. We will also examine in this book various theories of the nature of the firm and its moral or ethical responsibilities. We will, along the way, look at capitalism itself and also consider to what extent, if any, businesses should be regulated.

What Is Ethics?

Ethics is a science of human choice, concerned with the basic guidelines for how one ought to live one's life. It answers the question: How should I live?

Ethics presupposes that we are free to choose how we will conduct ourselves—that we can be deceptive or honest, courageous or cowardly, prudent or reckless. Without that freedom of the will, ethics would not make sense, either as doctrine or counsel. If you cannot choose how to act, it makes little sense to believe you ought to act one way rather than another. You will simply do what you have to do.[8]

Ethics also presupposes that an answer can be given to the question: How ought I to act, to conduct myself? In particular situations, of course, few of us refer to some well worked out ethical system—such as utilitarianism, hedonism, egoism, or altruism—as we make our decisions. Instead, we tend to act as reasonably as we can, by drawing on our innumerable resources: our history, parental teachings, what we learn from literature, television, movies, our religious upbringing, and such. It is likely that the right thing to do will be evident enough to us from such background education and, perhaps even more, from personal experiences.

Business ethics seeks to answer the questions: How ought I to act in my capacity as a commercial agent or professional merchant, manager, or executive? and What standards ought to guide my conduct as a businessperson?

Since "ought" implies "can," if one's will is tyrannized, regimented, and regulated, then the capacity to choose between fundamental alternatives is drastically curtailed; one often can act only as one is permitted to act, not as one freely chooses. Under such paternalistic conditions, the idea that one *ought* to act according to some standard is barely relevant. Behavior is determined more by law and public policy than by one's thoughtful choice between right and wrong conduct, that is, by ethics.

When we find ourselves faced with especially difficult choices, we may want to make consistent sense of how we act and should act. Here is where ethical theories enter, although few people have such systems in mind, at least not fully worked out. Besides, moral systems usually do not simply prescribe some course of conduct since the situations in which we act are often filled with elements no one has ever anticipated fully enough. So, while we may have some such system among the resources we can draw on to guide our conduct, we mostly act based on our character, that gradually formed tendency to do (or not do) the right thing.

Be it in business, medicine, athletics, child raising, or some other area of human conduct, what seems most important is a policy of paying attention and doing what we have come to believe would be the right approach. Discretion, good judgment, and being reasonable—that is, acting prudently, courageously, honestly, generously, moderately, justly, and so on—make it possible for us to deal with ethical challenges.[9]

No one ethical system is universally embraced, although different answers do overlap a good deal. Buddhists have certain teachings, as do Christians, Muslims, and Jews, as well as all the different schools of secular ethics. These differ not so much on what they would have us actually do, but on how they justify this by the priorities they assign to different principles, virtues, or rules and on the reasons we ought to follow these.

In any case, the sheer fact of disagreement among various schools of ethics does not preclude the possibility of discovering definite truths in this area (even if those truths might have to be amended as we gain new knowledge).

But even more important, decent people tend to rise to the occasion when facing ethical challenges. What makes this possible? Probably more than anything else, to be mindful and present to all that is relevant in the situations they face.

Since the most important thing is to do what is right, it makes sense to learn certain principles that will help us in this task. The basic presuppositions of ethics, the account of ethics that seems to be most promising, at least for the authors of this book, is the naturalistic one we inherit from Aristotle and the tradition of thinking he spawned. It holds that the good life is one that is lived according to human nature. This means that we ought to live reasonably, thoughtfully, and with our minds focused on the tasks we face. It is this with which we have a real, basic choice—we can, as it were, make ourselves pay heed and keep in focus. The approach can be summarized along the following lines: In nature, goodness arises in connection with living things. It is only for living things that some conditions are good and others bad. That's because life is contingent. The continued survival and flourishing of an organism depend on certain needs being met and certain dangers being avoided; and in various and diverse ways, every organism seeks to satisfy these needs and to avoid these dangers. For rocks or rain, which have no life to lose, nothing can possibly be good or bad.

Both external and internal conditions of an organism can be judged as good or bad by reference to a standard based on what kind of thing it is, its nature. Think of grocery shopping. Whether the apples in the bin are good, mediocre, or bad depends on how fully they have realized their nature as apples. This also applies when we judge a forest, a plant, or an animal. The same kind of judgments are made in medicine, as well, when doctors evaluate someone's heart or kidney. Is it fulfilling its natural function? Or is that function impaired (and thus threatening the well-being of the larger organism)?

With human life, however, a new dimension emerges: we have influence over our conduct. So, what is good, mediocre, or bad in the case of human life is for us to bring about. Our own choices affect how well we are doing. We can seek to actualize the potential of our nature in a way that nourishes our lives or we can default on this obligation. And this is where morality or ethics arises. To the extent that the goodness or badness associated with living a human life can be brought about by our own choices, we are morally responsible. Given this freedom of choice, we also need certain moral or ethical principles to guide our actions, especially when we face difficulties.[10]

What Is Business Ethics?

Business ethics[11] can be understood as the activity of drawing out the implications of the virtue of prudence. Because in business most often we seek to prosper, unless this virtue is one we ought to practice, what we do in business will not have moral value.[12]

Another crucial aspect of business and of business ethics is the institution of property rights. Business nearly always involves trade, the exchange of valued goods or services, for a consideration that has been agreed on. Someone writes a book and makes a deal with the publisher so it will be printed and sold to others. The publisher pays the author and the purchaser pays the bookseller who paid the publisher. These are acts of commerce and when made the task of special organizations such as firms, shops, stores, and so forth become part of the profession of business (which includes accountants, marketers, personal managers, chief executive officers, chief financial officers, advertisers, and the like). Without the right to private property being respected and protected in law, commerce and business are not possible, at least not as a common feature of a society. (Even without the institution of private property being legitimate, there can be black markets, underground commerce and business, as there used to be in the Soviet Union, which was officially a socialist and thus noncommercial society.)

We need to examine both of these underlying features of business ethics: the virtue of prudence and the institution of private property rights.

The Virtue of Prudence

If our life is a value worth sustaining, it is a moral requirement to take care that we live well and prosper. Although it is possible to prosper in many different ways, one prominent way is to attain some level of economic success. (Even those of us not so concerned about economic success depend in many ways on the efforts of those who are concerned with it.) Achieving economic success means engaging in commerce and developing the profession of business. There is little dispute that everyone ought to look out for his/her material welfare; economic preparedness is a necessity of survival. Business specializes in producing prosperity. It has moral standing because it institutionalizes the virtue of prudence.

Success as commercial agents may not be our primary responsibility in life, but it is one of them. Just as the profession of medicine emerges from the need to tend to one's physical well-being, and the profession of science from the need to understand the nature of our world, so the profession of business emerges from the efforts of those who earn their living by attending to prudential concerns: brokers, advertisers, bankers, consultants, and executive troubleshooters. These people specialize in making businesses grow, develop, and flourish. In so doing, they help themselves and others to flourish.

Even seemingly nonprudential values, like art and literature, are widely enjoyed thanks to the efforts of various profit-seeking businesspeople, such as printers, bookstore owners, the manufacturers of dyes and paints, and so forth. A kind of activity that nurtures and sustains every other kind of beneficial and praiseworthy human activity is surely proper and worthy of praise itself.

The Institution of Private Property

Business ethics is possible to practice only in relatively free societies. These are ones that uphold people's right to own things, including their own time, labor, and skills and what they manage to acquire directly or by earning money and purchasing what they want. The concrete expression of individual liberty in a human community is the right to private property.

One reason that the societies formerly under the jurisdiction of the Soviet Union are so sluggish in the development of business is that their legal infrastructure does not sufficiently protect private property rights and the integrity of contracts. Legal instability discourages investment. With most economic matters still in the province of government policy, business cannot flourish, and business ethics cannot be applied. A savvy investor isn't likely to take money to an illiberal country of the former Soviet Union, such as Russia, and fund a venture that the authorities can disassemble the next day.

Without a legal framework that identifies and protects the right to private property and the integrity of contracts, it is not possible to do business in any straightforward and reliable fashion. Instead, economic chaos prevails. In a communist society, where all property is collectivized, doing business may even be illegal. Then one must trade on the black market, relying solely on trust—or violence—with no legal framework to certify agreements and resolve conflicting claims in an orderly, civilized manner. Under such conditions, transactions cannot be conducted professionally.

In a collectivist system, everything is like the road in front of one's house: public property that one cannot sell or dispose of and everyone may utilize for purposes the government dictates. Public properties cannot be traded unless one has the authorization of "the public," either through the edict of a dictator or the democratic process or some blend of both.[13] Privately, nothing major can be traded.

By contrast, the United States is the one society in human history where the right to private property has been given wide and often diligent official protection. No, it's not uniformly and universally protected. Many criticize the legal order in the United States for too much regulation, too much arbitrary taking (as understood in the "takings" clause of the Fifth Amendment, arguably violated whenever property is expropriated in the name of eminent domain and the like). Still, despite considerable interference—greater and lesser violations of private property rights—Americans enjoy a relatively hospitable business environment in that private property rights and the integrity of contracts are relatively well protected. You can go into the market and say, "Here's my $5, I want that pen." And the merchant who owns the pen can then provide it to you for the $5. In other words, you each have authority over your own property, which is what is meant by having a right to private property.

This right authorizes business to thrive and makes considerations of its ethics possible and relevant. Honesty in laying out terms of trade, fulfilling one's promises, and dealing with business associates with integrity are all relevant in market transactions precisely because such transactions are protected by law. Such protections mean that promises made can in fact be fulfilled (rather than arbitrarily confounded by some bureaucrat). Not only that, when one receives a promise from a trading partner and one wants to certify and protect that promise so it cannot be abrogated with impunity, one can do so with reasonable assurance that future upheavals will not void the deal. The legal system, via property and contract law, preserves the arena of business conduct wherein business ethics is applicable.

So, in order for there to be business, as well as business ethics, there must be private property. Only when individuals have the right to the use and disposal of goods they honestly obtain and to direct their own labor can they make authoritative decisions about economic matters. And only when individuals can make authoritative economic decisions can their conduct be evaluated ethically or morally.

Since there is something morally right—prudent—about commerce and business, there must be something right about the private property system as well that they require.

Some Glitches in the System

We have said that business ethics is possible only when business itself is *made* possible with the type of legal infrastructure most Western societies possess. This claim needs to be qualified.

Nowadays, because of laws and regulations such as having to pay a minimum wage or providing disability facilities on the premises of one's business, people engaging in commerce lack full sovereignty. Government prohibits buying or selling labor at a price below the minimum wage, even if an upstart company requires cheap labor to enter the market at all. The terms of trade between willing parties have thus been forcibly constricted by a third party. The government has imposed restraint of trade.

Despite the many impediments to genuine free enterprise in the United States and other economically developed countries, they are arguably freer than most others in the world. Among these, the United States is closest to a free market system. In Europe, by contrast, even more regulations are in force not only from the national government, but also from the European Union. For example, once one is hired in Italy and Germany, the employer becomes legally obligated to take care of one's security for just about the rest of one's life. That is one reason unemployment is so high in Germany, Italy, France, and Spain. It is much more expensive for entrepreneurs to hire people under the burden of such an open-ended liability; they know they will be legally unable to lay off employees even when economic pressures would rationally require doing so.

One cannot make a rational business decision in such a situation. Given people's changing preferences, as well as innovations and the whole array of factors that can influence business, a firm must have flexibility, including the freedom to act. It must be able to say, "Look, we can no longer do business, so we must part."[14]

In a fully capitalist system, employees and employers would each be free to trade with the other either directly or through representatives. Without that flexibility (which is what private property rights make possible by providing as much freedom to remove your labor as to contribute it), the dynamism of the marketplace is stifled. At the very least, it becomes unnecessarily difficult to look for the best investment opportunities, take best advantage of them, bargain, and trade.

So, the institution of private property rights is a fundamental prerequisite of business and of business ethics. In order to pursue one's economic well-being, one has to be free to own things, including one's own time, resources, and labor. One can then trade them. Free trade means that nobody can dictate the terms under which one trades what is one's own.

Even if business as such is morally justified as a form of life-serving, prudential action, does that mean that every particular aspect of business deserves our acceptance and moral support? What about, for example, all those annoying ads?

In the rest of this book, we will touch on advertising, employment, government regulation, and other topics of business ethics. What will be unique in this treatment is that business will be taken to be an honorable profession, akin to medicine or teaching, not some rogue activity that needs to be tamed or held at bay.

Revisiting Prudence

We wish to stress, once again, that to embark on commerce and its professional arm, business, is prudent and morally proper. But prudence is just one of the virtues human beings ought to practice. Sometimes courage or justice are called for instead. But there is nothing wrong, ordinarily, in being prudent and, indeed, there is quite a lot that is right with it.

Prudence as a moral virtue isn't widely stressed in our time because for nearly three centuries it has been thought by many influential thinkers—Hobbes, Smith, David Hume, and Kant, among them—that prudential conduct is, as it were, guaranteed from us as a basic drive, instinct, or inclination, rather than as a virtue. It's our hardwiring, many have claimed, and thus in no need of encouragement or self-initiation.[15]

However, this is quite likely mistaken and remarkably so: People are far from automatically prudent and are, indeed, very often reckless, inattentive, and lacking in industriousness and ambition.

Granted, prudence is not always a priority—when one's country is under attack, courage and loyalty can be more important, so trying to profit by undermining national security, for instance, would be morally contemptible. But in normal times, certainly, and always to some measure, economic prudence is indeed a moral virtue, since it is undeniably good to take care of oneself.

If we are hardwired to care for ourselves and doing good for others is what counts the most, what remains as a moral requirement amounts to trying to extricate ourselves from our drives and be helpful to people. For example, John Rawls, the most influential moral philosopher in the last quarter of the twentieth century, regards us all as determined to be how we are by our upbringing or social class. The only means left for demonstrating some moral character seems to be whether we believe the right things, namely, that equality of conditions is the just way for a society to be designed.

The issue of which moral viewpoint is right cannot be explored, let alone established, at this early stage of our discussion. Yet, we need to have something at hand to help guide us in making good choices concerning our conduct in the course of commerce and business. So what are we to do?

As with other disciplines, so with ethics or morality: Apart from the highly technical and developed levels of understanding, there is also common sense. We are all commonsense physicists, chemists, sociologists, economists, moral philosophers, and political theorists—at least amateurs in these areas of concern. If we consider matters commonsensically, we can accept, at least provisionally, that business is an honorable profession and commerce a decent undertaking. Thus, prudence, which motivates these, is a moral virtue worthy for human beings to cultivate in themselves and teach to others.

It is with this in mind that the rest of this work is developed. Since much of business ethics in our time is warped by a misconception of the moral nature of commerce, some of the basics will be sketched in the introduction and discussed at greater length in chapter 1.[16]

Notes

1. Matthew 19:24.

2. August Bebel, speech in Zurich, 1892.

3. Thorsten Veblen, *The Nature of Peace* (New Brunswick, NJ: Transaction, 1998).

4. Eric A. Posner, *Law and Social Norms* (Cambridge, MA: Harvard University Press, 2000).

5. Peter A. Danielson, "Making a Moral Corporation: Artificial Morality Applied," Centre for Applied Ethics at the University of British Columbia, http://www.ethics.ubc.ca/pad/amcorp/amcorp.html.

6. Aristotle, *Nicomachean Ethics*, bk. 6, trans. W. D. Ross, in *A New Aristotle Reader*, ed. J. L. Ackrill (Princeton, NJ: Princeton University Press, 1987), 421. This isn't to say that Aristotle thought well of retail trade or of making money outright. He construed these as unnatural because they were not limited by some specifiable end or goal but let one spend for whatever reason on any number of projects. Much of this has to do with the belief, shared by Aristotle, in a closed universe, so trade had to be a zero-sum game, not a means to enabling one to improve one's lot or to stand ready to do so in the future (via the use of monetary resources).

7. Aristotle, *Nicomachean Ethics*, 420.

8. The gist of the view that it isn't true that "ought" implies "can" relies on a revision of what "ought" means. It is argued that "ought," say, in "you ought to tell the truth," means that one is being encouraged, supported, or urged to do this,

not that one has the moral responsibility to do it even if one chooses not to. For the skeptical position, see Paul Saka, "Ought Does Not Imply Can," *American Philosophical Quarterly* 37, no. 2 (April 2000): 93–105. However, see also Tibor R. Machan, *Initiative—Human Agency and Society* (Stanford, CA: Hoover Institution Press, 2000).

9. A good discussion of these points may be found in Stephen Toulmin, *Return to Reason* (Boston: MIT Press, 2001). His early book, *The Uses of Argument* (London: Cambridge University Press, 1964), is also valuable in gaining the kind of understanding of ethics we find to be sound.

10. This understanding of human life is much disputed by those claiming we can be fully explained by reference to various physical forces and properties and that indeed there really is no unique human self for any of us. This is the gist of reductionism, the belief that there is only one kind of being in reality and all differences are merely apparent. The idea is now propounded as implied by the successful scientific theory of Charles Darwin and is said to put to rest the hubris that there is anything more to our selves—you, I, or anyone else, from Mozart and Plato to the local postal clerk—than impersonal forces much like what makes computers behave as they do. Such ideas have always been in contention and are very inventive, serving thus to refute themselves by their renewed, if only minimal, originality. For more along these lines, see the works of Patricia and Paul Churchland, Daniel C. Dennett, and the psychological theories of B. F. Skinner.

11. We are discussing business ethics, not business law or public policy. We'll touch on those later. Law is a separate issue from business ethics, just as ethics is distinct from the law, although there is a relationship, an overlap. One can, for example, criticize gambling on moral grounds even though one would object to prohibiting it. The First Amendment of the U.S. Constitution clearly provides legal protection to everyone to say almost anything but that doesn't mean that anything one wants to say is good and that one should say it. All it means is that it shouldn't be prohibited. *Hustler* magazine, for example, may well be a despicable publication, but that alone would not justify banning it. So, there is a difference between law and ethics.

12. At times, we seek for others to prosper—we are simply providing our business acumen to help.

13. Actually, in most cases public stuff is traded at the behest of public authorities who effectively own these properties, with some restrictions in place (usually pertaining to accountability).

14. Often, critics of free markets insist that there is something wrong with "employment at will," that is, severing the employment relationship if one or the other parties no longer wants to continue it (provided contracts are honored). Yet, the objection is usually extended only against employers, not against employees who routinely leave employers for better opportunities. This is owing, mainly, to the widespread contention that employees lack bargaining power (a matter we shall discuss in more detail later in this book).

15. Richard Dawkins's provocatively titled *The Selfish Gene* (London: Oxford University Press, 1976) suggests this to many economists yet, in fact, when it comes to human behavior Dawkins isn't at all convinced that we are fully hardwired to act as we do.

16. For more detailed discussions, see Tibor R. Machan, ed., *Commerce and Morality* (Lanham, MD: Rowman & Littlefield, 1988); Tibor R. Machan, ed., *Business Ethics in the Global Market* (Stanford, CA: Hoover Institution Press, 1999); Tibor R. Machan, ed., *Morality and Work* (Stanford, CA: Hoover Institution Press, 2000); James E. Chesher and Tibor R. Machan, *The Business of Commerce: Examining an Honorable Profession* (Stanford, CA: Hoover Institution Press, 1999).

Introduction: A Potpourri of Business Ethics Issues

In this introduction, we are going to cover some basics of several areas of business ethics. We will later devote entire chapters to some of them. Here, we offer a brief and simple account of how business ethics applies to various areas of business activity.

Employment: Joining Forces in Business Enterprise

Employment is when a person with skills, time, or other value-producing resources cooperates with persons involved in some enterprise to produce goods and services, in return for a wage or salary, in order to help the enterprise profit and prosper (we talk about this at length in chapter 3). They agree to terms—typically, availability for skilled labor in exchange for salary or wages—and together produce something for the market. All parties are looking to achieve what they want through mutually beneficial terms of trade.

Prudence, then, should be the guiding principle of all trade; the focus of all parties ought to be on what does in fact contribute to their economic advantage, namely, the performance of work—skilled labor, management, and investment—that will result in profitable exchange in the market. This is one reason that hiring or firing people because of their looks, sexual orientation, or race is morally objectionable. Such conduct fails to heed the objective of business. It violates, as it were, the oath of the profession.

1

That doesn't mean incidental considerations can never enter the decision of whom to hire for a job. Obviously, given two equally qualified applicants and one is more personable than the other, it is not unreasonable to choose the one that is more personable. (To be sure, being personable may well be a substantive qualification itself, especially when it comes to customer service and other "people-related" functions.)

Bargaining Power

Ever since workers or wage laborers emerged from the feudal status of commoners or serfs—that is, from being practically owned by the upper classes and the king—they have had a somewhat confusing standing in political economic theory. At first, many were in dire straits and enjoyed little bargaining power. They had to take whatever job was offered to them. Lacking property of their own, they were, as Karl Marx and others point out, exploitable. Their vulnerability could be taken advantage of by those who did own property—mostly land, forests, mines, and such. Property owners didn't need the workers as much as the workers needed them; workers did not own capital that they could consume while waiting for a good deal or job. The impermissibility of organizing labor—which had existed in the United States until 1842 when Judge Shaw of Massachusetts overturned the common-law view that strikes constituted a harmful restraint of trade and could be stopped with the police power of the government—could pose an obstacle to workers in their bargaining efforts.[1]

However, this view of the worker as a downtrodden object of exploitation is inconsistent with the new relationship that was soon to be obtained by people, namely, respect for each person's basic rights to life, liberty, and property. Once workers could legally combine with each other, their bargaining power became equal to that of owners. After all, workers owned their skill and time and in sufficient numbers could paralyze any employer's enterprise, be it a factory, farm, or fleet of merchant marine ships. Furthermore, nothing in principle stops workers from forming their own professional corporations, just as doctors, attorneys, and others do in a free economy.

Unfortunately, the plethora of laws enacted to cope with the initial inequality of bargaining power—engendered perhaps by large doses of envy toward capitalists—has bequeathed a legacy of seemingly unavoidable conflict between labor and capital. The conflict is artificial in that nothing in the nature of work requires it. Yet, so conceiving of the relationships by political economists and other theorists has been very influential. It can lead to the enactment of laws and regulations as well as the shaping of popular opinion. So lawmakers can produce and sustain this artificial conflict, just as they can make women or Indian untouchables vulnerable and even facilitate their oppression.

Nepotism and Other Unjust Discrimination

To start with one of the less onerous ways the employment relationship can go wrong, consider nepotism, the practice of employing or promoting relatives in business relationships for reasons not related to the advancement of the enterprise. The term "nepotism" derives from the practice of early Roman Catholic popes who would father sons and then appoint them, as "nephews," to some post in the Vatican. Now it refers to preference peddling to relatives because they are relatives.

We witness nepotism all around us, mainly in privately owned firms—restaurants, laundromats, and other relatively small operations. And there may be nothing bad about this, given that the owners could well be fulfilling some other responsibility apart from what they owe to their business, such as giving assistance to a needy brother, daughter, or son-in-law. In public companies, however, where there is an obligation to produce profit for stockholders and other investors, nepotism is indeed a violation of business ethics. The practice distracts from the objective that's to be served.

Although unjust discrimination is now illegal, especially if it involves refusing employment or promotion to members of minorities because of race, color, sexual preference, ethnic background, and the like, the first issue is why it is unethical to practice it. Why is it wrong for an employer to hire whomever he/she prefers for whatever reason he/she might have? This is not the same question as whether the employer has the right to discriminate in these ways. Even if there is such a right, especially in the case of privately owned businesses where one is hiring to suit one's own business objectives, that does not dispose of the possibility of its being ethically wrong to hire and promote in that way. Just as there may well be a right to publish yellow journalism or otherwise morally objectionable writing, it does not mean one cannot be doing something wrong while exercising that right.

Basically, discrimination based on irrelevant factors is ethically wrong on the grounds of business ethics and on the considerations of justice. As for business ethics, to introduce irrelevant criteria when hiring someone for a job, under a reasonably specific job description, is to go back on one's word.

An applicant's being a woman, black, or from Poland has nothing to do with being able to work as an accountant in some firm. Thus, to introduce such a criterion is irrelevant to the employer's commitment to make the business succeed and violates that commitment.

Of course, such a practice can also be illegal, even apart from violating some federal or state law directing one not to do it. If a firm announces that it is seeking accountants but then rejects qualified people because they do not fit some irrelevant, unannounced criterion, this could be actionable on the grounds of some kind of deception. (The same would hold for unjustly discriminating against prospective customers.)

More generally though, unjust discrimination wrongly treats accidental attributes as essential. To reject a human being because of color, ethnic origin, or sex is to hold against a person what can't be helped, what the person didn't choose, and thus can't be blamed (or praised) for. There are exceptions: In personal relations, one may well need to serve some idiosyncratic taste or preference in order to be fulfilled, satisfied, and joyful, and these may well be traits that in another context would be irrelevant. For instance, consider choosing a date. Here, one is indulging one's preference and excluding numerous possible candidates but for a perfectly unobjectionable reason, namely, to enjoy another's company. And that could itself rest on custom, background, accident, familiarity, and such—all matters that are unobjectionable in decisions serving a personal purpose while objectionable when serving a professional one.

Comparable Worth versus Pay

Many in the marketplace are concerned with the evident disparity of wages and salaries between women and men. When a woman works as hard, long, and skillfully as a man, shouldn't she be paid the same as the man is? Not necessarily.

Clearly, the marketplace makes no provisions for equal work translating into equal pay. If a manager requires an accountant and can hire a woman for less than a man, this will surely be considered, even if some might think it to be unjust. Throughout the marketplace, such disparity is notorious—in fact most economic competition involves just such disparity. If one store sells a pair of gloves for less than another, a shopper would naturally purchase the less expensive of the two otherwise identical pairs. Indeed, one reason the price fluctuates is that merchants respond to competition by lowering their prices, just as they sometimes respond to increased sales by raising it. The labor market isn't different—those accepting a lower wage, say women, are likelier to get the job. But isn't there something morally amiss with this situation? It depends on what prices are, and we need to look at that briefly.

A wage or price is a sum of money that buyer and seller agree on to commence trade. In most cases of ordinary shopping, prices, salaries, and wages appear to be set, although occasionally one can challenge the apparently set amount and change it. There is nothing fixed about these sums—they are probably best viewed as something discovered between buyers and sellers, whatever is being bought and sold. If prices, wages, and salaries are the result of a process of discovering the amount it will take to commence a trade, then a "correct" or "just" price, wage, or salary would be what buyer and seller—actually millions of them interacting in the marketplace—ultimately agree to.

If it turns out that a company can usually hire women to do the same work as men but for less money, this is the result of the ebb and flow of negotiated wages. It is no more reasonable to demand that wages or salaries be adjusted to some desired level, based on comparisons between what members of different sexes tend to get, than it would be to demand that the spending habits of women and men have some desired level. Individuals are unique in these and other respects, bearing on their market relationships, and while there may be certain periodic trends, as well as trends resulting from collective bargaining, there is no right wage or salary for any group apart from what is discovered in the processes of trade. Consider what factors might be involved here. Lower wages for women could result from (a) there being more of them on the market than there is a demand for their work, (b) justified concerns about their not being on the job as regularly as men, (c) their own choice of not pursuing a career as ambitiously as men do, (d) idiosyncratic factors, and so on.

If a company wants to hire people in a cost-effective way and it happens that wages or salaries for that work are lower for women than for men, why should they not seize the opportunity? It is not the responsibility of employers to investigate and rectify the various more or less rational influences that play a role in determining prices, wages, salaries, and such. Besides, such a task would be impossible. By the same reasoning, consumers shopping for, say, shoes, are not responsible for ascertaining whether the lower price is the result of unfair wages for those who manufacture the shoes, or the result of greater efficiency at the plant where the shoes are made than that of their competitors, or due to the lower cost of materials or overstocked inventories, and/or a host of other possible factors too numerous and complex to weigh and balance.

This does not mean that no prejudice and related evils can enter the picture when wages, prices, salaries, and such are established. Of course they can. But this is true with any and all purchases—people can boost the price of X because, well, they irrationally prefer it to Y. But that need not be the case. And certainly, if one knows that injustice has produced the better deal, then one ought to go elsewhere.

If prices, wages, and salaries—indeed, all sums being charged for what can be bought and sold—are the result of a process of discovery (of the amount it will take to commence a trade), then there cannot be such a thing as a correct or just price, wage, or salary. It depends on what buyer and seller agree to.

It bears noting here that the concern in this kind of discussion is not with showing that all the results of market transactions are morally or ethically proper. It is rather with whether the process of market exchange is superior to alternatives such as regimented prices, wages, salaries, terms of trade, and so on. Is such a free market process, where sometimes ethically questionable conduct can and does occur, better than the unfree type that rests on the belief that some people may force others to behave properly, even granting that now and then the unfree-type system can produce results that ought to have been produced freely?

Corporations: Shareholder versus Stakeholder Theory

There is an old idea returning in new guise that challenges all of private corporate commerce. According to the stakeholder theory, a company does not really belong to individual, specific shareholders, investors, or families, but to all those who have "a stake" in the firm. This includes all the people who may have an interest in the firm's doing one thing rather than another—for example, staying put rather than moving to another town. On this view, if business, education, religious, charitable, and other local establishments would be adversely affected by the proposed move, the company has no right to do it. The stakeholder theory is set forth mostly by critics of capitalism and private property rights who are suspicious of autonomous and self-interested action to begin with.[2]

Some even advance the notion that company employees gain a proprietary stake in their jobs once they have worked at a company long enough. In other words, they "own the job" they hold.[3] This assumption is one reason that many who have worked for fifteen or twenty years at a large company like General Motors or Ford get indignant when they are laid off due to downsizing, especially when the company goes abroad to hire replacement workers at a far lower wage. They believe the job is theirs by right rather than by mutual assent.

Critics of free trade agreements, which uphold the right of companies to move if that is what they deem to be profitable, fret that "our jobs would be taken by Mexicans, Koreans, or Chinese." Such critics view employment as a kind of permanent acquisition. So when employees are let go, they've supposedly been robbed of something.

Of course, although critics regard employers as bound to the workers, they don't regard workers as bound to the employers. That would amount to championing involuntary servitude. Workers, in other words, are seen as owning their jobs, but the employer is not understood as owning the worker's labor. So when workers want to leave "their" jobs, this theory does not consider it wrong for them to do so. On this view, it seems okay to enslave the employer but not the employees.

The Friendliness of Hostile Takeovers

There is a villain of the Reagan era against whom many liberals love to unleash their moral indignation. This is the corporate raider, the financier bent on removing existing managers of firms by offering shareholders higher value for their stocks than what the current management is able to deliver. The new management then goes to work on squeezing more profit out of the enterprise, usually to the benefit of the stockholders.

It should be explained here that corporations are not separate entities. They are individual human beings who have united voluntarily, aiming for some common goal and committing themselves to certain rules in pursuit of this goal. Corporations are not persons any more than an orchestra, team, or family is, even if the law so treats them for certain purposes.

Commercial corporate efforts can grow quite large, as can educational, athletic, or scientific corporate efforts. Corporations have been given special advantages by various governments in the past. For example, they have enjoyed limited liability protection against plaintiffs' attempts to collect damages for harm done to them in the course of conducting business. These special advantages, however, are not a sound basis for treating corporations differently from other voluntary collective efforts. The remedy for unfairness is to remove it, not to condemn the institutions that have been favored.

Critics of corporate raiding offer a host of complaints. They find intolerable the lamentable, but by no means permanently avoidable, lot of employees of these firms, whose jobs are often in jeopardy from a hostile takeover. They bemoan the lot of the management running the targeted firm, as well as the suffering of some members of the community who have grown accustomed to the firm's presence. Other complaints concern the loss of tried and true products that the firm has provided to the market, the demise of old-fashioned business practices of the current management (e.g., being debt free), and the charming nepotism that often goes hand in hand with managing old firms. In fact, these complaints amount to refusing to accept the demands and consequences of living among free men and women whose patronage is never guaranteed and who are subject to a wide array of motivations, some of which are likely to be morally deplorable.

Corporate raiders are now a stereotype, having been endlessly characterized by critics as greedy, ruthless, heartless, callous, and indifferent to tradition, quality, and true values. Raiders desire nothing but greenbacks; they are mere self-interested brutes living by the principle of social Darwinism—the survival of the financially fit and clever.

The prevalence of this attitude no doubt has contributed to litigation by various states attempting to prevent corporate raiding. Certain lawyers and middle managers whose jobs are threatened, as well as adjacent businesses and other concerns, appear to be the greatest beneficiaries. They are attempting to gain the advantage of the law while the market is prevented from operating freely according to the law of supply and demand and the shareholders are made to subsidize these other objectives.

What fuels the "antihostile takeover" sentiment is a form of moral outrage that is hopelessly one-sided. Innumerable books and magazine pieces, election rhetoric, and Hollywood movies such as *Wall Street*, *Other People's Money*, and *Barbarians at the Gate* have nourished this sentiment. Employees and entrenched management are objects of sympathy, while stockholders are regarded as the unworthy beneficiaries of the process. But is this so?

The popular view overlooks some basic human virtues and vices. Once these are factored in, the actions of corporate raiders appear far more just than they presently do.

Consider the possibility that employees of inefficient firms expect security without innovation. An inefficient firm is one that, given the potential of the total enterprise, fails to operate so as to pay a return on its shareholders' investment. Employees of such firms want to keep their jobs without adjusting to the unalterable fact of human change and development.

Consumers need protection, say bureaucrats of the various government regulatory agencies, as well as "public interest" advocates such as Ralph Nader, Sidney Wolff, and, less stridently, Steve Kelman. But with respect to corporate raiding, it is consumers, including stockholders, who are too often neglected by the critics.

Some scholars in business ethics and law have tried to make a case for the lopsided attention being paid to those adversely affected by hostile takeovers by introducing the category of "stakeholders." These are people who can experience the negative effects of corporate behavior, people such as employees, members of the community whose economy is connected with the firm, and neighbors whose residence and environment may suffer from the disposition of the firm.

It has been argued, accordingly, that the concept of corporate responsibility should extend to include stakeholders to whom obligations of various kinds are due. Thus, a stakeholder would be "any identifiable group or individual who can affect or is affected by organization performance in terms of its products, politics, and work processes."[4]

Just how broadly one can interpret the vague notion of "affect or . . . affected" is suggested by the fact that some activists propose that every sizable corporation should be required to accept a consumer representative on its board. This would amount to a kind of in-house Ralph Nader, someone to represent the interests of stakeholders. In short, whatever such a representative deems pertinent will be pertinent. This clearly defeats the very function of private property rights in a society by blurring the distinction between "mine and thine," as well as the lines that demarcate the spheres of authority.[5]

These views, then, which are gaining momentum in our society, are a direct challenge to the institution of private property rights, a challenge reminiscent of Marx's platform for the abolition of capitalism: First abolish private property! All of this totally ignores the fact that stockholders have voluntarily invested (and thus risked) their own assets, intending to gain some future economic benefits and forgoing the use of these assets for other purposes in the meantime. In doing so, they have delegated to corporate managers the authority to act as a kind of financial agent, including the responsibility that comes with such a trust. Other persons who happen to take advantage of some of the side benefits of a firm's presence in the community are entitled to nothing else from the firm than a conscientious respect of their individual rights to life, liberty, and property.

In this instance, the rationale for regimentation is the belief that we should favor old technology over advanced technology simply because workers don't want to change and because members of the surrounding communities are going to be inconvenienced, perhaps even brought to suffer hardship. (The cause of such hardship may be found in the extensive dependence on the firm's presence or business that some people have often carelessly allowed to develop.) We are supposed to revere old firms instead of new ones because they preserve tradition and entrenched community values.

Consider, here, that all of this totally ignores the rights of people who have joined together freely and with no breach of obligation to anyone. They have done this in order to secure a better livelihood and enough wealth to help their children, fund their charities, purchase goods and services that they deem important, and so on. In short, those who actually own the resources that enable firms to operate and to create the values for which many people are willing to exchange their own wealth, are overlooked in favor of others to whom no direct promise of service was made by the corporation's officials. Thus understood, we can see a clear perversion of the idea of fiduciary duty, of social responsibility itself.[6]

Apart from this, there is also the issue of the benefits of modern science and technology. These, often translated into product safety and dependability, are thwarted, robbing consumers of advantages, commodities, and services that they might otherwise have enjoyed, including the very people in whose name the complaints against takeovers are made. This results in greater impoverishment and loss of values in contrast with the alternative.

Corporate raiders demand the highest quality and safety standards. They demand an efficient operation, which results in benefits to stockholders and consumers. Moreover, employees who are told the truth about the inefficiency of their firm are being treated with respect, not with the condescension of favors or special treatment. They deserve a fair return for their contribution to the production effort of the firm, as determined by what the free market—that is, consumers—will allow. The result is not always perfect. Yet, there is no reason to believe that bureaucrats would do better, especially since they wield legal power the abuse of which is more dangerous than any market failure.

So-called hostile takeover efforts or corporate raids are far more consumer and stockholder friendly than critics let on or perhaps even realize. And in the last analysis such friendliness could be deemed as a kind of "tough love" toward stakeholders as well.

Profits to a corporation are not, as the popular view would have it, more wealth to a few already rich, money-grubbing scum. Rather, the stockholders, the beneficiaries, are people preparing for the future by investing some of their resources, or people drawing on retirement investment, living off of mutual funds, hoping to increase the value of their life insurance and pension income, or even planning to contribute to charity and other worthy causes. Many of these millions of people are far from very wealthy and anything but greedy and callous.

Stockholders are quite unlike the stereotype projected by those who cari-cature capitalists as avaricious misers. The higher value of shares that a "hos-tile" takeover creates will go to finance college, a decent retirement, a trip to Rome, some additional compact discs for a classical music collection, pay-ments on a health insurance policy, a car, a business venture, a donation, and so on. To forcibly sacrifice the benefits stockholders obtain from their own decision to invest, for the sake of tradition and other people's needs, violates justice and common sense.

This side of the story is rarely if ever depicted on television dramas or in the movies, for that would seem to be siding with "big business," which makes for poor ratings and ticket sales![7]

The point here is not to defend the corporate raider by showing how help-ful he/she is to people. Rather, we should honor people's right to exercise pru-dence or good judgment in seeking a decent return on their investment. In doing so, they are also helping the rest of us by guiding firms to upgrade themselves as they seek our business.

The Moral Responsibility of Corporations

In discussions of business ethics, the idea of "corporate social responsibility" plays a prominent role, for example, in connection with environmental is-sues. Big companies in particular—chemical, manufacturing, logging firms, and so on—are often implored to pay attention to their social responsibili-ties. It's an interesting and even important idea.[8]

Notice, however, the selectivity of the admonitions, directed almost ex-clusively at business. Teachers, for example, are rarely enjoined to fulfill their social responsibilities apart from doing their work conscientiously. As long as they do so, they are morally respectable (i.e., already perceived as doing something worthwhile and responsible).

Why is this concern about social responsibility focused particularly on business? One reason is that business is highly engaged with the world—with customers, neighborhoods, government officials, and so on. So, many people who work in the field of business ethics believe that it is a part of a company's responsibility to improve and help the community.[9]

Some go so far as to say the companies ought to be legally *compelled* to serve society. This is a notion inherited from the feudal era, when corpora-tions were established by the king. Corporations were not formed as a result of people simply getting together on their own and starting a company, as they are now. They were a franchise from the Crown.

Because corporations received this franchise as an exclusive domain, it came with certain limitations of liability. That's where the concept of limited liability comes from and why in England companies are called "Ltd." Their liability was limited so that they did not have to pay the full cost of damages they may have caused at sea, for example. Or if a company ran down a horse, it would not have to pay all of the damage because it had received a dispensation from the Crown.

Indeed, state-granted limited liability is not appropriate for corporations that are *not* creatures of the Crown (i.e., corporations of today). The limited liability/monopoly had been given in exchange for performing certain duties for the Crown/society. The stage was set historically for the current idea that corporations must serve society by the origin of corporations as royal charters. As Nader is fond of pointing out, special privileges imply special duties and a moral obligation to act on behalf of society or the Crown rather than, as prudence would counsel, on behalf of the company and its shareholders.[10]

A further extension of this idea is the current argument advanced by some business ethics scholars, mentioned earlier, that shareholders should be deprived of their ownership rights and instead of this what are called stakeholders ought to have significant influence over corporate policy.

Corporation As an Arm of Government

People like Nader—who is called a "consumer advocate," somewhat question beggingly, we would argue—maintain that companies do not really belong to the people who established them. It's not the entrepreneurs who have the primary sovereignty over the company's doings, but "the public." So Nader, for example, advocates that all major corporations have a consumer advocate sitting on their boards as one way to ensure that companies are serving the public. According to this view, companies are just arms of the state. This is called the creature of the state argument.

By this account, business corporations are not private but public—not in the sense that they are sold on the public market, but in the sense that they are beholden to the authority of government that represents the public. Business corporations, therefore, ought to be directed to serve certain social or political objectives rather than profit-making business objectives.

Now, all of this doesn't usually affect small companies, but it does affect large ones: when they are told, for example, that they must engage in a certain amount of environmental cleanup—not necessarily because they have damaged anybody or created the mess themselves, but because they are a large entity in the community and possess the resources to do so. It is the philosophy of corporate social responsibility that enjoins corporations to devote their resources thus and that invites us as citizens to support the laws that compel them to do so. It is a philosophy that arguably stands in opposition to the very idea of private property rights and, thus, as argued earlier, against a fundamental principle of business and of business ethics.

With the kind of public policy Ralph Nader and Co. propose, there arises a heavy burden of government regulations that only large corporations can shoulder—via teams of attorneys and lobbyists—leaving some businesses at a great disadvantage. So indirectly Nader and Co. are supporting large corporate business and helping to undermine smaller firms.

Corporations As Just Profit Makers

A diametrically opposite position is put forth by Milton Friedman, the famous economist from the University of Chicago. Friedman holds that when a company gets established, it makes a promise to its investors and owners to bring a return on the investment and that this is the only ethical responsibility that corporate managers have. The sole social responsibility of companies, according to Friedman, is to make a profit. Everything else is out of court.

> Few trends could so thoroughly undermine the very foundation of our free society as the acceptance by corporate officials of a social responsibility other than to make as much money for their stockholders as possible. . . . If businessmen do have a social responsibility other than making maximum profits for stockholders, how are they to know what it is? Can self-selected private individuals decide what the social interest is? Can they decide how great a burden they are justified in placing on themselves or their stockholders to serve that social interest?[11]

Of course, Friedman does hold that making a profit should be constrained by basic rules of free trade and ordinary morality and law—of honesty and contractual integrity, the right to property, and the like. But within this set of elementary rules that apply to us all, corporate executives or managers have the sole responsibility of striving to turn a profit for the owners.

Humanizing Corporations

Some people argue that, yes, the primary responsibility of business corporations is to make a profit. But since they operate in human communities, it is judicious for them to also make sure that the community is nurtured, maintained, and preserved. They ought not to neglect the quality of the society in which they exist. Here is how Fred D. Miller and John Ahrens illustrate this point:

> Consider a case in which the manager of a corporation is trying to deal with the problem of alcoholism among his employees. The manager might be committed both to maximizing the profits of the stockholders and to treating the employees fairly and humanely. In . . . considering whether the company should finance a rehabilitation program for employees with an alcohol problem, he finds that it would be no more expensive to introduce such a program than to fire the employees and retrain new ones. He may also have reason to think that such a program would enhance the prospect for better employees in the future. The manager may introduce the rehabilitation program on the grounds that it is morally correct in terms of both profitability and the welfare of his workers.[12]

The principle is akin to that followed by individuals who accept the responsibility to enhance not only their own lives, which does come first on their list of priorities, but also, to a more limited degree, those of their neighbors who may request a cup of sugar or even more significant help at times. The morally healthy individual does not bark, "Hell, that's not my responsibility, go home!" Instead, such a person would respond: "I've got some extra here, so I'll help out."[13]

So, it is appropriate for companies to be socially engaged—not because they are instruments of the state, but because they are human organizations flourishing in a social context. In other words, when any human organization operates within a community, while its primary obligation is to fulfill its mission, it should exercise appropriate concern for other worthy tasks as well.

A major difference between this version of corporate responsibility (whereby companies ought, first, to strive for success but should also keep in mind other decent objectives) and the Nader version, is that no government coercion may be used to make it all happen. In this approach, corporations must *choose to do the deeds they ought to perform*. That is as it should be, since no good deed can be regarded as morally worthy if it is coerced.

The difference, in turn, between this last view and that of Friedman is largely a matter of degree. Miller and Ahrens agree that business is primarily responsible to make the enterprise prosper. They deny, however, that this objective stands by itself, independently of and in necessary competition with other worthy ones related to the workplace. Neither of these views implies, however, as does Nader's and that of the stakeholder school, that the government must compel business to act properly!

Which View Makes the Best Sense?

The view championed by Nader is based on the conception of society as being owned and regulated or guided by the government, as it used to be owned and kept in line by the king, a view that was rejected by the American Revolution. The fundamental thrust of that revolution is that it's not the Crown or government that owns us—we are not subjects like the people in England are (at least nominally). In the United States one is a citizen. One is not subject to the authority of the Crown or government; rather the government is instituted to serve citizens, to secure their rights.

In the United States, the legacy is that one owns one's life. One has an inalienable right to it. And as a result, the notion that government should determine what a company that citizens have set up ought to do is anathema to the U.S. political system.

The idea of involuntary servitude has been philosophically and constitutionally rejected. So Nader's argument rests on a historical fact long ago disowned. His view of what corporate commerce is depends on an older conception of government as the ruler rather than the servant of the people. This novel view makes better sense than the creature of the state idea, which rests on a conception of human nature that is compatible with the divine rights of kings, inherited status, and fundamental inequality of rights among people.

Friedman's view, that the sole responsibility of corporations is to make a profit, is closer to the truth. But it also lacks proper depth, in that companies are comprised, after all, of human beings who have concerns beyond simply trying to make profit, even as they take part in fostering corporate commerce. In a human institution like the business corporation, it makes sense that in addition to pursuing the bottom line, one would have other concerns as well.

So, the perspective advanced by philosophers Miller and Ahrens is the one that most people and companies can live with most fruitfully and most responsibly. Corporate managers ought to pay attention to their primary purpose of making the company grow, but not so much that they neglect where they operate, the people with whom they deal, and so on. Moreover, as Miller and Ahrens argue, "the question of what will enhance a corporation's profitability is ambiguous, and, consequently, so is Friedman's theory that the manager's social responsibility requires maximizing profits of the corporation."[14]

One may ask, however, whether the added responsibilities corporations have would be seen as over and above whatever reasonable social responsibilities they might have as private individuals, and whether the moral dimensions Friedman would agree should govern corporate policy do not actually subsume the presumptively more encompassing considerations Miller and Ahrens discuss. Also, it should be noted that the very existence of a productive, hiring company does much to benefit a community. The earlier comparison to teachers seems relevant here. Do teachers, other professions, small businesses, and so on also have the same social responsibilities as the big corporations? Arguably, teachers fulfill a similar obligation when they stay late at school to help a particular student. Or when they take on special volunteer work based on their professional skills. What is different is that many believe that businesses gain moral credit solely from such pro bono work, a perspective not widely embraced concerning the moral worth of other professions such as medicine, education, or science. The idea advanced here is that, on the contrary, business does something morally worthwhile when profit is pursued, when prosperity is its main objective, and the additional moral concerns should not be confused with this primary one.

Business and Government Regulation

Many who work in the field of business ethics believe government regulation of business is essential. They say that without regulation to govern advertising, trade relationships, aspects of the work environment that could affect safety and health, and so on, the marketplace would be a harsh arena. Business needs to be tamed and only the government can tame it.

To begin with, some hold that government regulation is justified in the U.S. legal system, at least, on grounds that it is one of government's official tasks to "promote the general welfare." Those who see government regulation as inconsistent with the ideals laid out in the U.S. Declaration of Independence, namely, that government is instituted to secure our inalienable rights, would note that this is a mistaken understanding of the "general welfare" clause. That means no more than that government exists for the welfare of the people, something that is achieved best by securing the rights of every citizen. Even if the clause were to amount to a more proactive view of government, government regulation of business tends to impede rather than enhance the general welfare, given its enormous cost and inefficiency.

Government regulation of business assumes the existence of a relatively free market. Under socialism or communism, no government regulation can exist since strictly speaking no business can exist in such systems. Even in fascism, where everything is run at the behest of the leader, government not so much regulates business as administers it (with more or less leniency).

But like socialism or fascism, government regulation is also a form of paternalism, deriving its justification from the belief that the state should relate to the citizenry as parents relate to their children. While the people are "allowed" some measure of freedom, the government must be able to trump their liberty, guide its use, and even veto it whenever the state deems it wise and necessary. Or, it is argued that the state is the only means by which difficult market decisions can be made.[15]

Yet, there are many differences between the relationship of parents and children and that of government regulatory bodies and the citizens being regulated. For one, parents are commonly held responsible for much of the misbehavior of their children. When a child breaks a neighbor's window or crashes the family car into some innocent people, the parents must pay and may even be legally penalized. Liability, in short, is largely assigned to the parental authority who is taken to be responsible for the child's conduct.

Not so with government regulatory bodies. Even though the Federal Aviation Association regulates airline safety, it is airline corporations or their insurance companies that must pay the damage awards from lawsuits filed by passengers or the next of kin. Even though in the United States the Federal Trade Commission (FTC) regulates a good deal of commerce, when such commerce is conducted badly and a company is sued, the FTC is never a codefendant or dragged into court as the primarily liable party. This is true even if the government's regulations could be shown to have impaired a firm's ability to fulfill its contractual obligations.

The same exemptions are enjoyed by the Occupational Health and Safety Administration, the Securities and Exchange Commission, the Environmental Protection Agency, and the rest. All these essentially paternalistic agencies keep imposing their innumerable rather intrusive rules and regulations—deemed to be so essential to keeping various industries morally virtuous—on the members of those industries. Yet, whenever there is an accident, malpractice, or product malfunction, the law ignores the central element of justice involved—that all parties, and especially the supervising agency, should be held responsible.

Regulation and the Law
The legal justification for the free pass for these regulatory agencies derives from the concept of "sovereign immunity." Basically, the idea is that a government cannot be sued because it stands for all of us, just as the military or the diplomatic corps stands for all of us when they conduct the foreign

policy of the country. Or as some put it, the government is us, and one cannot sue oneself.[16]

There are two other legal defenses of government regulation of business: the interstate commerce clause of the federal constitution and the common-law provision of the police power of government. The former constitutes a misguided interpretation of Article 1, section 8 of the U.S. Constitution, which provides Congress with the power to regulate interstate commerce. The clause was included because, prior to the formation of the United States, the colonies had engaged in various mercantilist economic practices—imposing duties on imported goods, restricting trade, and so on—that had to be stopped. Instead of leaving to the state governments the job of overturning their own trade restrictions, the federal government would harmonize commerce in the country. But later courts yielded to populist pressure to allow the federal government to meddle with free enterprise, thus undermining the very purpose of the clause: to remove, not impose, burdens on the free market.

The police power, in turn, is a legacy of feudalism, under which the king was responsible for how communities were shaped. This common-law provision had been imported into U.S. law from England and other European countries during the time that local law had not yet developed in line with the political tradition of individual rights. Any exercise of police power that goes beyond a night watchman function—namely, the protection of individual rights—is the relevant despotic legacy of feudalism. The king was responsible for how communities were shaped *under* feudalism and this responsibility was understood as part of *the police power* as constituted under feudalism.

But the government is not, after all, anything like one's parent, at least not as understood in the context of the politics sketched in the U.S. Declaration of Independence. The government is in principle akin to a hired bodyguard who acts on one's behalf and is confined to the role of a defense agent.

Regulation and Morality

As to the moral or philosophical support for government regulation, there are essentially four arguments: the creature of the state argument we have already discussed, advanced by Nader and his followers; two types of market failure argument invoked by, among others, John Stuart Mill and John Kenneth Galbraith; the positive rights-to-provisions argument advanced by such political philosophers as Alan Gewirth and John Rawls; and the judicial inefficiency argument proposed by the Nobel laureate economist Kenneth J. Arrow. Let's look at each briefly and see why they do not support the institution of government regulation, despite the belief in its absolute necessity by many very influential people.

Creature of the State

The first argument technically applies to virtually all businesses, since so many of them are incorporated. It asserts that corporate commerce is a creature of government itself, since corporations were brought into existence by acts of the British mercantilist government to enhance the wealth of the country. And governments still charter corporations.

Since government creates them, government is authorized and indeed ought to regulate corporations in accordance with the public purpose. If one has created something, one is morally responsible for it and may do with it what is reasonable and responsible. So government ought to regulate corporate commerce to the various good ends government sets out to promote—such as safety, social equality, racial and gender balance at the workplace, environmental purity, and so on, especially now that the goal of creating a wealthy country has been largely achieved. Government regulation is simply the rightful and responsible control of a creator over that which it has created.

Market Failures

Some have argued that although the free market is a wonderful provider of goods and services, sometimes it is needlessly inefficient, for example, when services like the provision of electricity or water are involved. John Stuart Mill thought that there were many uncontroversial instances in which government could take over functions that would be cumbersome for private individuals to perform.[17] (Or which they would perform with chronic irresponsibility, even when "perfect freedom is allowed to competition."[18]) Insofar as the free market should be limited in such cases—to avoid duplication of water or electrical lines, inept pavement of sidewalks, or whichever—companies should be awarded monopoly status or specific functions should be taken over by the state. The industry in question should be regulated by bureaucrats, not the market. And, indeed, throughout the world this view has led to the abolition of free markets in various industries and the institution of extensive government regulation of prices, wages, labor relations, and so on.

Others have taken this idea of market failure even further and argued that government must coercively correct the unwillingness or inability of markets to provide certain values. (John Kenneth Galbraith, for example, famously argues that the very abundance of private goods in an affluent society is "to a marked degree, the cause of crisis in the supply of public services,"[19] though why the missing public goods would be more abundant and robust in an impoverished society is unclear.)

An example of this type of market failure might be libraries. The argument for providing public varieties of this good is that the market simply will not furnish us with what we value here, namely, the opportunity to read on loan. Thus government must take over. The same basic argument is used to justify regulation of the workplace for health and safety—the market fails to ensure these in sufficient abundance, presumably, so government must step in. Affirmative action, minimum wages, fair trading practices, and the like are all supposed to be values the market fails to produce, albeit they are—or perhaps ought to be—widely wanted; so government must step in to fix things.

All government regulation, then, can be construed as the supposedly legitimate effort of the government to remedy what the market ought but fails to achieve. The animating idea here is utilitarianism: The central obligation of the state is to secure the greatest happiness of the greatest number, however that might be determined. When the market fails to achieve this, the state must step in with its remedial regulatory policies.

The Positive Rights Argument

Some argue that, contrary to the U.S. political tradition and classical liberalism—which upholds basic *negative* human rights not to be killed, assaulted, or robbed (i.e., upholds the rights to life, liberty, and property)— we in fact have the right to be provided with various goods and services by others.

Among others, philosopher Alan Gewirth claims that "all agents have positive rights to well-being and that the supportive state is justified as helping to secure some of these rights." He goes on to say that "well-being . . . signifies possession of a whole range of substantive general abilities and conditions needed for action and for successful action."[20]

For Gewirth and many others, including most who work in the field of business ethics, these conditions include specific goods and services. This does not consist of just the social condition of the right to liberty and its protection that enables us to *act to obtain* the goods we believe will further our purposes. Rather, we all are supposed to have the *positive* right to health care, social security, public education, unemployment compensation, safety and health protection at the workplace, and so on. Because we have these basic rights, and because government was (supposedly) established precisely in order to secure these rights, government regulation may properly be instituted to adjust private endeavors so that these provisions will be forthcoming.

As a matter of course, the argument for positive rights gains support by the weakening of the protection of negative rights.[21]

Judicial Inefficiency
Finally, there are some problems in society that not even the most vigilant effort to privatize could solve. Kenneth J. Arrow argues that many cases of pollution confront us with a situation that is "judicially inefficient." For example, "dumping wastes in a stream may ruin fisheries." So, "in a proper economic accounting, [such dumping should] be charged against the dumper, but it is impractical to do so."[22]

Let's say that A pollutes the air mass and B suffers as a result. A could not have sought out B first so as to secure permission, nor can B now find A so as to launch a lawsuit. So there is neither a market nor a judicial solution available to the parties. Ergo, government must take over and regulate the sphere of judicially inefficient human endeavors. It must set standards and establish some system of rationing and balance of cost and benefits arising from injury-producing activities not subject to litigation.

Actually, this is not so much an argument for government regulation of business as for government administration of what some view as unavoidably *public* spheres. Not all government oversight qualifies as regulatory: When government administers courts, public lands, roads, beaches, parks, and other facilities owned by "the people," that is not strictly government regulation but public administration. These lands are not privately owned and thus government is only handling what belongs to it or the people it serves, legally, at least, if not also rightfully.

When government dictates how the air mass, oceans, lakes, or rivers may be used, business must operate according to government's edicts when it interacts with these realms. So, to the extent public ownership of slices of nature is justified, so also is government regulation of business done therein justified.

Some Replies to the Arguments
What about these arguments, then?

Companies Are Not Created by the State
The creature of the state argument fails because the mere fact of a historically imposed claim does not establish the morality of that claim. States used to establish churches and printing presses, yet few in the West now defend their

authority and responsibility to do so, seeing that they should never have done so in the first place. When the state was sovereign, it was taken to be the initiator of nearly everything of importance in society. But when thinkers began to realize that the state's sovereignty simply meant the sovereignty of some people over the lives of other people, they began to recognize individuals as sovereign. At that point the state came to be regarded, by moral right, as merely a hired agent of the individuals it was to serve in certain limited capacities.

Now if individuals are sovereign, there can be no justification for regulating their lives, be it in commerce, religion, romance, or athletics. Barring any violation of another's rights to his/her own sovereign authority, every individual has a right to run his/her life as he/she chooses. Not that this choosing must always be wise or good, but it must be his/her own. The creature of the state defense of government regulation aims to restore us to a feudal time when the state was seen as a superior entity and its citizens as its subjects. Most wish to impose the feudal strictures selectively, for the most part on those engaged in commerce. But that is entirely arbitrary and unjust. When religion and the press are free, so should every other endeavor of human life be free. Indeed, it is a violation of the rule of law to do as we do now, namely, apply government regulation to business but respect the rights of others, for example, priests, authors, or poets, to carry on unregulated.

Market versus Political Failures

The argument for government regulation based on market failure is no more successful. The claim that because some inefficiency may occur in the market, we therefore ought to take a certain kind of productive activity out of the market, is premised on a kind of raw utilitarianism that ignores individual rights.

And what if a bit of inefficiency *were* inherent in certain market processes? Is getting rid of it so important as to sacrifice human liberty? But the argument actually depends on showing, also, that government regulation does not introduce its *own* set of failures, its *own* welter of inefficiencies. Market failures and government regulatory failures need to be compared. And there is ample reason to conclude, as the scholars of public choice have argued, that when one understands the nature of bureaucracy one can expect far more damage to society from government meddling than from alleged inefficiencies of the market.

When an industry is taken out of the market, competition ceases. Contra Mill, if a private company remains too inefficient for too long from the perspective of its customers, that inefficiency is an open invitation to competition. Customers naturally go elsewhere when they're dissatisfied. But a government monopoly doesn't have to worry about accommodating the consumer. There is nowhere else for the consumer to go. And in case of work stoppages or strikes the entire industry can be shut down, so that the only remedy is to impose legislative restrictions on the free movement of laborers. That is surely an awesome price to extract so as to obtain an illusory efficiency—an "efficiency" that is, indeed, far more inefficient than any occasionally unnecessary duplication or temporary mishandling of resources on the market.

As to the values the market does not always provide, it is once again dubious to suppose that government will supply them in the right proportion, according to a sound set of priorities, and effectively without enormous cost in the form of other goods that thereby must be foregone—the goods that people *would* in fact have chosen to produce and consume on the market had the resources not been diverted. Libraries are now nearly obsolete, except for a few people who could probably have been helped much better in other ways had they never been built. Economic decision making based on political sentiments expressed in the voting booth can be hazardous to our health inasmuch as such sentiments are merely voiced, but not reconciled in practical and prudent action with one's budgetary restrictions.

Furthermore, the creation of the common pool of valued resources results in the tragedy of the commons and the chronic overuse of resources that in a governmental context spawns huge debts and deficit spending. We all wish to advance our own objectives; when it seems we can do so without dipping into our own personal resources, many will try to even more vigilantly, hoping to get something for free. It would be foolish not to do so, especially if we are all being told that a good society must be run this way. The market failure that has been supposedly remedied—and that could have been corrected by the market's own mechanisms—is thus merely compounded. On the market, genuine failures to provide what the consumer wants yield loss, not profit.

Admittedly, in cases of negligence in the free market, there is always the instrument of liability and malpractice law, which focuses on punishing or seeking redress from actually guilty parties rather than punishing and obstructing everyone across the board by endless regulation.

The Myth of Positive Rights
We do not have positive rights unless we are owed servitude from our fellow citizens. Granted, our parents and perhaps some next of kin have some responsibility to help us reach maturity. But thereafter we ought to secure what

we need and want by way of voluntary exchange, not government protection of positive rights. Positive rights are impossible to protect consistently anyway, and attempts to enforce them would thwart the protection of our "negative" rights—our rights to life, liberty, and property. Assume both that doctors have the right to liberty and that patients have the right to be healed. Now if a doctor wants to, say, attend his daughter's graduation while someone down the street wants to be healed by him, we have a conflict of rights, one negative, one positive. Whose "right" prevails? And on what basis is that going to be decided, now that the system of rights is corrupted and incoherent?

Individuals have the natural right to their life, liberty, and property, to list just the main principles of proper social relations. Many other values are vital for them, but no one owes them these values, except, perhaps, parents and other intimates. Only children have positive rights, as well as those who entered into a contract of their own free choice. Thus, efforts to protect positive rights by way of government regulation are utterly misguided. That would hamper and in some cases even destroy the individual's ability to pursue his/her own values and sustain his/her own life, and force citizens into a relationship of subservience to one another. This is arguably immoral.[23]

Restoring Judicial Efficiency

Consider the troublesome case of judicial inefficiency. It's a real problem, but not one that can be solved by government regulation—which merely produces discontentment and injustice. Government cannot rationally decide which firm or individual should be entitled to dump harmful wastes onto the bodies and properties of others. It cannot establish collective priorities for individuals, who are diverse and may flourish in utterly different ways.

Accordingly, when we are confronted with the problem of, say, air pollution, the best approach to follow would be the one offered by classical liberals in their theory of basic human rights to life, liberty, and property. Dumping simply may not be undertaken when no permission can be obtained, unless it can be shown that the result does not increase the prevailing risk of harm to individuals. Manufacturing firms that pollute make use of other people who did not give their permission. The polluters avoid the full cost of their activities by stealing the resources, and sometimes even the lives, of others. The importance of one's own projects and the benefits they yield are not sufficient to warrant exploiting others in this way. Jobs are important, yes, and so is getting from one side of town to the other to attend the opera or the PTA meeting—but no matter how important such projects may be, they may not properly be undertaken at the expense of the rights of other people.

The way to control pollution, then, is by protecting personal autonomy and by privatizing as much as possible. In areas where this is difficult, we must follow a policy similar to that adopted in cases of highly communicable diseases: namely, quarantine. Those who cannot perform their important tasks without violating the rights of others must desist, period. A factory that can only operate by imposing serious harm on the surrounding population would not be permitted to exist, any more than a person with leprosy would be allowed to wander around the local mall. The most widely applied alternative of following the results of social cost-benefit calculations would violate the rights of many innocent persons.

So, the criminal justice system must develop means by which to determine when homicide, assault, negligence, and other forms of rights violation occur in such problematic areas and refrain from hoping that government regulation can solve the problem for it.

No Moral–Political Room for State Regulation
Generally, government regulation assumes that some people happen to be superior to others in intellectual and moral gifts, that these superior people can be identified, and that it is wise for them to exercise control over the daily lives of the rest of us.

When the government at any level regulates, it practices a form of tyranny. It is not the sort we usually dub by that term, like Soviet or national socialism, which were massive, totalitarian, and all-encompassing. Rather, it is tyranny by constantly nagging people in nearly every profession, one more petty, less dramatic, and less dire to be sure. But a tyranny of nagging is still tyranny. And sometimes it can be very destructive.

It is also unjust. Government regulation aims to prevent mishaps by forcing people to act in ways government experts believe are safer, fairer, and less difficult to understand than what government believes life should be. It is what we might call a form of preventative justice, by exactly the means that the criminal law prohibits—a kind of prior restraint. The regulations are imposed, sometimes at enormous cost to the regulated (as well as to the intended beneficiaries), prior to any evidence of any wrongdoing by the regulated parties. In other words, innocent merchants, producers, and others are being made to bear costs even though they have done nothing to deserve them. This is unjust.

The criminal justice system in a free society should not seek to restrain people because they *might* behave harmfully, injuriously, and/or dangerously,

LIBRARY
UNIVERSITY OF ST. FRANCIS
JOLIET, ILLINOIS

but only if they *do*—or are highly likely to—so behave. Everyone can choose to abstain from such behavior. Recognizing this, the criminal law of a free society ought not attempt to second-guess how people might behave and then restrain them on the basis of a prediction.

Yet this is, arguably, the kind of second-guessing that government regulation of industry, transportation, and various other professions amounts to. It does this when it treats people as if the government were a parent who is obliged to make sure we do not run any risks. But the government is not made up of superior people with the moral authority to guide what we do in life.[24]

Proponents of government regulation think government must prevent bad things from happening, even if our rights are violated in the process. But in a free society, only when harm has actually been done to others—or when there is a clear and present danger of such harm being done—does government have the authority to act against a person's plans, purposes, and wishes. The mere abstract possibility of harm is no justification for government action.

Norms of Doing Business Abroad

As our final example in this selection of topics in business ethics, we will take a brief look at the ethics of doing business abroad. The focus here will be on some of the troubling issues that sometimes arise in connection with doing business where labor is cheap. There are, of course, other business ethics matters that arise in connection with foreign trade. Environmental laws tend to be lax in Third World nations, and there is no protection offered against such practices as sexual or racial discrimination, even when these breach contracts and should be prohibited. Many taboos exist that may conflict with business objectives, so how might one deal with those if one finds them, especially if they are superstitions?

These problems will not be investigated, though the principles that emerge in our discussions ought to serve as guides to solving them. Instead, we will concentrate on labor topics. Putting it plainly first, an outstanding problem about doing business abroad for many companies is that the terms of employment are often very favorable for them but, it is of the near-conscripted kind.

This is one of the dilemmas facing major corporations, as well as all consumers, who are purchasing low-cost products made by workers in, say, China, Indonesia, Malaysia, Korea, or Mexico. This low cost arises from being complicit in the serious mistreatment of workers. Just how complicit and what might be done about it is morally quite problematic.

Clearly, some of these countries are, as the Soviet Union or South Africa used to be, tyrannies of a greater or lesser variety, ruled by an elite that has no concern for the basic human rights of the citizenry, including workers assigned to jobs involving trade with essentially capitalist, free market–type companies.

Some have dismissed this fact on the grounds that only Westerners, with their democratic bias, find something wrong with such systems, revealing, thereby, a cultural bias. As some of the leaders of these countries noted at the 1996 Vienna United Nations Human Rights Conference, the West is wrong to impose its measure of proper governance on all the countries of the world.

But the problem is not, as the expression goes, a matter of Asian (or Latin or some other) versus Western values.[25] At such a basic level, cultural differences are not relevant—the issue of how human beings need to be treated cannot be dismissed on grounds of cultural relativism. The plain fact is that many Western consumers wish to have it both ways—standing up for basic principles of human community life as citizens while benefiting from economic opportunities as consumers. These opportunities would probably be insignificant or nonexistent in many cases without the violations of basic moral and political principles in the countries where the cost of production, labor, transportation, and legal compliance are all quite low.[26]

No country is "pure of heart," that is, completely clean politically, let alone morally. But a country that tolerates or even supports, for example, slave labor is certainly worse than those that do not. That is elementary.

Still, the issue of how to relate to such a country cannot be ruled out since countries can change and even the worst of them have some valuable aspects that make contact with their people worthwhile. So we can ask: How should we approach doing business with the people of, say, China given the country's nature as a greater or lesser tyranny? Other professions are no less confronted with such issues: How should journalists deal with countries wherein the rulers censor the news to shield themselves from serious scrutiny and criticism?

It is the task of the discipline of professional ethics to examine the ethical challenges posed by distinct regions of human activity. In the field of business, this includes coming to terms with ethical challenges faced abroad. What special ethical problems arise for people—for managers and employees of companies, firms, and so on—while they embark on their commercial tasks in countries and cultures other than their own?

Laws are not uniform throughout the world, not even within one's own country. In the United States, a relatively free market tradition of business and trade prevails. This means that the laws within the United States, to a greater extent than elsewhere, tend to protect the right to private property and the integrity of terms of trade and contractual arrangements. This means that negative individual rights may not be violated with impunity. Government interference in the United States, and to a greater extent in other Western countries, is substantial but exists as something of an anomaly, an exception to the general ethos or style of doing commercial work. In short, in contrast to other societies, the United States is a near-capitalist economy, as are, to a lesser extent, many other so-called Western countries.

The governments of most societies are not based on liberal principles of social living—namely, respect for and protection of individual rights to life, liberty, and property—rather, they are frequently the owners and operators of business enterprises. This makes it possible to carry out trade while the right to freedom for the citizens is seriously compromised—for example, via the use of slave labor, heavy subsidization and monopolization throughout various industries, and a near-command economy that is loosened only because the government sees that as useful for a given purpose.

Professionals doing business have as their special goal to make their enterprise prosper and to earn a profit. They tend to focus on this goal as against others in their professional thinking and conduct. Of course, artists striving to express their visions do no less, or educators, scientists, and athletes. Normally, when no moral dilemmas arise from embarking on one's professional tasks, this is unobjectionable. When scientists search for truth in their specialty, it is not morally objectionable that they neglect, say, justice or generosity while wearing their scientist hats, as it were. Educators, even as they talk at great length about social problems, do not at that time do anything much about them. They are teaching others to think about them, who may or may not put this to practical use.

However, people often become single-minded and acquire "tunnel vision" as they fulfill some special role in their lives. Even as parents, friends, or citizens, we are often willing to overlook considerations bearing on our general, broad human—that is, moral—responsibilities in the course of pursuing our goals. The task of living a decent human life is often compromised by focusing so intently on special objectives. In business, as in other professions, this can result in being willing to achieve goals, for example, to make money, from circumstances that involve serious moral improprieties, even outright violations of basic human rights. When scientists use unwilling subjects for experimentation, educators metamorphose into indoctrinators, or those in business become, even if only indirectly, thieves or masters over unwilling subjects—they still see themselves as pursuing their professional goals but are, in fact, doing so at great moral cost. And if one realizes that the greatest and most important goal for every person is to excel as a human being and to maintain moral integrity, this comes to no less than self-betrayal, in the last analysis.[27]

Suppose some state firm in China, run by the military arm of the government, uses coerced labor and thus can produce various goods or services at far below market cost. Workers and managers are forced by their government to take low pay and the absence of organized labor makes collective bargaining impossible. Furthermore, the absence of a free market prevents wage competition that could lead to higher (or lower) pay.

The usual response to the claim that it is unethical to do business with such organizations is that if a given firm refuses to do business for various moral reasons, others will take advantage of the opportunities at hand. Or, alternatively, we are told that it would betray stockholders to forgo doing business abroad when facing clear economic opportunities. (Some invoke Friedman's thesis about the sole moral responsibility of business being making a profit, yet even Friedman modifies this by mentioning that this needs to be done within the rules of the game, ethics, and just law!)

None of the excuses offered are relevant to whether one ought to conduct business ethically, any more than it would excuse any other sort of conduct involving the violation of someone's basic rights. When a medical researcher, who uses unwilling subjects, intones about the greater good his/her results will reap for members of future generations, this does not justify treating his/her research subjects immorally. If one makes unwilling use of members of current generations for the sake of those in the future, those in the future are certainly at serious risk rather than being benefited. Stealing and other such violations of individual rights can often be economically or otherwise advantageous, at least in the short run. Muggers, plagiarizers, embezzlers, bank robbers, murderers, and so on all pursue their goals of obtaining wealth or other kinds of advantage but the means by which they do it are morally and thus decisively wrong. This is no less so when people in business abroad pursue policies that are complicit in violating the rights of human beings in foreign countries.

There is one way that such apparent complicity could be justified: If the gains made from such "business" are substantially devoted to altering or reforming the situation for the better or to fighting the policies that violate individual rights. Those who profited from doing business in the old apartheid South Africa from that unjust institution were exonerated if they also seriously contributed to abolishing apartheid. Without directing the profits in substantial measure to the eradication of the immoral policies that made them possible, those who reap the profits would be fully complicit in rights violations.

The bottom line, then, is that if businesses embark on commerce that involves otherwise unavoidable unethical elements, they must make up or atone for this by contributing to the abolition of those elements. Without that, their hands are seriously morally tainted. For although it is morally proper for people in business to focus on prosperity, that is, their professional commitment, it is not right to lose sight of other moral considerations. The end to which they devote themselves is morally unexceptional but the means certainly aren't.

All of this can get complicated but the fundamentals—abstaining from contributing to the violation of basic individual rights—must never be lost sight of.

Foreign and Domestic Trade Dumping

The matter of trade restrictions in international trade poses some thorny problems. When a country like France, Japan, or Germany subsidizes an industry, thereby enabling firms to sell their products to customers abroad for a price lower than the unsubsidized full cost, the specter of unfair trade or "dumping" raises its ugly head. This is often lamented by people who work in similar industries in the countries where domestic firms do not enjoy government subsidies. If some country gives tax breaks or subsidies to, say, shoe manufacturers so their shoes can be sold abroad for a lower price than domestic manufacturers can afford to charge, the firms in the country that do not get such breaks or subsidies will be understandably upset.

This is often the source of serious tensions among countries, at times leading even to outright war. Certainly, diplomatic relations suffer considerably, as they have done so, for example, between the United States and Japan. Because most countries engage in such interventions in the marketplace, including the United States, it is very difficult to fix blame precisely and to recommend remedial public policy. It is also tempting to escalate the tension by increasing tariffs, restrictions, quotas, and the like. Once you add to this situation the factor of diverse environmental regulations, labor laws, and so on, it is easy to see how things can get so muddied that no consistent solution seems feasible.

There are domestic analogies to the international situation that may assist our understanding. In a college town we know of, for example, there were several coffeehouses. One of these was seriously subsidized by the parents of the owner. It was reminiscent of some of the coffeehouses in New York, San

Francisco, and even Paris. It could not, however, carry its own weight at full-price trade since the business was sparse. Yet, because of the parents' initial willingness to fund the daughter's venture, the place managed to keep up, at least for some time, in the face of stiff competition from other more established shops.

Certainly, this could be taken as quite unfair: Why should the competing coffeehouses have to tolerate a competitor that does not really have to meet fully its own expenses? Maybe they should petition the city council and insist that the subsidized house be charged an extra tax because it receives the parents' subsidy. Perhaps the suppliers should be made to sell at a higher price to the subsidized coffeehouse.

Yet, none of that would eliminate the unfairness. More generally, customers often patronize an establishment, despite its higher prices, because they like the staff working there or because they enjoy the atmosphere or the decor. There are all kinds of "unfairness" that permeate the marketplace. Employers offer differential benefits and wages, and the locations of the workplace can be more or less convenient. Furthermore, those customers who simply like some establishment out of habit or prejudice can, as a result, keep patronizing it instead of going to the competitors that do not receive "unfair" breaks.

In international trade, too, the customers of some countries enjoy the benefits gained from domestic tax policies, subsidies, and the like. If restrictions are placed on the imported products, the customers will lose their opportunities for receiving what they want from these products at the price being charged.

To be sure, there are wronged parties involved. But who are they?

It seems clear that the only parties who are really wronged are the citizens of the countries that give the tax breaks or offer the subsidies, not the customers or even the firms in the countries in which the "dumping" occurs. For the firms might have stiff competition some other way—as when employees abroad charge a lower wage for their work or when customers around the world stick with some product for sentimental reasons and thus keep some firm in business even though its prices are higher than those of others. It is utterly futile for governments to try to establish some "level playing field" in trade, as in any other area of human life. This is evident from the fact that even in adjudicated disputes about product liabilities or malpractice, the process of fixing blame and determining damages is extremely hard, even with all the machinery of the judicial process at the disposal of the various parties. Certainly, governments have nowhere near the particular information and research facility brought to bear on a court case so as to figure out just where responsibility for injustice lies and what burdens should be imposed on the culprits.

In the end, the only way to create a reasonably fair international market is to set a clear example of free trade. It is not possible for the United States or any other government to change the internal policies of another country, given the principle of national self-determination. So what is left is insisting on the integrity of the market at home. In the end, this is what will teach them, nothing else.

Notes

1. We agree with Jim Sadowsky here who suggests that when workers who had been serfs before came into the city, they were disadvantaged by capitalists who often inherited their royal holdings rather than earned them through entrepreneurial effort. See James Sadowsky, "Private Property and Collective Ownership," in *The Libertarian Alternative*, ed. Tibor R. Machan (Chicago: Nelson-Hall, 1973).

2. For example, see Allan A. Kennedy, *The End of Shareholder Value* (Cambridge, MA: Perseus, 2000). See also the many articles promoting the stakeholder idea in publications such as the magazine *Business Ethics*.

3. This is the law now in much of Europe—such as Germany, Italy, and elsewhere—part of what is called the "third way," an economic system combining elements of socialism and capitalism.

4. Anthony F. Buono and Lawrence T. Nichols, "Stockholder and Stakeholder Interpretations of Business Social Role," in *Business Ethics*, ed. W. Michael Hoffman and Jennifer Mills Moore (New York: McGraw Hill, 1990), 171. It would be interesting to see if this criterion for what may be subject to government regulation would apply to, say, books, works of art, newspapers columns, films, and so on, which are all given firm protection against government intrusion by way of the First Amendment. Actually, some militant feminists argue that that is just what ought to be done when it comes to print or broadcast products deemed pornographic. See Catherine MacKinnon, *Only Words* (Cambridge, MA: Harvard University Press, 1994).

5. Despite what so many who follow Marx and Georg Hegel have argued, the principle of private property rights predates modernity by several centuries. Aristotle defended it, as did William of Ockham. For a discussion of its role in human community life in the fourteenth century, see Cary J. Nederman, "Political Theory and Subjective Rights in Fourteenth-Century England," *The Review of Politics* 58 (spring 1996): 323–344.

6. In a widely discussed essay, Milton Friedman argues that the sole responsibility of corporations is to their stockholders, provided the rules of the game are not violated (i.e., the law is followed). See Milton Friedman, "The Social Responsibility of Business Is to Increase Its Profits," *New York Times Magazine*, 13 September 1970.

7. It is blatantly unfair for popular television programs such as *LA Law*, *The Practice*, and *The West Wing* to feature nearly all corporations as villains and all plaintiffs as well as most government regulators of business suing them as heroes.

8. The magazine *Business Ethics*, now in its second decade of publication, is subtitled *Insider's Report on Corporate Responsibility*. The implication is that when companies do good business, this doesn't qualify as having fulfilled their corporate responsibility—they need to do pro bono work for that. Yet, why isn't this true of scientists, educators, or wage laborers?

9. Friedman objects to the idea of the social responsibility of corporations partly because corporate managers haven't a clue what socially responsible conduct, apart from fulfilling their fiduciary duties, would amount to. Friedman, "Social Responsibility of Business." It is a problem, in any case, to determine just what the public interest is.

10. Ralph Nader, Mark Green, and Joel Seligman, *Taming the Giant Corporations* (New York: Norton, 1976).

11. Milton Friedman, "The Social Responsibility of Business," in *Capitalism and Freedom*, by Milton Friedman (Chicago: University of Chicago Press, 1961).

12. Fred D. Miller Jr. and John Ahrens, "The Social Responsibility of Corporations," in *Commerce and Morality*, ed. Tibor R. Machan (Lanham, MD: Rowman & Littlefield, 1988), 156–157.

13. For more on this, see Tibor R. Machan, *Generosity: Virtue in Civil Society* (Washington, DC: Cato Institute, 1998).

14. Miller and Ahrens, "Social Responsibility of Corporations," 155.

15. See Steven Kelman, "Regulation and Paternalism," in *Rights and Regulation*, ed. M. Bruce Johnson and Tibor R. Machan (Cambridge, MA: Ballinger, 1983).

16. "'Sovereign immunity' is [the] doctrine precluding the institution of a suit against the sovereign [government] without its consent. "Though commonly believed to be rooted in English law, it is actually rooted in the inherent nature of power and the ability of those who hold power to shield themselves. In England it was predicated on the concept that 'the sovereign can do no wrong,' a concept developed and enforced by—guess who? However, since the American revolution explictedly [sic] rejected this interesting idea, the American rulers had to come up with another rationale to protect their power. One they came up with is that the 'sovereign is exempt from suit [on the] practical ground that there can be no legal right against the authority that makes the law on which the right depends.' 205 U.S. 349, 353" (http://www.lectlaw.com/def2/s103.htm).

17. "There is a multitude of cases in which governments, with general approbation, assume powers and execute functions for which no reason can be assigned except the simple one, that they conduce to general convenience. We may take as an example, the function (which is a monopoly too) of coining money. This is assumed for no more recondite purpose than that of saving to individuals the trouble, delay, and expense of weighing and assaying. No one, however, even of those most jealous of state interference, has objected to this as an improper exercise of the powers of

government." John Stuart Mill, *Principles of Political Economy*, rev. ed., vol. 5 (New York: Colonial, 1899), chapter 1. All we have to say is Mill, meet the modern libertarian movement.

18. "I have already more than once adverted to the case of the gas and water companies, among which, though perfect freedom is allowed to competition, none really takes place, and practically they are found to be even more irresponsible, and unapproachable by individual complaints, than the government. . . . In the case of these particular services, the reasons preponderate in favor of their being performed, like the paving and cleansing of the streets, not certainly by the general government of the state, but by the municipal authorities of the town. . . . But in the many analogous cases which it is best to resign to voluntary agency, the community needs some other security for the first performance of the service than the interests of the managers; and it is the part of government, either to subject the business to reasonable conditions for the general advantage, or to retain such power over it, that the profits of the monopoly may at least be obtained for the public. This applies to the case of a road, a canal, or a railway. These are always, in a great degree, practical monopolies; and a government which concedes such monopoly unreservedly to a private company, does much the same thing as if it allowed an individual or an association to levy any tax they chose, for their own benefit, on all the malt produced in the country, or on all the cotton imported into it." See Mill, *Principles of Political Economy*, 5:463.

19. "Our wealth in the first [the private sector] is not only in startling contrast with the meagerness of the latter [the public sector], but our wealth in privately produced goods is, to a marked degree, the cause of crisis in the supply of public services." See John Kenneth Galbraith, *The Affluent Society* (Boston: Houghton Mifflin, 1958). But is this not the doublespeak of the court intellectual?

20. Alan Gewirth, "Replies to My Critics," in *Gewirth's Ethical Rationalism*, ed. Edward Regis Jr. (Chicago: University of Chicago Press, 1984), 227–228.

21. See Henry Shue, *Basic Rights* (Princeton, NJ: Princeton University Press, 1980); Stephen Holmes and Cass R. Sunstein, *The Cost of Rights: Why Liberty Depends on Taxes* (New York: Norton, 1999).

22. Kenneth J. Arrow, "Two Cheers for Government Regulation," *Harper's* (March 1981): 20.

23. For more on this, see Tibor R. Machan, "The Non-existence of Basic Welfare Rights," in *Moral Controversies*, ed. Steven Jay Gold (Belmont, CA: Wadsworth, 1993), 413–419.

24. Kelman's claim that in some cases governments can achieve taking precautionary measures better than consumers and employees is true only if one forgets about the emergence of market-based cautionary institutions, such as watchdog agencies, consumer organizations, insurance companies, and so on. This is well known by many who support government regulation as evidenced by their insistence that they are acting "for the community," not to advance some private objectives. The use of "we" in this connection is telling.

25. For more on this, see Amartya Sen, "Human Rights and Asian Values," in *Business Ethics in the Global Market*, ed. Tibor R. Machan (Stanford, CA: Hoover Institution Press, 1999).

26. For more on the details of business ethics abroad, as well as this particular topic, see Tibor R. Machan, ed., *Business Ethics in the Global Market* (Stanford, CA: Hoover Institution Press, 1999).

27. This is where equality (being "created equal") is indeed vital in politics—no one has any justification for claiming more authority than over oneself and one's own.

CHAPTER ONE

~

Business Ethics—True and False

Expectations

In the former Soviet bloc countries, one often saw cartoons depicting Western "capitalists" as cigar-chewing fat cats, crushing workers and all beneath
them with their ruthless greed and reckless hedonism.[1]

Most people saw through this, of course, because they also read lots of U.S.
books, mostly fiction, which conveyed a very different sense of American
life. Zane Gray, Max Brand, Earl Stanley Gardner, Mark Twain, and the lot
depicted an American society in which most folks had a shot at doing well
in their lives or at least living life as they chose. It was well known, of course,
that this was fiction but many had the sense that those in the West and in
the United States, especially, at least aspired to those romantic ideals of individualism with a very human face.

Once these same people came West, they soon discovered that what
was caricature to the communists was actually serious conviction for many
Western intellectuals. It was a very shocking awakening to find that nearly
all of them, both Left and Right but for different reasons, had a demean-
ing view of commerce and business. This didn't make sense, considering
that business was also deeply entrenched in U.S. culture—nearly everything that needed financial support, from education to the fine arts, from
science to politics, and from athletics to recreation sought the support of
business.

Ethics and Law

To start with, the problem with many intellectuals lies with how they understand ethics or morality, not so much law. After all, law is more or less the explicit will of the governing body of a society—democratic, monarchical, dictatorial, what have you. But that will is shaped by ideas concerning what is right and wrong for people to do.

For example, beginning in 1920 alcohol was prohibited in the United States through a constitutional amendment because some believed it right to forbid others to consume liquor. More drastically, Jews were exterminated in Germany because many people accepted the leadership of someone who held that the purity of the race was a sufficient reason to murder people. In the Soviet Union the government abolished private property and herded millions to their death because powerful people believed it morally permissible to sacrifice human beings for the sake of what they took to be a future paradise on Earth.

So it is not law that's of primary interest in a discussion of business, but the more basic issue of ethics and the different ways human beings have answered the questions: How should I live, act, and conduct myself, as a human being? What are the correct standards of proper, good conduct for me and other human beings? If these questions can be understood and answered, then law would in the end take care of itself, especially in a nearly democratic country.

Ethics and Ethical Systems

Ethics is a field of inquiry that's quite problematic. When one says, "He is acting unethically," the meaning of this is hardly self-evident. There are competing ethical theories and systems, and this is evident in the widespread disagreement about what is the right thing to do. Among the philosophers who concentrate on ethics, there is just as much disagreement. Yet, there is also a good deal of overlap among the competing answers given to the question of ethics.

Some people, many in the social sciences, believe that ethics is a bogus field, like astrology, witchcraft, or demonology. We can see this view widely embraced today, even while others complain about ethical problems. For example, the *New York Times* ran a discussion a while back about how the human mind developed and only two positions were taken seriously: either we are hardwired and everything flows from our genetic makeup (nature), or our brains are flexible and the environment shapes them (nurture). The idea that individuals have something to contribute to their own thinking and, thus, behavior didn't even get one line in this report! So, the basis of the criminal law, namely, individual responsibility, seems for many to lack any scientific support.

But this idea is problematic. Many think that the hard sciences are the only rational field of study, so if we are to understand human life this understanding must use the methods (developed by Isaac Newton and others) that we follow in the hard sciences—or, actually, used to follow until recently. That means we need to explain what people do by reference to the various forces acting on them—genetic or environmental, for instance.

Then, also, even if this doesn't tell the whole story, it is completed once we add the (Kantian) idea that in the area of our "inner selves" we are free. We can intend to do well but that is all—it is the thought that counts and actual behavior is not really in our control. Free will is a kind of spiritual issue. So, what counts for the most, ethically or morally, is what someone intends or means—the categorical imperative our will accepts. On this view, what the person actually does and the behavior engaged in is morally irrelevant. "Feeling another's pain" is about all that can be done; doing anything to alleviate it is something else because in the physical, empirical areas the laws of nature dictate what happens and the human will is impotent.

From these kinds of thoughts, it emerges that those of our actions that produce good results for ourselves are morally irrelevant. Consequences do not count, only intentions. Moreover, such matters really cannot be dealt with scientifically, so they may even have to remain a matter of faith and religion.

This situation makes business unlikely to emerge as having any moral standing. Actually, not even medicine, nor indeed any other productive profession, can have moral standing if consequences do not matter. With medicine, though, one can focus on the fact that professionals mean well, are impartial, and are not focused on their own well-being. This is not possible to imagine about commerce, where people usually want to make a good deal to benefit themselves.[2]

Commerce and business, then, are seen to be primarily egoistic and self-interested, and so clearly not impartial. Business is concerned with prosperity, usually for the acting agent or those close to the acting agent. Such a moral outlook bodes ill for business. Prudence, which is the virtue in terms of which one ought to take decent care of oneself, lost its status as a moral virtue and became a kind of inner compulsion.

Now it needs to be noted that though prominent, this neo-Kantian view of what is right for us to do wasn't always in vogue and is no longer unchallenged. In ancient Greece, Aristotle thought that ethics was needed to guide us toward happiness. Oddly, it was Adam Smith who made this point most explicitly. In *Inquiry into the Nature and Causes of the Wealth of Nations*, Smith says:

> Ancient moral philosophy proposed to investigate wherein consisted the happiness and perfection of a man, considered not only as an individual, but as the member of a family, or a state, and of the great society of mankind. In that philosophy, the duties of human life were treated of as subservient to the happiness and perfection of human life. But, when moral as well as natural philosophy came to be taught only as subservient to theology, the duties of human life were treated of as chiefly subservient to the happiness of a life to come. In the ancient philosophy, the perfection of virtue was represented as necessarily productive to the person who possessed it, of the most perfect happiness in this life. In the modern philosophy, it was frequently represented as almost always inconsistent with any degree of happiness in this life, and heaven was to be earned by penance and mortification, not by the liberal, generous, and spirited conduct of a man. By far the most important of all the different branches of philosophy became in this manner by far the most corrupted.[3]

Now the ethics of Aristotle didn't quite include striving for prosperity as a major ingredient of striving for happiness because Aristotle was, well, an intellectual elitist. For him ultimately, only pure abstract thinkers could become happy.

Nonetheless, this is a major improvement on the ethics of Immanuel Kant who denied that happiness was the goal of ethics. Once we revise Aristotle's ethics in light of a humanistic, naturalistic perspective, and add that not just the intellectual life but human life in all its fullness, including its economic dimension, should be part of happiness, it follows that productive professions such as business also have moral standing. After all, what do people in business do but strive to achieve prosperity? While prosperity may not be all there is to human happiness, it is clearly a part of it—just ask the poor!

So, we have two different ideas of what it is to be ethical: the first says we must be indifferent to good, earthly things for ourselves, even for our intimates, and worry only about following impartial rules. Egalitarianism is the result of this for politics and law—as the work of John Rawls shows. Since business is competitive—so that some do very well, some a bit less so, some moderately, some not well at all, and others outright badly—business does not fit into this view of human morality. The only way those in business can redeem themselves is if they engage in pro bono activities, philanthropy, "socially responsible" projects, and the like.

The second view, however, implies that business is an honorable profession, no less so than medicine, art, or science: it aims for some ends that contribute to human happiness.

But this view is out of vogue today, especially among many academic philosophers, including many of those who teach business ethics. Instead, they embrace the Kantian view and regard prudence and caring for oneself, including economically, at best amoral, but more likely greedy and callous.

Assumptions of Business Ethics

Suppose we reject the Kantian idea and contend that business is indeed an honorable profession? Does this mean that people in business can do no wrong?

Clearly not, but they would generally be quite worthy of respect and even admiration when they carry out their professional tasks conscientiously and successfully. Even without any extracurricular deeds of charity or generosity, those in business, as those in education or science, could be seen as embarking on morally worthy tasks.

There are, however, pitfalls in business, as in any other profession, which is why business ethics is an important field of study, a subfield of professional ethics. Under the Kantian view, though, business ethics is what so often is said about it, an oxymoron. For anything so directly concerned with self-promotion couldn't possibly be justified as being motivated impartially.

With business as an honorable profession, it can now be appreciated that the field has some unique tasks where one faces temptations to go wrong, to become corrupted, but no more or less so than in medicine, art, science, and education. Yet, this is not how most ethicists see the field.

Business ethics is taught in our time mostly as a kind of business bashing. What the courses and books teach is that business needs taming because it is a kind of wild beast, driven by a motive of self-regard and profit. Such amorality needs to be civilized and socialized.

Thus, much of so-called business ethics focuses on public policy—law and government regulation. What in other fields may be taken to be ethical pitfalls are, in business, addressed by some government regulatory agency. This isn't so, evidently, with religion or journalism, at least in the United States, because our system of law prohibits the regimentation of professionals in these fields. But then those fields do not face the obstacle of having prudence as their main justification.

However, if we acknowledge that business is honorable and does not require constant paternalistic government intervention, we run afoul of political thinking predominant in academe. The reason is not difficult to see.

Ethics assumes that people have free will and that the choice between right and wrong conduct must itself be free, not coerced, compelled by others. That precludes a great deal of government intervention—what is tantamount to prior restraint—now on the books. Even more controversially—and here many in business join the skeptics—there would have to be firm, stable standards by which business conduct can be guided and evaluated. Some things might well be wrong to choose, even though they could not be subject to prohibition.

One could argue, for example, that racial prejudice in business is morally wrong, not just unlawful. Sexism, bigotry, unfairness, callous management, stereotyping customers in advertising, peddling risky stuff to children, taking advantage of political favoritism, exploiting tyrannical systems abroad so as to get low-cost labor, and so on are all likely ethically objectionable, but that many people in business might not wish to give up because of the temporary benefits gained from them.[4]

If one regards business as lacking moral standing, then ethics is irrelevant and everyone in business looks at most only to what is legally permitted. If China has favorite nation status, then dealing with it is permissible, never mind any slave labor being used in its manufacturing plants. If South Africa is not under official sanctions, then why not take advantage of the cheap black labor there? If the law permits lobbying for protectionism, then William F. Farley, the chief executive officer of Fruit of the Loom, can exclaim, "I make no apology for fighting for the interest of Fruit of the Loom's shareholders and the American workers we employ," as he asks the government to deploy restraint of trade against foreign importers. Never mind that this is really nothing other than sending extortionists to "level the playing field."

Bottom Line and Other Goals

Let's take a brief look at what business ethics actually comes to, seen from the neo-Aristotelian perspective we sketched earlier, wherein ethics is a life-enhancing system of guiding principles.

To start with, the professional task of people in business is to make the enterprise prosper, first and foremost. Why? Because they are usually hired to provide this service to consumers who, in turn, are practicing the virtue of prudence in making sure they are prospering in life.

Thus, for people in business to do their jobs well is itself morally praiseworthy, not simply shrewd and clever. But, if one pursues business affairs in terms that are irrelevant to furthering the success of an enterprise—such as suiting one's racial or sexual prejudices, nepotism, or bigotry—one violates business ethics, for such indulgences undermine the objective of the profession.

Accordingly, keeping the bottom line in focus is a moral, sometimes even a legal, responsibility, not just a "natural drive" in business. Losing sight of the bottom line, that is, that goal of prosperity, is itself a kind of moral negligence and betraying it is morally wrong and a form of malpractice.

But business ethics isn't the only area of ethics about which people in business need to be concerned. This holds for any other professional ethics because we are not just professionals but human beings who ought to live morally whatever we do and wherever we do it. In business, the bottom line is the first but not the only consideration. People in business, as in other fields, also have family obligations, citizenship responsibilities, fraternal duties, and so on.

So, while business ethics is important to follow, it is not all that matters for those in business. However, from the Kantian perspective, people in business are already condemned to doing something at most amoral but probably morally shady, for their motives are deemed morally tainted.

Since it is proper and commendable in business to focus first on the bottom line, those who teach the contrary betray a disdain, moral contempt for the field, not a concern for its ethics! The claim that profit can be used for good or ill—so how can it be a good thing?—can be answered, but keep in mind that medicine, law, science, and all other professions can also be misused to support what is wrong. Yet, because they generally and basically foster good ends, they are all honorable.

Entrepreneurship and Ethics

A serious temptation of those in business arises because entrepreneurial initiative requires assertiveness. This drive, though proper, can get corrupted from lack of care and degenerate into aggressiveness and reckless disregard for other objectives about which human beings should be concerned. Again, this is true of artists who, aside from being tempted by plagiarism or repetition, can also neglect their families, or of scientists who fudge evidence and also become so absorbed that they neglect politics and friendship, or of politicians who serve special, vested interest rather than the true public interest that has the security of every citizen's rights in focus.

What might be termed "excessive eagerness" in business, however, is quite visible, so it is easy to focus on it unfairly. When artists cheat by copying the styles and ideas of fellow artists, hardly anyone knows. Even scientific fraud is very tough to spot as is the misconduct of some educators who exploit their captive and vulnerable young audiences by pitching their favorite doctrines, rather than teaching the students to think critically in their disciplines.

Conclusion

So why is business approached so hypocritically? People place it under a moral cloud but fervently wish for its fruits: Praise Mother Teresa and then hit the shopping mall?

Part of the answer is that many people haven't understood that ethics must guide our lives to success as human beings here on Earth. The "hereafter" is essentially out of our hands, a matter of mystery and perhaps God's grace. What we are responsible for is to achieve our human form of happiness here on Earth. The various professions, including business, can be instrumental for that purpose. Thus, business must be given its due, as are science, art, medicine, education, and the law. Once this is understood, then a bona fide ethical perspective on business will become possible.

Before concluding this discussion of the basic framework of business ethics, mention should be made of the position often appealed to by business ethics scholars, namely, David Hume's influential moral conventionalism.[5] This is the idea that there are no firm ethical principles by which to guide human conduct and institutions. Instead, all we have are the various practices and customs in the regions where people live and conduct their affairs, including commerce.

Hume advanced this view in correct opposition to the prospect of a rigid rationalistic ethics, one that gives strict guidance every step of the way to human beings embarking on some activity. He thought such a deductive approach to ethics is hopeless since one cannot logically derive how one ought to act based solely on the things one knows about the world.

However, Hume's alternative yields the problem that conventions are so different in different places around the globe. How can there be the needed measure of common ground when conventional beliefs are all that one has to go on? This would be akin to expecting the same cuisine or type of dance to be practiced everywhere.

A better analogy to ethics would be medicine or nutrition. Ethical principles cannot be relative to a culture the way cuisine, style of dress, or music are, not ultimately. Otherwise, a cross-cultural understanding of what is the right way to do business would be impossible. Yet, we see that such understanding is at least approximated widely, explaining why international business is conducted reasonably successfully. Complaints about unethical conduct and proposed remedies can be quite intelligible.

It is human beings, after all, who are engaging in commerce, a rather constant, ongoing activity throughout history. Commerce isn't unique to some particular culture, except perhaps in its levels of intensity or degree of complexity.

In any case, the conventionalist approach to ethics rests on quicksand—conventions differ between families, regions, countries, ethnic communities, religions, and the like. Just as medicine cannot rest on convention, neither can ethics.

Thus, to judge whether people in business are conducting themselves ethically we need to consider the virtues that arise from an understanding of human nature. How should people act? To answer this, we need to ask what kind of beings they are. They are volitionally conscious, rational animals.[6] From this it follows that a reasonable life of prudence, courage, honesty, moderation, generosity, and justice, among other virtues, is what is best for them.

As we have seen, prudence is what supports commerce and the profession of business and it is in that light that problems in the sphere need to be analyzed.

Notes

1. Arguably, not all people in business are bona fide capitalists, any more than all doctors practice bona fide medicine—some are quacks. In business, too, there are those who do not observe even the elementary standards of bona fide trade.

2. Although it is a fair assumption that most business deals are done to benefit the dealers, it is probably more accurate that they are done to enable the dealers to pursue their own chosen goals, even if these be mainly charitable, generous, and kind rather than primarily benefiting themselves.

3. Adam Smith, *Inquiry into the Nature and Causes of the Wealth of Nations* (New York: Modern Library Edition, 1927), 726.

4. That many in business actually do not wish to take all such shortcuts is evident from the fact that 26 percent of the 544 largest U.S. firms have not up until recently given money to political candidates—for example, IBM, Campbell Soup, and Gillette.

5. For example, see Norman Barry, *Business Ethics* (West Lafayette, IN: Purdue University Press, 1999). Barry finds nothing inherently untoward about business as a profession and doesn't engage in the customary business bashing that characterizes so

many other works in the field. For more on this, see Douglas J. Den Uyl and Tibor R. Machan, "Recent Work in Business Ethics: A Survey and Critique," *American Philosophical Quarterly* 24 (April 1987): 107–124. Barry, working from what might be called a Popperian framework, is eager to eschew any hint of essentialism, ergo his conventionalist sympathies.

6. For the most recent defense of this view, see John Searle, *Rationality in Action* (Boston: MIT Press, 2001).

CHAPTER TWO

~

Capitalism

Capitalism is the political economic system in which the institution of the right to private property is fully respected or at least protected. There is dispute about the label, of course, mostly because its definition is often a precondition of having either a favorable or unfavorable view of the system. Capitalism is also the political economy that's most hospitable to commerce and business. In economics, for example, the social science that studies commerce and business, capitalism is the default system in terms of which commerce and business are to be understood. Any departures from that system are treated as impediments to commerce and business and are in need of justification.[1]

By itself, capitalism is an *economic* arrangement of an organized human community or polity. Often, however, entire societies are called capitalist, mainly to stress their thriving commerce and industry and the legal infrastructure that make these possible. But more rigorously understood, capitalism presupposes but is not itself a type of legal order governed by the rule of law in which the principle of private property rights plays a central role. Such a system of laws is usually grounded on *classical liberal* ideals in political thinking. These ideals may incorporate positivism, utilitarianism, natural rights theory, and/or individualism, as well as notions about the merits of laissez-faire (no government interference in commerce), the "invisible hand" (as a principle of spontaneous social organization), prudence and industriousness (as significant virtues), the price system as distinct from central planning (for registering supply and demand), and so on.

Put differently, "capitalism" refers to that feature of a human community whereby citizens are understood to have the basic right to make their own decisions concerning what they will do with their labor and property. Thus, capitalism includes freedom of trade and contract, free movement of labor, and protection of property rights against both criminal and official intrusiveness.

The concept "freedom" plays a central role in the understanding of capitalism. There are two prominent ways the nature of freedom is conceived as it pertains to human relationships. The one that fits with capitalism is *negative* freedom, namely, the condition of everyone in society not being ruled by others with respect to the use and disposal of themselves and what belongs to them. Citizens are free, in this sense, when no one else has authority over them that they have not granted of their own volition. In short, in capitalism one enjoys negative freedom, which amounts to being free *from* others' intrusiveness. In the U.S. political tradition, government is charged with the primary if not the sole task of securing the rights to such negative freedom— to life, liberty, and the pursuit of happiness.

The other meaning of "freedom" is that citizens have their goals and purposes supported by others, via their government, so as to prosper. Under this conception of freedom, one is free to progress, advance, develop, or flourish only when one is enabled to do so by the efforts of capable others. Government is charged with the task of arranging the securement of such freedom via taxation and wealth redistribution.

In international political discussions, the concept "capitalist" is used very loosely, so that such diverse types of societies such as Italy, New Zealand, the United States, Sweden, and France are all considered capitalist. Clearly, however, no country in our times is completely capitalist, nor has there ever been one. Of course, this is true of all other political economic systems, which are more or less faithfully approximated in various societies.

No country, accordingly, enjoys a condition of economic laissez-faire in which government stays out of people's commercial transactions except when conflicting claims over various valued items are advanced and the dispute needs to be resolved in line with the due process of law. But many Western-type societies protect a good deal of free trade, even if they also regulate most of it as well.[2] Still, just as those countries are called "democratic" if there is substantial suffrage—even though many citizens may be prevented from voting—if there exists substantial free trade and private ownership of the major means of production (labor, capital, intellectual creations, etc.), the country is usually designated as capitalist.

Of course, there are somewhat different versions of substantially capitalist countries; Japan, for example, enjoys a great deal of free trade. Yet, corporations are not free to pursue profit as the managers choose but must serve various social goals. They are required, for example, to heed the welfare of stakeholders—those whose lives are influenced by the decisions of corporate managers even if they lack any proprietary rights—for example, shares—in the company.

A similar situation applies in Germany, where many corporations are legally required to provide extensive benefits to employees and often may not even lay them off, even when this would be economically prudent. This is sometimes referred to as the "third way," a type of compromise between capitalism and socialism, the completely free and the completely planned economy.[3]

The most common reason among political theorists and economists for supporting capitalism is the system's strong support of wealth creation.[4] Such theorists also credit capitalism with other worthwhile traits, such as encouragement of progress, political liberty, innovation, and so on.

Those who defend the system for its utilitarian virtues—its propensity to encourage the production of wealth—are distinct from others who champion the system—or the broader framework within which it exists (what F. A. von Hayek called *The Constitution of Liberty*[5])—because they consider it morally and politically just.[6]

The first group of supporters argues that a free market or capitalist economic system is of great public benefit, even though this depends on private or even social vice, such as greed, ambition, and exploitation. As Bernard Mandeville, the author of *The Fable of the Bees*, puts it, this system produces "private vice, public benefit."[7] Many moral theorists see nothing virtuous in efforts to improve one's own life. Some believe, however, that enhancing the overall wealth of a human community is a worthwhile goal and also worth the price of a substantial measure of vice.

Those who stress the moral or normative merits of capitalism say the system rewards hard work, ingenuity, industry, entrepreneurship, and personal or individual responsibility, and this is all to the good. This alone makes the system morally preferable to alternatives. They also maintain that capitalism is a morally preferable system because it makes possible the exercise of personal choice and responsibility, something that would be obliterated in noncapitalist, collectivist systems or economic organizations. The point isn't that in capitalism everyone gets to choose the morality he/she likes, but that the right thing to do, whatever that really is, has to be chosen by a person, that one isn't forced by others to just behave in certain ways deemed to be proper.[8]

The most influential critic of capitalism is the nineteenth-century German thinker and social activist Karl Marx. He did not oppose capitalism, but he argued that it occupies only a specific period of humanity's development. Capitalism, as Marx saw it, is the adolescent period of humanity, as it were. Socialism is the young adulthood, while communism is full maturity. Marx believed that supporters are wrong to assume that the system has universal relevance and validity. Instead, Marx held, the system must be accepted as a temporary fact of the life of humanity—two hundred or perhaps four hundred years long.

In response, capitalism's defenders have argued that economic liberty is best suited to human beings because human nature is reasonably stable over time. Human beings, in turn, tend always to be motivated by self-interest or they will always want to be rewarded for their work and will not likely develop into creatures who are loyal primarily to humanity or society, never mind their self-interest.

Others have responded to Marx by claiming that not only is his position untenable, but that it is also morally despicable. The vision of human life Marx champions cuts directly against what is best about human beings, namely, their individuality, uniqueness, and resulting multifaceted creativity, that is, their often single-minded vision. Capitalism accords more with the idea of human excellence exemplified by the great artists, scientists, and industrialists of the world, not the vision exemplified by members of a stagnant commune.

Capitalism is an economic organization based on some very limited rules or principles. People are at liberty to do anything except intrude on the sovereignty of other human beings and what they own. As such, it is a system said to be well suited to human nature, whereby one may embark on various tasks and do well or badly at them but avoid intruding on others. This is best done when one's own sphere of authority—one's private property rights—is clearly identifiable.

With the 1989 collapse of the centrally planned economy of the Soviet Union, the debate about the ultimate merits of capitalism has heated up once again. It had been somewhat lukewarm earlier because of the dominance and apparent success of the welfare state. But that system began to falter from the malaise of stagflation, that is, both inflation and recession at the same time. Such East European scholars as Janos Kornai have argued in favor of moving toward a full-fledged free market system,[9] instead of attempting to institute the welfare state, mainly because they believed that the latter is only possible, at least for a while, in robust economies that can support the redistribution of wealth. But Kornai argued that the East European countries—indeed, all those with serious economic deficiencies—require robust economic activity, something the welfare state tends to stifle.

Others have urged that a "third way" be found, such as communitarianism or market socialism. They argue that capitalism is too harsh a system to be fully adopted in any decent society, echoing what earlier critics said about the system (e.g., John Maynard Keynes in *The End of Laissez-Faire*[10]). Indeed, one such warning comes from Robert Kuttner, himself the author of a recent book (coincidentally?) entitled *The End of Laissez-Faire*.[11] In all of these criticisms, despite protestations to the contrary, the conception of capitalism the critics embrace differs little from Marx's. What differs are the proposed solutions, which are closer to the pre-Marxist utopian socialist solutions.

Marx had argued, in his *Das Kapital*[12] and other works, that although unavoidable, capitalism leads to the alienation of the members of its community, not to mention the exploitation of the working class. In the end, this will also be the immediate cause of its necessary demise, namely, workers' disenchantment. Marx also argued that capitalism, as all societies prior to socialism and communism, is essentially a class system, so that the working and the capitalist classes are locked in an irresolvable conflict that will result in fundamental change, namely, a revolution (either peaceful or violent) leading to a socialist system.

The more recent critics wish to forge some kind of hybrid between capitalism and socialism. But the welfare state is just that hybrid and it is suffering from the inconsistencies that such systems wish to live with but that also haunts them. Trying to preserve both negative and positive liberty is futile. The disorder of allotting a portion of one to some and a portion of the other to others tends to slow everything down. By only partially protecting private property, for example, the welfare state or market socialism or communitarianism instills major uncertainties into people's lives, some of whom set property aside only to find it confiscated for some public cause just when they wish to make it useful for themselves and possibly others. In such a system, it is the state, rather than individual property owners, that has the final say.

Those who champion capitalism have different answers to Marx and the welfare statists. Mainly, they argue that although capitalism permits some harshness of treatment, such harshness is neither inherent in nor unique to capitalism. Nor need economic and social classes be rigidly formed—people travel from one economic level to the other more often than the critics imagine and certainly more so under capitalism than its alternatives. Exploitation is really just a way to meet the needs of differently positioned members of the community—some need certain goods and services more at one time than others, some have too much, some lack even elementary survival resources, but it is still best to leave things to the marketplace of free trade.

Capitalist theorists also note that most critics of capitalism demean wealth. Indeed, they virtually attack the pursuit of human well-being itself and, especially, luxury anytime there are needy people left anywhere on Earth, as well as, more recently, if any portion of nature is overrun by human beings (as if they were not natural creatures). But, the champions of capitalism argue, this stems from utopian thinking and has the consequence of begrudging anyone a measure of welfare, since some people will always be poor some of the time and nature will continue to be transformed by people.

Yet, the capitalist advocate need not be seen as reckless toward the environment. Indeed, arguably the strict and consistent institution of the principle of private property rights—through, for example, privatization and prohibition of dumping waste into other private as well as public realms—may solve the environmental problems we face better than any central planning champions of the environment tend to propose.[13]

Finally, critics of capitalism do not credit owners of wealth with any moral virtues—not even for their industry and prudence (often denying that these are virtues at all). This, its champions maintain, is a grave and indeed tragic mistake. We all depend on the wealth created by our fellow human beings, even as we try to produce wealth ourselves. Despite this, the activity is rarely appreciated, leaving business with very bad press, indeed.

In order to be effective navigators of our lives, we require what Robert Nozick, a philosopher at Harvard University, calls "moral space."[14] We need some sphere of exclusive jurisdiction, sovereign power, and a certain measure of autonomy. Thus, for some of the most crucial decisions of our lives, other people must ask permission to participate. We have a veto power—the only way that our moral worth can be developed and recognized by others as indeed our worth.

If we do not act in some measures as independent, sovereign agents, then we are like conscripted members of committees, in every decision we make; every bad or good decision is really the forced labor of a group, and no one is responsible.

Then the rapist is not responsible; nor the architect, Mozart, Beethoven, Albert Schweitzer, Mother Teresa, or even Osama bin Laden! They are all simply products of some large or small committee: a tribe, a clan, a community, or a society. And the committee itself is but a product of forces over which no one has control, responsibility, or accountability.

If one denies this measure of individual initiative and this social requirement of moral space, of a sphere of protected private jurisdiction, then no one can be held responsible, admired, or faulted for anything. Despite the widespread view that no one is responsible, there is also the widespread view that, for example, whoever creates pollution or waste should clean it up, or at least pay for it.

To the extent that individualism and the economics of capitalism are rejected, we have what we would call the moral tragedy of the commons: the inability to distinguish between those who are deserving and those who are not deserving, fundamentally, of moral recognition or praise. If everyone is a victim, then there is no room for either culprits or heroes. The institution of private property rights is a concrete, legally implementable manifestation of this concept of moral space.

The first issue of politics is or should be: Are we going to be able to act as moral agents in a social context? Though we are surrounded by countless others, is there going to be some place where we are sovereign judges? The principle of private property—which assigns to me those things that are justly and naturally mine, to you those things that are yours, from a watch to stocks and bonds, to business firms, to novels or computer programs—defines the arena where we are responsible. Here, other people may enter only at our discretion and with our consent. If that place is not secured for us, then our moral agency is not secure and we do not operate as independent, sovereign, and moral agents. Then we are mere subjects of the will of others who have taken power over us, be that a king, a tribal chief, a democratic assembly, or a central committee of a ruling political party.

If other people have legal authority to coerce us to use our private property and if they can impose their rule on us, then our moral responsibility is seriously diminished. For example, consider how environmental problems arise in any society. They arise, in part, because many firms utilize the commons without being fully accountable for how they behave there. It's the politicians who give them permission; it's the judges who rule in favor of a certain public ground being utilizable by the people! Firms get blamed all the time, but the firms cannot justly regard themselves to be guilty because they don't know how much of that public ground they really own and are responsible for. How much of it is at their disposal to rule, to navigate, and to manage? They just say: "Well, they tell me I can throw my soot into Lake Erie. I will do so," because the law says they are doing what everyone has the right to do, namely, take advantage of certain entitlements. The same with people who lobby for public funds for the arts, sciences, education, business, or whatnot. They all regard the public realm—for example, the treasury of their governments—as for their special use.

Most people who criticize firms don't realize that managers of firms are convinced that their activities are perfectly honorable and when they utilize the public realm, the legal system has said, "Yes, it's available for you to use."

So they don't, indeed, cannot see, themselves as exploiters and defilers. They see themselves as responsible people, having utilized whatever resources are legitimately available to them to advance a goal that they pursue as a matter of their professional duty. This is the goal of maximizing the profits of their stockholders, who include pensioners, teachers, nurses, and thousands or millions of people who trusted them with the responsibility of giving them a return on investment.

Similarly for all those who utilize government funds for their various projects (which, of course, they tend to characterize as "being in the public interest"). They all have causes they believe in and want to promote. If the public coffers are there for them to use, they believe it is their right and responsibility to do so. This then leads to more and more people using the resources regardless of which portion if any should go to their cause. That is something no one can tell. Thus, the tragedy of the commons!

From this perspective, one can see that blaming business or any other segment of society seeking public resources—including regions of the wilds publicly owned and managed by government—is quite unjust. It's the system that makes it possible; a system that has socialized a great deal of resources and made it impossible to distinguish between what is one person's realm of operations and what is someone else's. Just compare Disneyland to a public beach and the picture becomes clear. Or consider one's private budget, which when exhausted, is immediately evident, in contrast with utilizing public support!

On the public beach, many people thoughtlessly litter and often leave without cleaning up. Meanwhile, Disneyland stays cleaned up. Why? Because it's privately owned and people know how to take care of that, or at least have a greater propensity to do so.

This is one function of private property rights, to enable people to operate their lives with the sense that they alone are responsible for it. It also allows others to notice when someone intrudes or takes advantage without permission. So, one very important and systemic element of the morality of capitalism is that it enables people to be moral agents.

Capitalism has experienced widespread disrespect in part because throughout human history there has been a powerful intellectual tradition of *otherworldliness*. In the Bible, Jesus decries wealth acquisition when he asks, rhetorically, "For what shall it profit a man, if he shall gain the whole world, and lose his own soul?" And, again, the Bible states that sooner will a camel go through the eye of the needle than the rich man enter the kingdom of heaven. Socrates, Plato, and even Aristotle tended to denigrate wealth production, regarding trade and commerce as lowly and base. Throughout much of Western history, taking interest (i.e., earnings from lending money) was deemed usurious, hoarding, miserly, and avaricious. Marx's criticism was different not in the standards he employed to judge the system but by his claim that it is a necessary evil soon to be superseded evil and nothing more.

Some supporters of the system argue that this view is untrue to the facts of human nature and has misled us about the moral merits of commerce and business and, thus, of capitalism itself as a vital human institution. Because of its challenge of some central ideas of the past, it is arguable that capitalism is far more radical than even communism. The commune has always existed, in its relatively small versions, and it has much in common with the prominent social organization of primitive times, namely, tribalism (both as idealized and as actually manifest).

Capitalism, however, rests in large part on the belief that human beings are essentially or by nature sovereign individuals and a society's laws must value individuals above all else. Contrast this with Marx's conservative view that "The human essence is the true collectivity of man."[15] Most historians of ideas admit that whether the importance of human individuality should have been recognized in earlier times, it certainly was not much heeded until the modern age. Even in our time it is more often that groups—ethnic, religious, racial, sexual, national, cultural, and so on—are taken to have greater significance than individuals. The latter are constantly asked to make sacrifices for the former. In capitalism, however, the individual—for example, as the sovereign citizen or the consumer—is king. Undoubtedly, a capitalist system does not give prime place to economic equality among people, something that group thinking seems to favor since in groups all are deemed to be entitled to a fair share.

Capitalism's champions take it as more reasonable that people may differ in their abilities, talents, and willingness pertaining to economic achievement. So what is crucial is that they should be *equally unimpeded by the aggressiveness of others*—whether criminals or bureaucrats—in their access to the marketplace or, indeed, to any other place in a human community whenever they gain permission to enter or reach satisfactory terms of agreement. From this, it is proposed that they will not only benefit in the long run, collectively, but will have their individuality as human beings with dignity and choice, more respected than in alternative systems.

Capitalism tends to be favored most by academic economists, even more so than by members of the commercial community (who often do not understand and may even wish to subvert the system). They are unique in the academic world and are often met with severe criticism from outside their field.[16]

The most prominent academic economists who champion capitalism are known as members of the neoclassical or Chicago School. Another that stands foursquare behind capitalism is the Austrian School.[17] Others include the well-known Public Choice and the law and economics theorists. With certain variations in their approach, all these believe that capitalism is well suited to people living in communities, mainly because any other system places obstacles before the natural inclination of human beings to advance their own lot and thus improve the world.

But is that enough? An economic organization of society needs to appeal to what people believe is just and proper; it may not offend moral sensibilities. Unless supporters of capitalism reconcile their vision of economic life with the demands most people make for their society to conform to a sound view of justice, they will not succeed. Despite the demise of centrally planned socialism and the great deal of skepticism about socialism of any kind, capitalism is by no means the hands-down winner in the race for the hearts and minds of people in the world regarding the kind of community they ought to support.

Notes

1. Even in welfare states or mixed economies, the provisions making them such are dealt with as departures from the default system of commerce and business.

2. The extent of such regulation in the United States alone, thus the divergence from pure capitalism, is chronicled in Jonathan R. T. Hughes, *The Governmental Habit*, 2d ed. (Princeton, NJ: Princeton University Press, 1991).

3. Some economists note that one reason for the high unemployment rates of countries that practice the "third way" is that to start a business is extremely difficult and those who attempt it take on enormous costs independently of whether what they do is purchased by consumers.

4. See Adam Smith, *Inquiry into the Nature and Causes of the Wealth of Nations* (New York: Modern Library Edition, 1927); Milton Friedman, *Capitalism and Freedom* (Chicago: University of Chicago Press, 1961); F. A. von Hayek, *The Road to Serfdom* (Chicago: University of Chicago Press, 1944).

5. F. A. von Hayek, *The Constitution of Liberty* (Chicago: University of Chicago Press, 1960).

6. For example, see Ayn Rand, *Capitalism: The Unknown Ideal* (New York: New American Library, 1966); John Hospers, *Libertarianism* (Los Angeles: Nash, 1970); Robert Nozick, *Anarchy, State, and Utopia* (New York: Basic, 1974).

7. Bernard Mandeville, *The Fable of the Bees* (Indianapolis, IN: Liberty Classics, 1988).

8. The point here is that some argue that morality is subjective and capitalism makes possible doing what one subjectively feels one ought to do. But while this is possible, if there is an objectively right way for one to act, the action is morally worthwhile only if it is chosen. And in a capitalist society, because one enjoys substantial sovereignty and autonomy, one has the right to choose to do the right thing or, of course, to choose not to do it. So there is a risk, admittedly, but without choice the very possibility of moral conduct is eliminated.

9. See Janos Kornai, *The Road to the Free Economy* (New York: Norton, 1990).

10. John Maynard Keynes, *The End of Laissez-Faire* (London: L. and Virginia Woolf, 1926).

11. Robert Kuttner, *The End of Laissez-Faire* (New York: Knopf, 1991).

12. Karl Marx, *Das Kapital* (New York: International, 1967).

13. In this connection, see the works of such free market environmentalists as John Baden, Richard Stroup, Fred Singer, and Tibor R. Machan.

14. Nozick, *Anarchy, State, and Utopia*, 79.

15. Karl Marx, "On the Jewish Question."

16. For example, see Amitai Etzioni, *The Moral Dimension* (New York: Free Press, 1988); Kenneth Lux, *Adam Smith's Mistake* (Boston: Shambhala, 1990); Andrew Bard Schmookler, *The Illusion of Choice* (Albany: SUNY Press, 1993).

17. For a collection of nontechnical essays by such thinkers and others who favor capitalism, see Lawrence S. Stepelevich, ed., *The Capitalist Reader* (New Rochelle, NY: Arlington House, 1977).

CHAPTER THREE

~

Self-Interest, Egoism, and Business

Self-Interest and Commerce

Among the various troublesome features of business is the fact that economists, who study it as a social science, believe it runs based on self-interest. In this chapter, we will examine what this means for economists and how to understand it apart from their technical language. We will also explain what egoism is, the view so often associated with commerce.

Even apart from that technical language, many believe that crass egoism is at the heart of free market capitalism. Consider the following, by Michael Lewis, as an example: "The beauty of free market capitalism is that it does not require anything more than ruthless self-interest from its most ruthless self-interested citizens. When the system works properly they enrich us all by enriching themselves without giving the matter a great deal of thought. If that is no longer true it is a sign not that they are less moral, but that the invisible link between private gain and the public good has been severed."[1]

This observation uses the concept of "self-interest" in a way that does not quite do justice to what economists mean by that term. We shall see why that is so.

Some economists who champion the free market embrace some version of the idea Lewis relates. For example, Milton Friedman holds that "The private interest is whatever it is that drives an individual."[2] This use of "self" or "private interest" is not the same as Lewis's. For Lewis, economists believe that the free market system rests on the assumption that when people act, they want to benefit only themselves, in contrast to benefiting others. But this isn't so, as the quote from Friedman suggests. In Friedman, the idea is simply that everyone does what he/she, not others, wants to do. The sort of freedom enjoyed in free markets makes this possible because others do not have the authority to order one to do various things. All (legal) conduct must be voluntary, arising from the choices of market agents. It may be misleading to call such conduct "self-interested" or the "private interest," because in nontechnical language these suggest that we all do indeed act only to benefit ourselves and not anyone else. For the economists, however, that isn't the point, not, at least, as most use the term.[3]

What Is Self-Interest, Really?

From the time of Plato there has been a serious debate as to whether self-interest means "doing what one wants" or "doing what one actually benefits from (by some objective standard of what benefits a person)" or, again "doing whatever one is doing." Now, there is nothing remotely "ruthless" about doing the second, while the first is in effect tautological or redundant: People who are free act as they do because, well, they want to act as they do.

To invoke "self-interest" as ordinarily understood, namely, acting to benefit only oneself, does not do the economist justice. Of course, economists sometimes do use the term as if they meant what Lewis has in mind. But at that point they are inadvertently suggesting that they have in mind some (objective) standard of what counts as being of benefit to oneself. Yet, most economists do not believe there exists such a standard and so to benefit oneself means to them no more than doing what one *wants* to do, something valued subjectively (whether this be getting wealthy, helping the poor, or furthering the fine arts).

It is the last way of understanding self-interest that most technical economists mean: when people do things, they are pursuing their self-interest. By this account, both Michael Milken and Mother Teresa—and indeed we all and always—act from self-interest. But this leaves unresolved the issue of what differentiates those who work to satisfy others' welfare more than their own, from those who focus on their own before anyone else's or indeed those who have some other goal in mind entirely—say, saving wildlife or preserving historical relics.

The Economist's Idea of Self-Interest

The economist's concept of self-interest may be captured by the ordinary claim that *we all have our own motives from which we act when no one is coerc-*

ing us. Those motives vary a great deal. To understand them and the conduct they lead to, it is the differences that are of interest, not the common fact that everyone does what he/she chooses to do. Knowing that we all want to do what we are doing isn't going to tell us much about why we want to do it. Being called "self-interested," as the economists understand that term, is not at all informative even though it appears to be when taken in its ordinary sense.[4]

Lewis's claim assumes we all know what it means for some system of political economy *to work properly.* But there is a great deal of dispute about that, too. Does a system work properly if it enhances justice? Or economic prosperity? Or equality of well-being, stability, order, or peace? Or does a system work properly if it fulfills God's purposes, as gleaned by reference to Scripture, the Torah, the Koran, or some other good book? Or all of these?

When Does a System Work?

Indeed, those who talk along the lines Lewis exemplifies may well have some hidden idea—even from themselves—of what "works" means, usually, advancing some ideal they hope they share with their readers. But that assumption is a mistake. In this age of multiculturalism, especially, there are too many competing social ideals afoot and by some accounts we aren't even supposed to ask which is better and which has greater validity.

Yet, without addressing that issue, there simply is no way to determine what system of political economy works. For example, it needs to be shown that a system that achieves mainly equality of opportunity, aggregate prosperity, the protection of individual rights, or spiritual enlightenment is to be preferred over all those that achieve some other objective. Yet, when public discussion ensues concerning what kind of system works, these various possibilities are usually left untouched and only one is considered, and that one depends on who is considering the issue.

Must Moral Conduct Be Altruistic?

Lewis's claim also seems to assume that being moral consists of doing things not for oneself but for the public interest, whatever that means. There is in his remark an implied schism between private gain and the public good.

Yet, why should we accept that this is the way to be moral and/or ethical? After all, if the public is worth benefiting, why would not private citizens also be worth benefiting, even from their very own actions? For one, the public is comprised of the private and for every private individual there are probably many more private than public concerns that matter that might benefit the person. In the U.S. political tradition, it is taken that the *sole* bona fide public concern is the securing of the inalienable rights every individual has by nature. Other concerns or interests tend to be special or private, not public, and these are best pursued without treating them as if they were public. The latter may lead to treating some people's private or special interests as if they were public ones, thereby creating privileged status for some citizens.

Perhaps, we should prefer interests that are widely shared? But that assumes that mere numbers make something worthy for us all.

Even simple altruism poses a problem. Why is benefiting others good but benefiting oneself is not? After all, isn't the agent also a person with needs and wants just as worthy of serving as those of others?

Does Prosperity Depend on Vice?

The invocation of the Smithian doctrine, so aptly expressed by Bernard Mandeville, namely, "private vice, public benefits," is instructive. It shows that we still embrace the conflict between the individual and common good that has given rise to many of our troubles. Mandeville's insight is that what is deemed to be immoral individual conduct may result in widespread benefits. The implicit suggestion is that people might even exonerate themselves morally when doing something that is to their benefit if this is done so that others also benefit. However, even then one isn't gaining moral credit, only escaping moral blame. For if one does not mean to benefit others while benefiting oneself, then one's action lacks redeeming moral worth. All that can be said for it is that somehow, rather oddly, a shady deed turns out to be of value to the public.

The view that others and not only oneself ought to be the beneficiary of action leads to a harsh opinion of business professionals, as well as anyone else who undertakes commercial tasks. It condemns business professionals for lacking in moral worth simply because they seek to benefit themselves.[5] This tends to treat people in business who are not guilty of any moral wrongs as lacking in positive moral achievements as they carry out their business successes.

Yet, nearly all artists, scientists, educators, athletes, and others do what they do because they benefit from it. They find it rewarding and fulfilling. Their feats are no less worthy or moral because of this.

Few great artists and athletes set out to serve others; rather, they have a vision or personal goal they want to realize. The greatest scientists likely do not engage in their work to benefit humanity but because they are deeply intrigued by some problem. Nevertheless, countless others may benefit from their efforts. So, it is not only people in business who strive to realize something important to them rather than to others. But, as with scientists, artists, and many others, what's important to them may well be something that benefits others even more than themselves.

The same view of what is moral that condemns people in business to moral irrelevance also condemns nearly everyone who isn't a martyr or saint. This alone should call the position into question. What needs to be addressed is what counts as doing the right thing in the various fields of human endeavor and what kind of political economic system would be most hospitable to such endeavors.

Selfishness Rightly Understood

If selfishness is understood as striving to make a good human life for oneself, then selfish people need not apologize. Nor would a system of political economy in which this can be done most effectively be shameful. That system is laissez-faire capitalism, associated with the view that we all do things out of selfishness.

But if "selfish" means something else, then, as we have noted earlier, the term is ambiguous and invites confusion. Simply signifying by it that one wants to do what one wants to do says nothing informative and sheds no light on the quality of the deed, contrary to what the critics who focus on the economist's use of "selfish" suggest.

A final note: When bona fide self-interested conduct is condemned, this amounts to an indictment of what and who we are, of our human self or ego. And if that is justified—if we are really no good by nature—then all is lost since any doing for others would be done by someone morally corrupt.[6]

Because selfishness is so closely linked with the psychological and ethical systems of egoism, it will be useful to examine egoism more closely.

Varieties of Egoism

The term "egoism" is ordinarily used to mean "exclusive concern with satisfying one's own desires, getting what one wants." Dictionaries tend to support this. They call "egoism," for instance, "1. selfishness; self-interest. 2. conceit."[7] The term "egotist" is often a substitute, although it's defined differently, for example, as "excessive reference to oneself." The ego is the self. But we should distinguish first between "selfishness," "self-interest," and "interest of the self." They usually mean, respectively, "concern exclusively and for indulging one's desires," "consideration based first on what is good for oneself without the exclusion of others," and "that which motivates an autonomous person." These will help us appreciate what follows. (See also rational choice theory.)

"Egoism" is also used in ethical considerations of how human beings do or ought to live. It is thus often qualified by such terms as "ethical" and "psychological." So what determines the most sensible meaning of the term? It is crucial, first, to ask, what the *ego* is. If it is the unique identity of the individual human being or self, what exactly is this?

Some argue that everyone is, to use Karl Marx's term, a collective or specie-being. Others hold that the human being is related to a supernatural God and has a body (which is of this Earth) and a soul (of the spiritual realm) combined in one person. Some others say a human being is an integral and unique whole, comprised of many diverse facets. Egoisms differ depending on which of these is taken to be true.

Psychological Egoism

Some hold we are all automatically selfish. So just as it is constitutive that we have certain physical organs and functions—a heart, brain, liver, blood circulation, and motor behavior—so it is that we *will* act to advance our own well-being and attempt to benefit ourselves at all times. In short, we are supposed to be instinctively moved to act selfishly. Or, by a different sense of self- or private interest, we all will do just what we want, what suits us.

Lewis appears to embrace the former idea. Here is one expression of the latter: "[E]very individual serves his own private interest. . . . The great Saints of history have served their 'private interest' just as the most money grubbing miser has served his interest. The *private interest* is whatever it is that drives an individual."[8]

But egoism actually concerns *benefiting oneself first, though not exclusively*. This means providing oneself with the wherewithal for flourishing, excelling, and developing in positive ways. Different explanations of what that comes to can be given.

For example, some hold that to benefit oneself is to become satisfied, to obtain whatever one would like to have, or to do what one wants to do. As Thomas Hobbes put the point: "But whatsoever is the object of any man's appetite or desire, that is it which he for his part calleth good: and the object of his hate and aversion, evil. . . . For these words of good and evil . . . are ever used with relation to the person that useth them: there being nothing simply and absolutely so; nor any common rule of good and evil."[9]

Yet, the previous quote paradoxically implies that if someone were to desire something obviously self-destructive, the person would be benefited! This suggests that being benefited is different from having one's desires satisfied or one's wants fulfilled. If so, then psychological egoism would mean that everyone does what one benefits from in terms of some objective standard of well-being, not based just on what one desires or likes.

For example, if being physically healthy were a primary good—such that whenever one's physical health is enhanced, one would be benefited whether or not one chose it as a priority—then psychological egoism would imply that everyone is always acting to enhance his/her health. Whatever the standard of goodness or well-being or being benefited came to, psychological egoism would mean that one is always motivated to act to fulfill this. Yet, this seems wrong since people clearly do not always aim to benefit themselves by some standard of goodness or well-being. They often slack off. So psychological egoism means that we do what we desire or want, quite apart from whether it benefits us.

But might we make this more sensible by adding that what we desire or want is always something *we take to be* of benefit to ourselves? When we take a job, go on a vacation, seek out a relationship, or, indeed, embark on an entire way of life, we may be doing what *seems to us best*. Is this what is meant by the view that we are necessarily selfish?

Yet, what is meant by "what seems to be best"? If one says, "This *seems* to me to be a vase," we know what is meant because we know what it *is* to be a vase. So could one tell what *seems to be of benefit* to oneself, *seems to contribute to one's well-being*, without any standard independent of what one desires or wants and determining what *is to one's benefit, contributes to one's well-being*? No.

Some argue that despite its troubles, we can make good use of psychological egoism as a technical device, for example, in the analysis of market behavior—of how people act when they embark on commercial or business tasks. By assuming that's how people act in markets, we can anticipate trends in economic affairs. In fact, however, when these estimates are made, certain assumptions are often invoked about what *in fact is of benefit to us* (usually, an increase of available resources). So even as an analytic device psychological egoism by itself seems difficult to uphold as a cogent doctrine. Nor can it be of use to guide our own conduct or to understand the conduct of others.

So, by this doctrine we act as we do because we want (which tells us nothing), or that we act as we do because we take it to be of benefit to us (which is often false).

Ethical Egoism

Ethical egoism states that one *ought to* benefit oneself, first and foremost. This by no means tells it all, as we have seen in connection with psychological egoism. The precise meaning of ethical egoism also depends on what the ego is and what it is to be benefited.

Subjective Egoism

The most commonly discussed version of ethical egoism differs only in one basic respect from psychological egoism. According to this, subjective egoism, the human self or ego, consists of a bundle of desires (or drives, wishes, or preferences) and to benefit oneself amounts to satisfying these desires in their order of priority, which is itself a subjective matter, something entirely dependent on the feelings of the individual. This is still a type of ethical egoism because everyone is supposed to *choose* to satisfy the desires he/she has— that is, one *ought to* attempt to satisfy oneself.

This view is said to have serious problems, too. First, if John desires, first and foremost, to be wealthy, next, to be famous, to find a beautiful mate, to please some of his friends, to give support to his country, to conserve resources, and finally to assist some people who are in need, John ought to strive to achieve these goals in this order of priority. But how John ought to rank these goals cannot be raised. (Here is where the position is similar to the first version of psychological egoism: the desires are decisive in determining what benefits John.) Yet that's crucial in ethics.

Next, a bona fide ethical theory must be universalizable (i.e., it needs to apply to all choosing and acting persons), unambiguous (i.e., it provides clear guidance as to what one ought to do), consistent (i.e., it does not propose actions that contradict one another), and comprehensive (i.e., it addresses all those problems that are reasonably expected to arise for a person). Subjective egoism fails to satisfy these conditions. Even for an individual desires often conflict. Mary may desire to be a conscientious mother as well as a successful attorney, but both desires are not always possible to satisfy. Basing decisions on desires alone will not help her.

Any ethical theory must avoid the problems just cited. Subjective egoism is, thus, often used as an example of a failed ethical theory.[10]

Classical Egoism

A more promising ethical egoism states that each person should live so as to achieve his/her *rational self-interest*. (This can be called "classical" egoism to indicate its pedigree in Aristotelianism. It is also captured by the term "eudaimonist ethics.") Accordingly, as living beings we need a guide to conduct and principles to be used when we cannot assess the merits of each action from the start. As living beings, we share with other animals the value of life. But life occurs in individual (living) things. And human living, unlike that of other animals, cannot be pursued automatically. We must learn to do it. And the particular life we can pursue and about which we can exercise choices is our own. By understanding *who and what we are*, we can identify the standards by which our own life can most likely be advanced properly and made successful and happy.

In short, this ethical egoist holds that one's human life, the basis of all values, is to be lived with the aid of a moral outlook. Since (the value of) one's own life is the only one a person can advance in a morally relevant way (by choice), each person should live it successfully within that person's own context (as the individual one is, within one's circumstances). Thus, people should pursue their own individual happiness, and the principles that make this possible are the moral principles and virtues suited for leading a human life. The benefit one ought to seek and obtain is, then, not subjective but objective: it is one's own successful, flourishing human life.

The prime virtue in classical egoistic ethics is rationality (or being reasonable and sensible), the uniquely human way of being (conceptually!) aware of and navigating through the world. Success in life or happiness for any human being must be achieved in a way suited to human life. Accordingly, being *morally virtuous* consists of choosing to be as fully human as possible in one's circumstances, *to excel at being the human being one is*. Each person is a human being because of the distinctive capacity to choose to think and to attend to the world rationally (by way of careful and sustained principled thought); therefore, to succeed as a person, everyone should make that choice. All the specialized virtues in egoism must be rationally established (or at least capable of such establishment).

Classical egoism, unlike other ethical positions, considers morality or ethics itself the way of pursuing one's best possible life—not, however, pathological self-centeredness (egotism). Pride, ambition, integrity, honesty, and other traits that are by nature of value to any human life are considered virtues. It is with regards to the sort of self that is proper to a human being that one ought to be selfish. (Indeed, whether selfishness is to be thought of as good or bad depends on what the *self* is.) The worst, most reprehensible way of conducting oneself is to fail to think and exercise rational judgment, to evade reality and leave oneself to blind impulse, others' influence, the guidance of thoughtless clichés, and the like. Since knowledge is indispensable for successful realization of goals, including the central goal of happiness, failure to exert the effort to obtain it—thus fostering error, misunderstanding, and confusion—is most disastrous to oneself and, hence, immoral.

Finally, in classical egoism the goal, one's happiness, is something that should be sharply distinguished from pleasure, fun, or thrills. This type of egoism sets as our primary goal happiness, which is a sustained positive reflective disposition, resulting from doing well in one's life qua the individual human being one is.[11]

Egoism is rarely advocated, yet, many act as if they accepted egoism for their ethical system. People often strive to be happy, to succeed in career, school, marriage, and the numerous projects they undertake. Inventors are usually devoted to success, as are financiers, politicians, doctors, and most productive people. Being rational is often acknowledged as a significant virtue, as when people express dismay with unreasonableness and with their own failure to think, saying, for example, "I am sorry, I just didn't think!"

The details of any bona fide moral outlook are not amenable to philosophical discussion any more than specific medical advice can be given in a medical treatise. Only very general moral principles can be identified, which must be interpreted and implemented by individuals who, thus, either gain or lose moral credit from how they act.

Criticisms of Egoism

The critics have much to say about egoism—often dismissing it as not even a bona fide, let alone *the* successful or correct, ethical theory. They condemn it for its allegedly naive view of human nature—the idea that we are born without destructive impulses and that we should simply go about achieving our natural goals. They say egoism leads to self-centeredness, egotism, and the ruthless pursuit of wealth and power, prompted by the complex and often destructive motives that lie deep within us. (In a way, altruism is *the* criticism of egoism!)

On a more formal level, classical egoism as a moral theory is thought to disallow universalizability, a criticism we noted in connection with subjective egoism. For example, if asked by another person what he/she should do, where in fact it would be good for him/her to take a job that would also be to one's own benefit or best interest that he/she not, could a consistent egoist give the correct advice? Doing so seems to be undermining oneself. Thus, egoism apparently cannot be universalized to everyone. So egoism appears to set people at odds for lack of a coordinating principle. The criticism charges egoism with generating contradictory plans of action: people both should and should not do certain things. Thus, it fails because it leads to the view that what one should do *cannot* be done!

A further objection pertains to classical egoism's focus on happiness. Just what is this happiness anyway? By saying that it is the awareness of ourselves as being successful at living as people—that is, rationally—this position prejudges that rational living will lead to something we ought to achieve. But is it not possible that something else besides this "happiness"—which seems very self-indulgent anyway—is worth pursuing? Could there not be far more important goals (e.g., political liberty, social justice, or being a productive member of society) that overshadow happiness? Furthermore, many rational, scholarly, and artistic achievers such as scientists, lawyers, and writers have been notably unhappy. However, some of the most irrational, whimsical, and haphazard people retire in luxury to Miami Beach to live out their lives in bliss.

Rebuttals for Egoism

In response to the charge of naiveté about human nature, the egoist will claim that egoism is concerned only with the essentials. Egoism focuses on the morally relevant aspects of every person, the capacity to freely choose to think. The misery, neurosis, cruelty, and self-destruction that often characterize human life are explainable in terms of people's refusal to think through the requirements of their lives and their willingness to meddle in the lives of others (always for others' good, of course). Were people to stick to doing good for themselves, much of the disarray would disappear. Also, such factors do not show inherent conflict in human nature. As long as there are well-integrated people who live with peace of mind and are happy, this possibility is established for all human life.

The criticism that advocating or publicly affirming ethical egoism is often self-contradictory is answered by distinguishing between conduct one undertakes as a moral theorist versus what one should do when embarking on some contest or economic competition. The former role commits one to advancing the general truths of ethics, the latter does not. But if one rationally elects to be a moral theorist, then it will be to one's benefit to do so. No conflict need arise.

Conflicts of desires and wishes aren't decisive, the egoist will say. If living one's life rationally is the first principle or virtue of egoism, the appropriate course is to deal with the question: What should we do when desires conflict? For example, if two people, even friends, have applied for the same job, their desires may be in conflict; nonetheless, each may sincerely wish the other the best and even offer good advice. The rational course would be to understand that the best candidate deserves the position, an honest attempt to gain it should be made by both, and then let the chips fall where they will. Such a perspective is fully consistent with ethical egoism.

The difficulty of *defining* happiness is not a problem of ethics but of epistemology. This difficulty faces any complex system of ideas. It is enough to note, according to the egoist, that being happy does seem to be different from being satisfied, pleased, contented, thrilled, or fun-filled. It is, rather, the realization (and its corresponding feeling) of having carried on well in life and of having lived as a human being lives best. To be successful in the broadest sense means to do well at what people are uniquely capable of doing: guiding their lives rationally. We do not always do this, which explains regret, but that does not mean that it isn't good to make the attempt. That, in a nutshell, is what ethical egoism says we should do.

Egoists grant that rational conduct will not *guarantee* a long and happy life; accidents can happen. The position is rather that a rational life makes reaching success more likely than does any alternative. It is wrong, moreover, to compare one person's rational life with another's irrational life without making sure that the two people started from essentially similar points. True enough, some who have lived irrationally could be comparatively well off in contrast to others who live rationally but in extremely different situations. In any case, it is highly unlikely that a person is well off because of living irrationally.

What is crucial to ethical egoism is that by living rationally each person would very likely be happier, and certainly savor a better self-concept, than by living irrationally. Moral theorists who advocate egoism propose that this is what needs to be examined to learn whether living rationally is indeed the most promising path to happiness.

This is as far as we can go here.

Business Ethics and Egoism

Egoism is relevant to business ethics both in assessing how people in commercial and business endeavors ought to act and in determining what kinds of public policy should govern business and industry. Capitalism is an economic system closely linked to versions of egoism. Adam Smith, the founder of modern economic science, advanced something like a psychological egoist position about human motivation (although in his *The Theory of Moral Sentiments* he advances a different position). Many neoclassical economists incline toward psychological egoism when they discuss why people behave as they do, although their referring to "utility maximization" rather than "the pursuit of self-interest" sometimes makes it difficult to classify their position.

If commerce and the profession of business are moral endeavors, then some form of egoistic principle must be included among the virtues human beings ought to practice. Thus, some argue that *prudence* ultimately gives moral support to commerce and business.[12]

Unless room is made for egoistic conduct as morally praiseworthy, commerce and business may have nothing morally significant about them. In terms of classical egoism, commerce is a morally worthwhile undertaking and business an honorable profession. They are to be guided by both the general moral principles of human living and their specific professional ethics. The latter posits the creation of wealth as its primary objective, to be pursued without violating principles of morality and through the effective achievement of prosperity with the appropriate enterprises selected accordingly. A banker ought to earn a good income from safeguarding and investing the deposits and savings of his/her customers, honestly, industriously, and with attention to the need to balance these undertakings with others that morality requires. So should an automobile executive, the chief executive officer of a multinational corporation, or the owner of a restaurant. And this requires the institution of the right to private property and freedom of enterprise, lest the moral component—self-direction—be missing from how those doing business comport themselves.

Notes

1. Michael Lewis, "Lend the Money and Run," *The New Republic*, 7 December 1992. This is a review essay of books by Nicholas von Hoffman, *Capitalist Fools: Tales of American Business, from Carnegie to Forbes to the Milken Gang* (Garden City, NY: Doubleday, 1992) and James Grant, *Money of the Mind: Borrowing and Lending in America from the Civil War to Michael Milken* (New York: Farrar, Strauss and Giroux, 1992).

2. Milton Friedman, "The Line We Dare Not Cross," *Encounter* 47, no. 5 (November 1976): 11.

3. Of course, a problem arises from the belief of most mainstream economists that what one wants to do is just what is in one's own interest. This position has a long, albeit controversial, perigee. It is expressed in ordinary discussions by way of saying: "Well, isn't everyone selfish—when you do something, don't you do it because, well you want to do it, it makes you pleased to do it?" This is confused but not anything close to the idea that "ruthless self-interest" motivates people in the marketplace.

4. This analysis is disputed in J. C. Lester, *Escape from Leviathan: Liberty, Welfare and Anarchy Reconciled* (New York: St. Martin's, 2000). For a more detailed defense

of the contention that the explanation from self-interest is either false or trivially true, see Tibor R. Machan, *Capitalism and Individualism: Reframing the Argument for the Free Society* (New York: St. Martin's, 1990).

5. Often, they are actually seeking monetary wealth so as to help other people or to contribute to various causes!

6. It is for this reason that Ayn Rand titled one of her books *The Virtue of Selfishness: A New Concept of Egoism* (New York: New American Library, 1964), so as to indicate that there is something seriously wrong with regarding selfishness as bad, untoward.

7. *Webster's New World Dictionary* (Englewood-Cliffs, NJ: Prentice Hall, 1982), 149.

8. Friedman, "Line We Dare Not Cross," 11.

9. Thomas Hobbes, *Leviathan*, edited with an introduction by C. P. Macpherson (Baltimore, MD: Penguin, 1968), 120.

10. For a discussion of this and other forms of ethical egoism, see Tibor R. Machan, "Recent Work in Ethical Egoism," in *Recent Work in Philosophy*, ed. Kenneth G. Lucey and Tibor R. Machan (Totowa, NJ: Rowman and Allanheld, 1983), 185–202.

11. See Rand, *Virtue of Selfishness*; for a somewhat different treatment, see David L. Norton, *Personal Destinies: A Philosophy of Ethical Individualism* (Princeton, NJ: Princeton University Press, 1976).

12. See Douglas J. Den Uyl, *The Virtue of Prudence* (New York: Peter Lang, 1991); Tibor R. Machan, "Ethics and Its Uses," in *Commerce and Morality*, ed. Tibor R. Machan (Lanham, MD: Rowman & Littlefield, 1988).

~

CHAPTER FOUR

Employment Ethics

It is hardly possible in contemporary U.S. society to talk about moral issues that arise in the workplace and in the employment relationship, apart from legal considerations. Discussion about workers' rights, hourly wage, safety on the job, overtime pay, benefits, hiring and termination practices, and so on inevitably involves reference to various state and federal regulations, laws, and guidelines. Such is the pervasiveness of government that it has become not only the rather visible hand that directs the various aspects of employment, but shapes, as well, the way we think and talk about it. Consider the questions: What is a fair wage? How many hours a day or a week ought a person be expected to work? Who is responsible for injuries to a worker on the job? Is it right for an employer to hire whomever he/she wishes despite qualifications? What may an employer expect of an employee in terms of effort, honesty, loyalty to the company, and so on? What may an employee expect from an employer in terms of protection from workplace hazards, job security, additional pay for especially productive work, and freedom from unwanted or disrespectful treatment such as sexual harassment, acts of prejudice, bias, exploitation, and the like? These, and many related others, are legitimate moral questions well worth exploring, but the purely *moral* dimension of these questions has given way to legal answers brought about, at least in part, by political, that is, coercive, as opposed to social or moral, pressures.

And so, a "fair" minimum wage is established by Congress, while the Occupational Safety and Health Administration oversees worker health and safety. For many workers, hourly employment that exceeds forty hours per week, eight hours a day, or some such number must be paid a premium; workers must be given at least one ten-minute break for every four continuous hours of work (or some such formula); there is an extended family leave provision guaranteed by federal law, and so on. The laws, rules, and regulations overseen and enforced by the U.S. Department of Labor cover every conceivable aspect of employment and number into the thousands.[1] In addition, there are countless state laws and regulations that govern or impact employment. It is fair to observe that these many laws and regulations are designed to protect the worker from abuse and neglect by employers, on the assumption that workers generally do not have sufficient power to persuade employers to provide them with the desirable wages, benefits, and conditions that these laws and regulations mandate under threat of force through penalties and other deterrents.[2] In other words, the perceived justification for these laws and regulations are the social benefits of the increased well-being of workers—that is, an overall reduction of human suffering that, the reasoning goes, would have existed but for these laws. Thus, a moral end (in this case, utility and increased happiness) serves as a rationale for the legal mandates. Now, a historical case for the necessity of state involvement in the workplace can certainly be made, citing, for example, the abysmal working conditions of early industrialization. That such conditions existed are beyond dispute, though whether state, and thus, coercive solutions were (and presently are) the best moral response is surely debatable.[3]

Putting this aside, and granting that suffering is in fact reduced by government regulation and statutes, and granting further that laws generally serve to prevent suffering, it still does not follow from these facts alone that such regulations and laws are morally justified. For example, a law prohibiting the eating of junk food or requiring daily exercise, if strictly enforced, would likely reduce human suffering, but would hardly be justified and would certainly be unwelcome even by many of those who exercise and have healthy diets. It is arguable that there are limits to the proper intervention of law and that some matters ought to remain private and left to the discretion of the individual.[4] Where the lines are drawn is, of course, a matter of dispute, as evidenced by major political differences between, say, liberals, conservatives, and libertarians with respect to the extent to which government ought to direct the affairs of its citizens. In fact, there is hardly a dimension of human life, hardly a possible human relationship, that escapes the directing force of law and regulation. Thus, contemporary life is profoundly shaped by the law, with individual deliberation, choice, initiative, and discretion largely determined by government and thus political, rather than moral, in quality. To the extent that this is so, then the moral space within which decisions are made is quite small, with little room for genuine moral struggle, discovery, and the expression, even growth, of character that such struggle makes possible.

What all of this means is that, contrary to appearances, the employment relationship is fundamentally and essentially moral rather than legal, social rather than political, and personal rather than institutional. The purpose of this chapter is to revisit employment, to explore the employer–employee relationship from a moral perspective, and to determine which principles ought to guide the employer–employee relationship as well as to settle conflicts that arise in the workplace. Such principles should enlighten us as to the limits and proper application of laws governing employment. In short, we wish to address the question: What are the ethics of employment?

Clearing the Way

Discussion of employment ethics should begin with an account of the nature of employment and of the relationship between employer and employee. At once, we come across a possible obstacle as the roles of employee and employer are subject to a widespread cultural mythology that tends to conceive of the relationship as inherently adversarial and unfair, with one side, employer, enjoying all of the advantages that accrue to a favorable differential of power. And so the employee, the worker (as though the employer does no work!), is considered something of a servant, slave, or property of the employer, who is pictured (quite unabashedly, in the popular entertainment media) as the master, the boss, who rules over all and whose word is law. The employee is seen as the often helpless overworked and underpaid victim of the often tyrannical and stingy employer who reigns as master to slave or lord to serf. This picture derives much of its power and plausibility from the historical origins of labor being forced on slaves, and of the long period of feudal serfdom, followed by the industrial revolution of the early modern era, which saw all manner of worker suffering and abuse. It is also supported by the intellectual movement of liberalism beginning with the Enlightenment, branching off into suspicion of anything less than complete egalitarianism, and culminating in the form of Marxist thought.[5]

However understandable and rooted in history and intellectual tradition, this view of the employment relationship is not adequate for our purposes. To begin with, the slave–master model, which is inherently immoral, can hardly serve as a model for the employment relationship. There can be no serious answer to the question: What are the ethics of slavery? Second, whatever vestiges of slave, feudal, and early industrial abuses exist in contemporary society are just that—vestiges and residual features of an earlier time that are no longer applicable to present circumstances. We should be aware, however, that this picture of the employment relationship still holds many people captive as they talk about employment, that it is as metaphorical as our talk of the sun rising and setting, but with greater social consequence. Assuming, then, that the popular model is deficient, let's return to the question of the nature of the employment relationship. What do we see?

In contrast with the rest of the animal kingdom, human beings must work in order to live. Among the earliest of the Babylonian myths is the story of the victory of the god Marduk over his divine adversaries. From the blood of the defeated gods, so the story goes, Marduk fashioned out human beings to perform labor for him. This myth answered the ancient but enduring question: Why must man labor? Clearly, the answer "because Marduk wanted someone else to do the work" is hardly satisfactory, but it does point to an inescapable fact of human life, that we must work. Even today, with the assistance of technology, few people escape this fate. Given the various necessities, not to mention the amenities, of life, most of us must work for their procurement. The principle of the division of labor, championed early on in the modern period by Adam Smith, illustrates how inefficient it generally is for individuals to attempt solitary production of whatever will satisfy all of their needs. This was discovered in prehistoric times and developed into a full-blown, widespread practice with the advent of modern technology, industrialization, and insight into the sources of the creation of wealth.

Now, since solitary production is on the whole unsatisfactory, we have the option of working in relationships with others. This can take a variety of forms: partnerships, cooperatives of various sorts, including corporations, trade, and, of particular interest here, employment. These various relationships are all commercial, involving, in one way or another, the exchange of goods, services, or labor for the sake of securing, from the point of view of all participants, something valued.

Thus, commercial activity, including employment, is, from its origins to its ends, normative in character. We engage in work and enter into commercial relationships, including employment, in order to realize valued ends. Furthermore, though necessary for human life, whether to work at all, to what extent, and in what way is volitional, a matter of choice. Unlike animals, who are driven by nature to do what they do, human beings recognize that they have a choice even in whether to exert effort to do what it takes to live, to be, or not to be. This capacity to choose includes, inherently, the choice of the very standard according to which choices are to be made. Were this not so, human efforts to encourage others, to remonstrate with them, to argue, and to praise and blame would be idle ceremonies.

These two basic features of commercial life, value and choice based on a standard, which are features of all human activities, make employment and the employment relationship fundamentally moral. That is, one enters into an employment relationship voluntarily and with the aim of benefit to oneself by offering the other party to the relationship something, such as one's labor, skill, or talent, that the other values and sees as of benefit. Were it not voluntary it would be slavery, and calling it "employment" would be a euphemism at best. Were there no expected value, one could hardly explain the proposed exchange. Of course, it may well be that the choices available to one side or the other are few or great, and this will likely affect the value of what is offered for exchange, as well as the terms of the exchange itself. If what one has to offer is in great supply, one ought not expect its exchange value to be as great as if the demand were much greater than the supply, and vice versa. This is so for either side of the exchange. For example, when it comes to employment, a worker who has relatively few skills to offer will, to that extent, have fewer opportunities for employment; the employer who has relatively fewer benefits or lower wages to offer will, to that extent, attract fewer qualified workers. This explains the quite common (and commonsensical) advice that elders give to the young about getting a higher education, or, if not that, of acquiring skills that are in demand. It also explains why employers, in search of the best candidate for an opening, are (or anyway ought to be) willing to pay a premium wage and additional benefits.

What affects the relative worth of labor, services, wages, benefits, and so on is a complex matter beyond the scope of this discussion. Suffice it to say that, whatever the sources affecting supply and demand, the matter of concern here remains clear: The employment relationship is entered into voluntarily, if not always eagerly, and with the understanding of mutual benefit, if not always mutually acknowledged.

The Employment Contract

In essence, then, the employment relationship is a contract, an agreement by each side to offer the other something that the other values. This establishes moral boundaries and provides a guide for the proper workings of the relationship. That is, the nature of the relationship, that it is voluntary and mutually beneficial, along with the particular details of the contract agreed to by both sides to provide the criteria by which the actual workings of the relationship are to be assessed, conflicts resolved, changes made, and in the end the relationship terminated.

In short, the ethics of employment are grounded in the model of employ-ment as a contract between consenting, mutually self-interested adults. Clearly, this relationship can take a number of forms, and the particulars of the contract may vary widely depending on the parties involved, the work or service to be performed, the conditions under which the relationship oper-ates, and other factors. One party may offer to provide labor or some other service for a set fee or in exchange for something else of value. This could be as simple as one party offering to haul trash for another in exchange for, say, $50, or as complicated as one party offering another financial advice on a business venture in exchange for, say, an hourly rate on a sliding fee based on some agreed to standard and/or a percentage of the profits of the business, a share in ownership, or some other arrangement contingent on one or another specifiable condition among many.

It is not always clear whether a commercial relationship is an employment relationship or some other commercial arrangement, since it is not always clear who has hired whom, and what counts as hiring. In one sense, a home-owner who contracts with, say, a roofer to replace his/her roof for a specified amount has hired the roofer, who in turn is in the homeowner's employ. The roofer, in turn, may have workers to do the actual labor in exchange for an hourly rate. Though the homeowner has hired the roofer, the roofer's work-ers are not thought of as employed by the homeowner, since their agreement is with the roofer, and not the homeowner. Had the homeowner contracted directly with the workers, he/she could properly be said to have hired them and the workers could then be said to have been in his/her employ, at least for the duration of the job.

But suppose that, in the first instance, the roofer had agreed to provide a roof not for money, but in exchange for the homeowner's providing, in re-turn, say, so many meals at the homeowner's restaurant or so many auto tune-ups from the homeowner, a mechanic. Who has hired whom? Who is in whose employ? What should be stressed here is a feature of employment that is often overlooked and that this question brings to surface: The nature of the employment relationship, being grounded in voluntary agreement to a mu-tually beneficial exchange, is essentially reciprocal, one of moral equality. What is significant here are the terms of the agreement and the extent to which each party honors those terms. One can be employed by another in exchange for an hourly rate, for a fixed salary, for so much produced, for a commission, for a share in the profits, for an indefinite number of other var-ious considerations, or any combination of these. In other words, employment can take many forms and questions appropriate to one form of employment may not be appropriate to others.

Now, the usual conception of employment, and certainly the one that figures in most discussions of the employer–employee relationship, is where one party, the employer, hires another, the employee, to work for an hourly wage over an extended period of time, usually understood as extending into the indefinite future. It is generally pictured that the employer is a firm, company, or private business offering products or a service to customers. (Let's leave aside public employment, which raises unique questions not relevant to our concerns, not the least of which is that the employer of a public employee is, ultimately, the tax-paying citizenry, which includes the employee![6])

Given this necessarily general understanding of who is employee and who is employer, let us now address some basic questions about the nature and moral aspects of this relationship.

The Ethics of Employment

The employment relationship is essentially contractual, reciprocal, and entered into by both parties on equal terms. This last feature, equality, does not mean that each party is equally in need of the particular other for the benefit sought, nor does it mean that each has equal opportunity, resources, or desire to otherwise secure that which an employment agreement would bring. The facts of supply and demand determine which side has the bargaining advantage, exactly as they would in any other commercial transaction. Generally speaking, the employer has more resources and usually more candidates to choose from than the prospective employee, who likely has more competition from other prospective employees. (This, as we note later, is not always so, as in circumstances of a labor shortage, which are frequent enough in modern industrialized societies.)

In short, it is generally the case that there is a greater supply of prospective employees than of employers. This of course means that for any given employer, any particular prospective employee is less significant, less necessary for the realization of the employer's ends. Any one of among many potential employees may well satisfy the employer's needs. On this matter, the employer clearly enjoys more of the power that comes from having greater opportunities. In general, to terminate an agreement with any given particular employee is less traumatic and threatening to the employer's ends than the reverse would be for the employee, whose opportunities for alternative employment may be comparatively few.

Now, these general facts are not unique to employment; they prevail in all commercial transactions to varying degrees, depending ultimately on the law of supply and demand. Furthermore, whether supply and demand favors the employer or the employee is also variable. In some instances, for example, in certain dynamic and rapidly growing industries such as computer programming some years back, or Web-based communication technology more recently, the demand for qualified employees may exceed supply. It may also be the case that an employee will make more money than his/her employer, and it is certainly the case that some employees, such as certain salespersons, earn more money than a good many employers, such as owners of corner markets and other modest businesses. So, contrary perhaps to the popular view, simply because someone is an employee does not, of itself, guarantee that the person is at any disadvantage with respect to his/her employer. Thus, though the power differential may in general side with the employer, it does not always, which means that there is nothing in the employment relationship as such that favors either side. To repeat, each side is free to accept (or refuse) the employment terms of the other, each enters into the relationship voluntarily and self-interestedly, and each recognizes the mutually beneficial value of the agreement. Each is also free to terminate the relationship (subject to the terms of the agreement). In the end, the employer and employee enter the relationship as moral equals, equally bound to honor the terms. That is, in coming to terms, each recognizes the rights and obligations of the other to abide by the terms. They could, of course, make their agreement a legally binding contract, the violation of which would put one at legal risk, but this goes beyond the moral dimension of the relationship and of our present interests.

The Terms

So, the contract or agreement creates the employment relationship and sets the terms that establish the boundaries within which each side must act. Nothing can be determined in advance about the specifics of the agreement apart from certain very basic prohibitions against criminal conduct on the part of either side. Particulars bearing on the employer–employee relationship are bound to vary from time to time, place to place, and from person to person.

For instance, what counts as a fair and attractive wage will vary not only from industry to industry, but also from individual to individual, depending on a host of personal, economic, and social factors. It is impossible to specify what the terms or their limits ought to be, apart from an actual context. In general, the terms agreed to will be determined by what each side has to offer and by the value of those offerings as perceived by both parties. Now, though the particulars of the terms may vary widely, there are general *moral* limits to what may be offered by either side as well as to what each side may accept. These limits, in turn, may vary depending on the moral perspective, philosophy, or principle that serves as a guide. For example, what is permissible from, say, the utilitarian perspective may not be permissible from the Kantian, egoist, or theistic perspective.

However, though these schools of thought differ in some fundamental way from each other, they are in general agreement about many features of morality. For example, they agree about the importance of the virtues and the principle that human beings should avoid harm to innocent others whenever possible, that one ought to keep one's word, and so on. These in turn imply a host of corollaries that form an interlocking web of guiding principles that are the source of everyday, commonsense morality. Much of which, not surprisingly, is consistent with the principles of the major moral theories.

When persons enter into agreements as moral equals, such as when they enter into an employment relationship, this web of principles provides the limiting conditions within which the terms of the agreement are morally acceptable and binding. Many of these principles are so entrenched in and inherent to common social life that they rarely rise to the level of consciousness. For example, that in general people are expected to, and in fact do, tell the truth and keep their word. Were this not so, we would hardly do any of such countless ordinary things as asking a total stranger for directions to the airport!

Human social life abounds in practices, institutions, and behaviors that would be quite inexplicable and empty were it not for shared assumptions that, when made explicit and analyzed, are seen to be moral in nature. The widely acknowledged notion of the "reasonable person," as well as the related notion of "consenting adults," implies a vast array of justifiable assumptions, among them the web of common moral principles. It is from this web that moral philosophies arise and against which moral theories are in part tested.[7] The ethics of employment, beginning with the initial creation of the employment relationship, are also grounded in the common moral web. And so, we can apply not only commonsense moral thinking to the area of employment, we can also apply the insights offered by fairly well-developed moral theories.

Employment and Moral Theories

Now, how does all of this apply, theoretically, to the ethics of employment at the level of abstraction? Put generally, the terms of the employment agreement must be (i.e., are implicitly understood to be) offered by both sides in good faith, free of fraud, without threat of coercion, and open to acceptance, rejection, or possible revision or negotiation. These features are almost always taken for granted and become explicit only under special circumstances or when at some later date conflict occurs and the original agreement is brought into question. The employment relationship is essentially a relationship of trade, with each side offering the other something of value in exchange, the most typical arrangement being some form of labor in exchange for a wage. The trade feature of the relationship means that employment is inherently tied to self-interest. That is, each side seeks to benefit from the trade, otherwise the proposed agreement would make no sense. Thus, the employment relationship has an inherently normative, indeed, moral feature, for it concerns human beings choosing so as to add value to their lives, recognizing that the other is doing likewise. For example, Smith chooses to offer his/her labor in exchange for a certain wage, believing that he/she shall benefit therefrom, and offer what he/she believes the other will perceive as of benefit to him/her. And, just as Smith would see it as an injury or loss to him/herself were the other to misrepresent what he/she offered, so too must Smith recognize his/her misrepresentation as an injury to the other. Smith's understandable resentment toward the other's misrepresentation means that Smith expected to not be so treated, and this expectation arises from the very nature of trade, that it generally serves to be mutually beneficial. But it could hardly have this feature if people were not generally forthright when trading.

This reciprocity feature implicit in the employment agreement is consistent with Kant's second formulation of the categorical imperative, commanding that one treat others as "ends in themselves"—that is, as like oneself in morally relevant ways. Genuine trade, trade befitting of human beings, Kant might say, is possible only among parties that acknowledge and respect one another's autonomy. Fraud, threat, distortion, coercion, and the like corrupt and undermine the essentially moral basis of trade.

The self-interest feature of trade and of the employment relationship makes the moral philosophy of ethical egoism relevant to employment ethics. As we have just seen in the previous chapter, ethical egoism—or moral individualism—holds as its central principle that one ought to act so as to bring about one's own best (or enlightened or rational) self-interest.[8] Clearly, as one enters into an employment agreement, with so much typically

at stake, it behooves each party to be thoughtful, prudent, and as knowledgeable of relevant factors as possible, so as to maximize the securing of
terms that are as beneficial to oneself as possible. From the employer's perspective, for instance, it would be prudent to consider an offer that would
secure him/her the most return in productivity and profits with the lowest
expenditure in labor costs. There may indeed be a going wage for the type of
work offered, including typical benefits, to be adjusted by a variety of other
factors including particular working conditions, hours to be worked, likelihood of continued employment, additional benefits, pay raises, and so on, all
open to bargaining.[9] The same considerations apply to any prospective employee. As in other aspects of life, there is no denying the wisdom of thoughtful consideration. Acting in one's own best interest means acting prudently
and responsibly.

The "mutually beneficial" aspect of the employment relationship is consistent with the utilitarian principle, which praises actions in proportion to
the happiness they produce. Employment brings about benefits to both parties, not to mention in many cases to others, such as customers, and can
thereby be seen as contributing to the "greater good." Granted, the principle
of utility can be interpreted so as to obligate the party that has the greater advantage, to give more than he/she may otherwise be willing to offer, but such
an interpretation, if employed widely, would result in the overall decline of
productivity and would also undermine the free trade feature of the employment relationship, the feature that presupposes the moral autonomy of both
parties. The terms of employment would no longer be determined by the rational and voluntary efforts of the parties; rather, an egalitarian calculus
would prevail. Such is the case with the planned economies of socialist
states, resulting in national bankruptcy as well as in the moral weakness of a
citizenry that depends on the state to make decisions that properly belong to
the individual. On utilitarian grounds, then, the employment relationship as
conceived in this chapter is fully justified.

The employment relationship is also a model of Social Contract Theory.
According to this view, variously understood by thinkers such as Hobbes,
Locke, and Rousseau, society comes into being by means of agreement
among individuals. Social, legal, and cultural rules are justified because of the
consent or agreement of the parties involved. Thus arises the idea of "consent of the governed," which, in terms of the employment relationship,
means consent to the terms mutually agreed to. And, as in Social Contract
Theory, the agreement defines the relationship, is binding, and is rationally
grounded because the goal that motivates the autonomous agents to enter
into the agreement is the expected benefit derived therefrom.

According to theistic ethics, as embodied in the Judeo–Christian–Islamic tradition, the employment relationship is as we have described. This is implicit in the Old Testament, but made quite explicit in the New Testament, where, in the gospel according to Matthew, Jesus offers the parable of the vineyard owner in need of workers. The owner strikes a bargain with some men early in the day, and as the day progresses makes the identical bargain several times with other men. At the end of the day, all of the workers discover that they have been paid the same sum, to which they had initially agreed, regardless of the hours worked. Those who worked the least were paid the same as those who labored for the entire day. Those hired earliest complained of unjust treatment. To which the vineyard owner replied, "Friend, I do thee no wrong; dids't not thou agree with me for a penny? . . . Is it not lawful for me to do what I will with mine own?" In contemporary U.S. society, the aggrieved workers would cry "exploitation" and take the owner to court. But, from a moral point of view, the complaint is groundless. No one entering into an agreement is entitled to more than the terms agreed to. No doubt Jesus had a loftier lesson in mind, but this story illustrates the main points stressed in this chapter about the nature of the employment relationship. The story also underscores the practical wisdom of thinking for oneself in matters of employment. We can imagine the aggrieved workers making additional inquiries before entering into agreements thereafter, especially with the likes of the vineyard owner.

The principles of the major moral theories are, for the most part, consistent with common moral understanding and practice. Furthermore, these theories can enlighten us about the nature of employment and can offer deeper and more sustained accounts of what ought to be done and why when various problems that arise in employment are complex or particularly significant. Consider for a moment the fact that there is widespread agreement, at the commonsense level of morality, about the following: Given that the terms of the agreement that give birth to the employment relationship are voluntarily and mutually acceptable, and given that the agreement creates a reasonable expectation that each party will abide by the terms, it is prima facie wrong for either party to fail to meet the terms, and prima facie right that the terms be honored. This seems clear, obvious, and unobjectionable. In the end, it amounts to saying that one ought to keep one's word. Now, since there are terms to be kept on both sides, the ethics of employment necessarily require approaching employment questions and problems from two perspectives. Let's turn, then, to the question of how this moral base, supported as it is by moral theory, applies to some issues that arise in the area of employment.

There are some commonly held beliefs that employees are morally entitled to such things as a "fair" wage, equal pay for equal work, job security, and safe and healthful working conditions, as well as a variety of benefits including sick leave, paid vacation, rest breaks, maternity leave with guaranteed reemployment, and so on. There are also beliefs concerning hiring and firing, such as nondiscrimination rights, equal pay for equal work, advance notice before termination, severance pay, and so on. These topics merit discussion.

Hiring and Firing

The employment relationship begins when a bargain is struck and the terms of employment are agreed to. The question arises: Are there moral constraints within which an employer must operate when it comes to hiring and to letting an employee go? In other words, may an employer hire and fire "at will"? This question usually means: May an employer hire whomever he/she wishes for whatever reasons and fire an employee whenever he/she wishes and for whatever reasons, without violating morality? If so, then an employer may discriminate on the basis of race, gender, sexual preference, and so on and may fire an employee to make room for, say, a relative or in favor of someone whose looks the employer prefers. From the perspective of all the major moral theories, the answer to this question is "No," but with qualification.

Just as an employer clearly has a right not to hire anyone at all, and even not to offer work in the first place, he/she also has a right to hire whomever he/she wishes and for whatever reasons. However, the conceptual preconditions that the employment agreement be free of coercion, hoax, or fraud morally preclude an employer from advertising a job opportunity publicly, knowing that some otherwise qualified applicants will not be seriously considered because they do not meet the employer's personal, extraqualification preferences.

For example, should an employer advertise a job opening for, say, a sales clerk at his/her store, knowing that he/she will not hire from a minority group, then morally he/she ought to make this clear.[10] Otherwise, qualified minorities, having reasonable expectation of being seriously considered on application, would be victims of deliberate deceit. The advertised opportunity would, to that extent, be fraudulent. Unless otherwise advertised, all candidates with the job-related qualifications ought to be seriously considered. Of course, in actual life, many employers consider all manner of personal characteristics that may not be strictly job related, such as age, race, sex, physical appearance, and so on. No doubt as well, many employers sometimes hire in favor of their preferences and can do so with impunity. It would be absurd to expect an employer to advertise all of the nonjob-relevant preferences he/she might have with respect to an employee. So, this requirement that the agreement be nonfraudulent seems to be a moot point. But the question here is what an employer ought to do, not what in fact some may do or have done.

Many, perhaps most, people believe that an employer seeking to hire ought to be guided only by the job description and the extent to which applicants meet the qualifications. Thus, the "most qualified" applicant ought to be hired. After all, this is what one would want for oneself, should one be a candidate. Anything less seems to be making significant decisions on irrelevant grounds. But is this necessarily so? From the employer's point of view, the job requirements may not be all that matters. Certainly, he/she is looking for someone who can do the job, but he/she may also desire an employee that has a pleasant personality or a quiet demeanor, or one that does not smell of tobacco or perfume. The employer may be considering the social aspects of the work environment and the effect that a prospective employee, however otherwise qualified, may have on coworkers, or on the employer him/herself, not to mention on customers or clients, vendors, and others who might interact with the employee as a representative of the employer's business.

For obvious reasons, employers are as a rule guided primarily by the need to fill an opening with the most qualified applicant, and, as a rule the specified job requirements include relevant experience, skills, knowledge, training, and education. But, depending on the position to be filled, certain qualifications may outweigh others, and rarely are applicants identical in all relevant respects. Furthermore, it may well be that the "most qualified" applicant lacks a sense of humor, has an annoying mannerism, or an otherwise distracting or unpleasant characteristic. Depending on the context, this may be a minor or a serious consideration. The employer is likely in the best position to determine this. Thus, the employer must have latitude and discretion, though he/she may be guided by the job requirements. Were the employer morally bound to hire the "most qualified" no matter what, this would, on at least some occasions, result in the employer hiring someone he/she judged to be a less promising prospect for his/her business than a "less qualified" candidate. But this would contradict the very purpose of hiring someone to begin with, namely, to find someone whom the employer deemed most suitable for the job. On analysis, it is not so evident what the boundaries are of a relevant qualification, much less that an employer ought to hire solely on this basis.

The conclusions reached thus far are supported by appeal to the nature of the employment relationship, and reinforced when considered from the perspective of the applicant. By nature, both employer and employee expect to gain from the employment, or else agreement to terms would be irrational. Suppose that the employer is offering what would otherwise be attractive job-related terms, such as an attractive wage, benefits, hours, and so on, the counterpart to job qualifications. In other words, the employer, by his/her offer of terms, has met the job-related qualifications. Is the applicant morally bound to accept the terms? Suppose, further, that despite the terms the applicant finds certain features of the prospective employment personally distasteful or otherwise not meeting his/her personal preferences, such as the employer is very ugly, has noticeable body odor, is a bit loud and brusque, or some such qualities, or the place of employment is unattractive, other employees are seemingly unfriendly, traffic to work would be burdensome, parking a challenge, or many other possible unwelcome factors. Under some such description, suppose that an applicant declined a job offer in favor of another job with less pay, fewer benefits, and so on, that is, a job with less qualifications because it met his/her personal nonjob-related preferences. Clearly, this is well within the person's rights. No one would hold that the applicant must accept a job simply because the terms offered met his/her expectations and qualifications. By parity of reasoning, it follows that an employer is not morally bound to hire the "most qualified" applicant.

When it comes to terminating an employee and ending the employment relationship, the employer has much less latitude than with hiring. This is because the employee, though having no right to the job as an applicant (the employer could have decided, without moral blame, not to hire any of the applicants after all), does have a right, based on reasonable expectation established by the employment agreement, to remain employed so long as he/she meets his/her end of the agreement and so long as the business continues to require his/her services. The employer may not, morally, fire at will. However, should it eventuate that the services of the employee are no longer required, the employer is not morally bound to continue the relationship; otherwise he/she would become slave to his/her own employee! The employer is, though, morally bound to serve advance notice as early as is possible and prudent. This obligation is reciprocal: the same applies to an employee about to quit his/her job. It is wrong for either employer or employee to terminate the employment relationship without reasonable advance notice, since the welfare of the other to whom one is bound by moral agreement, is at stake. Such eventualities (among others) can be anticipated and ought, if feasible, to be addressed by the terms of the original agreement. Prudent forethought can prevent much avoidable grief.

Fair Wage and Benefits

It is commonly believed that every person is entitled to a fair wage. The idea here is that persons have a right to a decent life, to at least the minimum that is required for survival, and then some, should resources be available. What counts as just with respect to the distribution of resources is explored in the area of philosophy called distributive or economic justice. It has been argued that an economically just society is one where each citizen receives an equal share of society's resources, is guaranteed at least the basic necessities, or receives a share proportionate to his/her productive input, as determined by market demand.[11] Depending on one's view, an economically just society will be somewhere on a continuum of socioeconomic models from laissez-faire, to varying degrees of welfare statism, to communism. Now, regardless of the merits of the various positions taken on the questions of distributive justice, it is safe to say that the more one's model of distributive justice includes a guarantee of wages and benefits, prior to the employment agreement, the less will there be of the moral feature of employment. That is, the more that what would have counted as the terms to be negotiated are presupposed, perhaps even coded into law and backed by threat of force, the less room there will be for careful and deliberate choice by either party.[12]

How is a fair wage to be determined? Indeed, how is a minimum wage determined? In the simplest sense of the term "minimum," such a wage would be the lowest that a prospective employee would be willing to accept, and this would vary from person to person. If Jones is willing to work for a lower wage than is Smith, an employer could hardly be called unfair and unjust in hiring Jones, anymore than Jones could be accused of unjustly depriving Smith of the job by accepting a lower wage.

Furthermore, the idea of a fair wage, understood as anything other than the wage freely agreed to, is a conceptual error. The wage that an employee is willing to work for depends on a host of other factors that the employee (ought to and usually) has taken into account: in contrast with available employment options, the hours to be worked; the prospects of long-term employment; the prospects for advancement, pay raises, and fringe benefits such as a retirement plan, health plan, vacation, and sick days; distance from home to work; conditions at the workplace, including safety features; conveniences; possible social relationship; and other factors will determine a fair wage—that is, the wage that a person will be willing to accept. Thus, $10 per hour, everything considered, may be acceptable to one person, a boon to another, and woefully inadequate for yet a third. No one can determine in advance, prior to offers being tendered, what a fair wage will be for any job. We can, of course, answer the empirical question of what the going rate is for many jobs, but that fact tells us only what people are typically or on average being paid for that kind of work. Such facts have little, if any, moral implications.

In terms of the basic features of employment, a just or fair wage would be one that each side agrees to, so long as there is no misrepresentation, fraud, or coercion, just as a fair or just price for some property one wishes to sell is the price that seller and buyer agree to. This does not mean that each side will be equally benefited by the exchange, but a resulting inequality does not mean that either party acted unjustly. One might have acted prematurely, impulsively, ignorantly, or without sufficient forethought, or perhaps unknowable factors were at work to account for the inequality. Regardless, so long as the terms agreed to come by way of bargaining in good faith, one cannot say that the wage is unjust. Now, it may be indecently low, meaning that the employer may be quite able to offer more without sacrifice to him/herself, but instead refuses to pay any more than a desperate prospective employee is willing to accept. Some may call such a situation coercive. After all, the worker has no power, no alternatives, is at the mercy of the employer, and the subsequent working conditions may likely amount to exploitation. Such circumstances fuel talk of workers' rights, the idea that, given the typically disadvantageous position of the employee relative to the employer, the worker is morally entitled to certain special consideration, including such benefits as health and safety provisions. In other words, *were* the worker to actually be on equal bargaining terms, these benefits would be among those that he would bargain for. On this reasoning, it is only the difference in power, favoring the employer, that accounts for the lack of benefits that the employee would otherwise enjoy.[13]

This view certainly has merit and given the exigencies of supply and demand many workers, particularly the relatively unskilled, have little to offer as bargaining chips. They are, so to speak, at the mercy of employers. No wonder that the acquiring of education and of marketable skills is so much a part of common wisdom. The very concept of a "marketable" skill suggests that those workers whose skills are in demand are likelier to secure desired benefits than those without such skills. This appears to be an inherent feature of free markets and of human life, not of the employment relationship as such, and only an external force such as government mandates could make it otherwise. Thus, the appeal to a special set of workers' rights based on the power differential between employer and employee has the following oddity: the "rights" exist just to the extent that the power differential exists, and in direct proportion to the difference in power. In other words, the rights would be going in and out of existence, and would fluctuate in force with shifts in the market. In turn, the converse of the power differential is also possible: An employer unable to offer sufficiently attractive terms may have to settle for a less skilled, experienced, or desirable applicant.

Furthermore, even in those circumstances where the employee is at the mercy of the employer, it is an error to call the terms or the conditions unjust, however deplorable the conditions. The employer who is capable of offering more but refuses to is acting within his/her rights and within the boundaries of moral obligation. He/she owes the employee(s) only what was agreed to; he/she is not (we assume) responsible for the employee's desperate circumstances, and he/she is no more obligated to pay beyond what is agreed to than he/she is obligated to offer a job in the first place. If an employer were morally bound to offer a particular wage, then, at least to that extent—which would be considerable—the fundamental nature of the employment relationship as described earlier would be so altered that we could not call it an agreement at all. In short, the free exchange feature of the employment relationship would be lost, just as if, in the market, one were prohibited from deciding for oneself the value or worth of a product or service and from bargaining over the price. One casualty of this would be the elimination of each party's acting prudently, intelligently, and thoughtfully about a matter of significance to his/her life. The view that there could be a morally obligatory wage or other employment benefit would, ironically, rob the employment relationship of the very feature that makes it a moral matter in the first place!

Many people believe that there is a minimal standard of living tolerable in a society with sufficient resources, and that, at the very least, employers ought to offer a wage no less than would provide the worker with such a living. On this view, a fair or decent wage is presumably determined by the cost of living within a community or a society. Something along these lines is the rationale for our national minimum wage law. But the guarantee of such a wage prior to an employment agreement is not consistent with the nature of employment in its basic moral sense. Such a guarantee would be a politically mandated coercive action requiring state involvement. Our concern here is with the moral dimension of employment, which presupposes that the terms are a matter ultimately to be decided between the prospective employer and employee.

Everything said earlier with respect to wages applies as well to benefits. In years past, anything in addition to the wage, such as overtime and vacation pay, insurance, and the like, was referred to as a "fringe" benefit, underscoring the primacy of the wage as of value to the employee. Given the growth of wealth in recent decades, the influence of labor unions, and the expansion of public employment, which includes extrawage benefits as part of a total employment package, it is now commonly expected that at least some benefits in addition to the wage will be offered by employers. This, of course, makes the idea of a "fair" wage even less definitive. Clearly, the more that an employer is willing to offer in the form of a wage, the less will he/she be willing and able to offer in the form of benefits, and vice versa since benefits, like wages, are a cost of labor to be assumed by the employer. There can be no ideal or objectively determined balance of wage and benefits apart from a context that includes particular persons, places, and circumstances, all of which are bound to vary.

Now, to say that there is no morally well-grounded claim to workers' rights and that an employer does not have a moral obligation to provide anything more than the market will bear does not mean that employees are never exploited or that such employers are free of moral blame. Morality includes much more than rights, duties, and obligations. In particular, morality consists, perhaps essentially, in the expression of virtues and avoidance of vices. Among the virtues are charity, compassion, and kindness to others. These human excellences are not *duties* such as others can be said to have a right to them from others, but they are constitutive of human character and expressive of human goodness, such that failure to be virtuous when called on is cause not for punishment or redress, but for moral censure. Failure to act virtuously does not so much bring on one judgment of guilt, as it does judgment of shame.

Now, the idea of workers' rights is likely motivated by genuine sympathy for the plight of others, and the tendency to respond in the language of rights is understandable but misplaced. There is indeed cause for moral outrage at exploitation, whether in employment or elsewhere, but the moral failure is the lack of charity, compassion, kindness, and human decency. The language of rights and duties has the practical advantage of offering justification for legal protection, backed by threat of force in the form of punishment such as fines or incarceration. By comparison, moral censure typically fails as a catalyst for change, ironically, as morality collapses into law and the difference becomes obscured. Such has been the direction of our culture, of most social democracies: The more that morality is legislated, the less genuine morality will there be.

Job Security

Without doubt, one of the most disruptive and personally threatening events for most people would be to lose a job. A recurring complaint aimed at "corporate America" is that it treats employees as expendable, and that the disruptions caused by downsizing, closing plants, relocating, and using mass layoffs in the name of "the bottom line" are an undue hardship on ordinary workers. A theme of the recently emerging communitarian view is that companies have an obligation to the communities in which they do business, including an obligation not to relocate nor to practice large-scale layoffs. It is often argued that workers have a "right" to job security. Setting aside the more general question of the obligations, if any, that a company has to the community in which it operates, we can address narrower questions: Does an employer have an obligation to see to the continued employment of his/her employee(s)? Does an employee have a right to job security?

Clearly, a worker has a reasonable expectation of continued employment so long as he/she meets the terms of the employment agreement, and in this sense he/she does have job security. This seems to be implicit in the original agreement. Thus, if the employee is meeting his/her end of the terms, it would be wrong for an employer to dismiss him/her without just cause. As part of common understanding until quite recently, a person was thought to be secure in his/her job to the extent that he/she was a productive worker, loyal to the company, honest, and otherwise an asset to the business. Secure, that is, so long as the employer could afford to honor the terms of the employment agreement. A job is only as secure as the business is thriving. Lately, the idea has been gaining currency that workers have a right to be secure in their jobs and to be free of the worry of losing their jobs to the whim of the employer or to downturns in the economy. As noted earlier, an employer may not morally dismiss an employee without just cause, but the guarantee of security, independent of factors such as the health of the business, would essentially turn the employer into an indentured servant, thus undermining the voluntary feature necessary to the employment relationship. To say that the employer must continue employing a worker "no matter what" is logically equivalent to saying that the employee must continue working for the employer "no matter what," which of course is absurd. Should the employee get a better job offer elsewhere or learn that relocating would likely improve his/her career prospects, no one would seriously argue that it would be immoral of him/her to terminate his/her employment.

An employer can hardly be morally expected to provide an employee continued employment for a position that is no longer serving the needs of the employer. In this sense, a job is only as secure as there is a market demand for it—just as a business is secure only to the extent that there is a market demand for its products or services. Without customers who are willing to pay for the product or services, there would be no need for workers. To the extent that one person's job is guaranteed secure, through, say, protective legislation, someone else's job or freedom will be curtailed.

Health and Safety

Matters of health and safety in the workplace ought to be major considerations to both employees and employers. On the one hand, some might argue that an employer has a moral obligation to see to the health and safety of his/her employees. Since the employee is under the direction and supervision of the employer, is working on the premises of the owner, and is usually using the tools and equipment of the owner, it is up to the employer to see to it that the working conditions, including the equipment, are safe. Additionally, the employer is generally more knowledgeable about such matters relevant to his/her industry and is therefore in a better position to anticipate dangers than are employees. There is, after all, a general moral duty to avoid harm to others, and health and safety protection are clearly preventive measures. On this view, the employer is morally obligated to provide a safe and healthful working environment.

On the other hand, appealing to the nature of the employment relationship, it can be argued that the employer has no obligation apart from the terms to which he/she has agreed. If anyone should attend to matters of health and safety, it is the employee him/herself, since it is his/her own welfare and interests that are at stake. It would be imprudent of an employee to assume that the employer will see to these matters. The view that it is the employer's duty, not the employee's, misplaces the burden, discourages caution, and thus puts the employee at even greater risk than otherwise. As for the moral duty to avoid injury, this is a negative, not a positive, duty. It admonishes one from acting in ways that, if avoidable, bring harm or injury to innocent others, unless a more morally compelling duty cannot be met without such injury. In other words, this duty does not require that the employer provide anything special by way of health and safety protection.

All this said, there is nonetheless very good reason for the employer to see to health and safety in the workplace. It is in the employer's best interest to provide a working environment free of undue risk of injury or illness, since productivity is directly and negatively affected by injury and illness. Just as it makes good sense for a prospective employee to assess the safety conditions of the workplace as part of his consideration of the merits of the job, so too does it make sense for the employer to attend to risk of injury and threat to health in the workplace of his/her business.

But health, safety, and risk are relative and must be understood contextually. Different industries pose different dangers and to varying degrees. Even with elaborate precautions, some jobs are inherently more dangerous than others. Over time, various industries have gathered data, assessed risks, and provided "industry standards" to inform and guide the decisions and behaviors of those within the industry. Understandably, these standards must themselves be adjusted to relevant differences in location, as well as to changes in and accessibility to relevant technology, new discoveries, and economic conditions. Generally speaking, lowering the risk of injury or disease is technology dependent on a continuum from somewhat effective to "state of the art." Additionally, the more effective the protection, usually the greater the cost. It is also a fact of life that some people are willing to run greater risks than others and to assess risks differently.

In other words, though both employee and employer have a vested interest in the safety of the working environment, the degree of interest, as well as the degree of risk that anyone is willing to take or expect others to take, cannot be quantified or predicted. Thus, even with industry standards, individual preference, assessment, and judgment are called for. One prospective employee may be willing to run a greater risk for the same pay or to perceive the risk differently than another. One employer may assess the productivity implications of certain preventive measures as more promising than another, and so on.

What all of this means is that, though neither employer nor employee have rights against or duties toward one another over and above the employment agreement, they can and ought to include health and safety considerations among the specific terms of the employment contract, if there is special reason to do so. It should be noted here that there are certain widely expected standards of health and safety for workers in various industries, and for the most part these are already generally provided by employers, such as adequate heating, lighting, and ventilation. Over time, given technological advances, greater knowledge, and reduced costs resulting from economies of scale in response to increased demand, what at one time may have been prohibitive and thus rare health and safety protection, may become reasonable and customary. What passes for safe today, or in this or that industry, may, from some future vantage point, be seen as deplorable or reckless by comparison. In any event, the employer has an obligation to provide working conditions that meet common expectations or to inform prospective employees if he/she does not. But since continued advances and new knowledge seem ever unfolding, there may always be thresholds and gray areas about which thoughtful people may disagree as to what is reasonable or customary.

Organized Labor

Given the generally social tendency of human beings, especially the tendency of people with like circumstances to associate with one another, it is hardly a surprise that workers would find it in their interests to associate as workers. Such associations can take various forms, from loosely structured, informal social gatherings, to clubs, to unions with dues, elected representatives, and bargaining power. There is strength in numbers, in solidarity, and in sharing resources, ideas, and problems, and doing so in an organized way is inherently more productive, efficient, and effective than to do so haphazardly. So, some degree of labor organizing would seem inevitable, especially as the number of employees in a business increases. Nor is it the case that employee organizations are inherently adversarial with respect to management. Indeed, both employer and employee can benefit from organized labor since the organization can serve as a resource of information and as a vehicle of communication between employer and employee, which can enhance relationships between labor and management.

The employment relationship typically continues over an extended period of time, during which many factors affecting employment are likely to change and to raise employee concerns. Through an employee organization, workers can more effectively voice employment concerns and increase their influence on management decisions. All of this can be accomplished amicably and to the mutual benefit of employer and employee. Under conditions of good faith communication, where all parties are willing to listen and are resolved to work together toward mutually agreed to solutions, it is likely that participants will consider matters from other points of view, thus reducing the chance of misunderstanding, resentment, and entrenchment, which result in warring camps.

Admittedly, this view of the employment relationship runs counter to the widely held attitude that workers must unite "against" their employers lest they be exploited in the employer's greedy pursuit of profits. Historical appeals to the working conditions of the early industrial period support this perception, as do appeals to the advances made by labor subsequent to forceful strategies by labor unions in the first half of the twentieth century. But, even granting this interpretation of labor history, the apparent premise underlying the common attitude is that the employment relationship is inherently adversarial. This premise does not hold up under analysis.

However compelling its historical origins, the adversarial view too rigidly identifies people with their roles and tends to stereotype these as well. It treats accidental features of employer and employee as though they were essential features of the employment relationship. This error creates the very division that the adversarial view holds to be inherent in the employment relationship. In other words, the common attitude begs the question.

We saw earlier that the employment relationship is essentially a matter of morality, which requires that we treat people as persons who are rational and able to make choices for themselves. There is nothing inherent in one's social or economic class, or in one's employment circumstances that precludes one from treating others morally. It is simply social or economic prejudice to assume, as does the adversarial view, that employers are inherently evil, that is, unwilling to treat employees with moral respect. Immorality is a feature of individual human beings, not of a social class. Without doubt, some employers are stingy, disrespectful, exploitative, and uncaring. But not all. Those who are have come by it on their own, not because they are employers. Likely the same persons, as employees, would continue to be stingy, disrespectful, exploitative, and uncaring, as no doubt some employees are. Human faults and frailties find a home in every social and economic class.

In a number of industries, such as mining, steel, auto, and trucking, unions have become the predominant mode of organization for workers. The exact nature of a union is not easy to define and distinguish from other forms of labor organization, but generally a union appears to be a relatively highly organized association of workers, complete with dues for membership, a hierarchically structured administration with elected positions, and agents who represent the membership.

In bargaining for wages and benefits, the larger and more powerful a union is, the greater is employee leverage in bargaining for desired wages and benefits, mainly because the threat of work stoppage, or strike, poses considerable disruption of commerce within the industry or business.

Many people believe that, short of government mandates, unions are the best assurance that workers will be treated fairly.[14] It is also widely believed that unions are a major cause of the improvement of working conditions, wages, and benefits, though there is dispute about the overall desirability of the bargaining power of unions.

For example, it has been argued that unions ultimately work against the consumer because the additional cost of labor secured by union bargaining results in higher prices of goods and services to consumers.[15] What this means is that the gains to union employees may come at the expense of other workers.[16] Much the same could be said about strikes, which effectively curtail or altogether stop production.

A strike suspends the employment relationship, with the end result of compelling the employer, by virtue of economic pressure, to agree to certain terms. On its face, this seems inconsistent with the original description of the employment agreement, which requires that there be no coercion. However, this requirement applies to the origination of the agreement.

Once an employment relationship exists, a union is in place, and bargaining reaches an impasse, a strike is the temporary termination of the relationship, not a violation of the terms, unless the terms of the original agreement included a no-strike provision. Apart from this, there is nothing in principle wrong with employees refusing to work and circumstances are conceivable where this would be the most effective and reasonable strategy for workers. Such a strategy amounts to the workers quitting and/or terminating the employment relationship. But, under these circumstances the employer is hardly morally bound to rehire the employees. Unless the employer has breached the terms originally agreed to, or has otherwise acted fraudulently or coercively, a work stoppage is equivalent to quitting one's job. An employer's obligations to an employee end with the termination of the employment relationship.

Everything said thus far is within the context of morality. There exist a host of laws and regulations relevant to employment, unions, and the legal rights of workers that may or may not be consistent with the moral view sketched in this chapter. A considerable body of literature exists that explores the relationship between employment laws and morality, as well as the social, political, and economic implications of protective legislation. A final word: Since the employment relationship is essentially moral in nature, employment legislation that diminishes the freedom and responsibility of individuals to make decisions regarding their own welfare is morally questionable.

Notes

This chapter derives from one, similarly titled, in Tibor R. Machan, ed., *Morality and Work* (Stanford, CA: Hoover Institution Press, 2000).

1. For a "mission statement" and legislation data relevant to the U.S. Department of Labor, go to http://www.dd.gov/dol/public/regs/main.htm.

2. Other factors may also contribute to the existence of such laws, such as promises of benefits to large blocks of voters in exchange for votes. What may be

questionable, both morally and economically (e.g., a mandated minimum wage), becomes the expected, the valued, the norm of decency, and so on once it gets legal sanction and enjoys the respectability of having come into being through the democratic process.

3. See James E. Chesher, "Business: Myth and Morality," in *Business Ethics and Common Sense*, ed. Robert W. McGee (Westport, CT: Quorum, 1992), 45–65.

4. An irony of contemporary politics is that the very moral principle that is often appealed to for justification of government spending and the limitations on freedom created by regulations, namely, utilitarianism, was given sharp limits ignored in wholesale fashion by the very people who invoke action in the name of the greater good. John Stuart Mill, in his famous essay "The Tyranny of the Majority," argues that there are moral limits to what can be mandated. In other words, Mill himself argued that majority rule, or majority benefit, does not in itself justify action that brings it about; there are some actions that even the majority may not rightfully impose. Examples abound.

5. For a discussion of Karl Marx's influence on the myth of worker as slave, see Chesher, "Business," 59–61.

6. There are political factors inherent in public employment, as well as problems unique to the public sphere, that would require lengthy treatment beyond the scope of this chapter. Additionally, government employment necessarily involves complex legal and bureaucratic considerations that would unnecessarily complicate our inquiry, which focuses on the moral aspect of employment. In short, not every legal obligation, right, or limitation is a moral one. However, generally, what we say about the ethics of employment should apply to public employment, though with a host of qualifications.

7. By "in part," we mean that moral theories must, in the end, not conflict with our most fundamental and general prephilosophical moral intuitions. There are, of course, other requirements of a moral theory, that it be internally consistent, broad in scope, applicable by the ordinary person, and so on. This fact of human life may account for the phenomenon that nearly everyone takes his/her own moral opinion about something quite seriously, if not always reflectively. After all, in addition to the acquired cultural and social prejudices we are subject to, and that may vary from time to time and place to place, there is also a moral wellspring of principles, virtues, and values that can be traced to human nature itself, to the fact that we are rational beings, language bearers, and self-interested agents. Failure to understand the values implied by our nature, coupled with a failure to distinguish between behavior and meaning, leads often to cross-cultural moral assessments that are off the mark and compound conceptual confusion with normative error.

8. The terms "best," "enlightened," and "rational" are to be understood in this chapter as synonymous. The basic idea of moral individualism is that each individual human being flourishes or tends toward the realization of his/her potential *as a human being* just to the extent that he/she lives thoughtfully and intelligently so as to live fully and happily. Moral individualism sees the commonly recognized virtues of

courage, honesty, generosity, prudence, patience, and such as not only definitive of human excellence, but also as essential elements of happiness and the good life.

9. This assumes the moral context of a completely free exchange, without the interference of the state with its mandated regulations, minimum wage laws, overtime restrictions, and so on. The more state involvement here, the less freedom either prospective employer or employee has, and the less room there is for individual initiative, creativity, and responsibility for the terms of the relationship.

10. It would, of course, be illegal today to do this. The point here is that, from a strictly moral point of view, an employer's job offer is an extension of his/her right to property.

11. For a brief overview of three positions on this question, including a defense of the social welfare state, see Trudy Govier, "The Right to Eat and the Duty to Work," *Philosophy of the Social Sciences* 5 (1975). For a brief defense of the free market view on this question, see Irving Kristol, *Two Cheers for Capitalism* (New York: Basic, 1978).

12. Rather strong support of the view that increasing state involvement undermines the volitional, and thus, moral feature of employment, comes from France, where recently companies that violated the zero-tolerance no-overtime work faced fines sufficient to disincline employers and employees from agreeing to mutually beneficial overtime arrangements. As a result of the inhibition created by threat of fines, some companies in France are finding it hard to compete with companies from other countries that have no overtime restrictions.

13. For a defense of workers' rights, see Patricia H. Werhane, *Persons, Rights and Corporations* (Englewood Cliffs, NJ: Prentice Hall, 1985).

14. Today, labor organizations are highly regulated and protected by a considerable body of legislation. For a discussion of the history of unionized labor and regulations, see Tibor R. Machan, *Private Rights and Public Illusions* (New Brunswick, NJ: Transaction, 1995).

15. For an elaboration of this point, see J. T. Bennet, *Does a Higher Wage Really Mean You Are Better Off?* (Springfield, VA: National Institute for Labor Relations Research, 1985).

16. See William Hutt, *The Strike Threat System: The Economic Consequences of Collective Bargaining* (Indianapolis: Liberty, 1975).

CHAPTER FIVE

~

Advertising and Ethics

Advertising is the most morally chided aspect of doing business. Hardly any-body admits to liking advertising and even advertising professionals say nasty things about it, judging by all the exposés published by former advertising ex-ecutives. As for junk mail, most of it is thrown away. No one likes telemar-keters, either, who call at 6:00 P.M., during dinnertime.

But what is advertising? It is a form of promotion, plain and simple, every bit as necessary and defensible as other kinds of promotion. Advertising is a sort of plea, like a job application, from people who are trying to make a liv-ing. They're hoping that our interests and theirs can coincide at some point. To find out, they are shouting at everyone, as it were, with their message that they can do this or that for us, and sometimes the message does hit the tar-get.

Advertisements are often chastised for revealing less than the whole truth.[1] But this is no moral lapse: Advertisers do not tell the whole truth about their products, but no one with any sense should *expect* to be told the whole truth, especially within the span of a fifteen-second television com-mercial or a single glossy magazine ad. (Just as a résumé is neither intended nor expected to tell the whole truth or an attractive garment to reveal the whole person.) One does not list faults on promotional literature but leaves it to buyers to discover them, perhaps by purposeful inquiry of one's own or the employment of business firms specializing in gathering such information. In any case, gaining that knowledge is the buyers' responsibility.

Advertising is not primarily a means for conveying the whole story about products or services but for *calling attention to their availability for sale*. Common sense is important here. When the Toyota guy jumps into the air and hangs there suspended, we are not being told, "Hey, we here at Toyota can levitate," so that if in fact they cannot, they may be sued for misrepresentation. That's a misconception. Instead, advertising is best understood as a sometimes colorful, sometimes silly means of catching the attention of potential customers.

Consider what personal endorsements try to accomplish: An Elizabeth Taylor, a Bob Dole, or a Tom Selleck pitches something and we recognize the face; our attention may thus become engaged. Or perhaps gimmicks are deployed that have nothing to do with the product or service for sale. The gimmicks may well snag the attention of those who aren't thinking of buying anything, but might be persuaded to consider a purchase if only they were to pay heed. Hence the romantic tales, adventures, jingles, and skits that segue into pitches for beer, batteries, and bras. Some of these commercials are masterpieces of misdirection, but nobody with a bit of wit misconstrues the nature of the product once the true point of the ad is revealed.[2]

Like makeup or shoulder padding, advertising aims to enhance the image of a product or service. In doing so it neither lies nor tells the whole truth. Rather, it parades the possible advantages that a seller may have to offer, with a little bit of ornamentation. Most of us know that the goal of advertising isn't primarily the dissemination of information. And, of course, it is always possible to gather more information about a product before buying it. At very least, one's initial purchase of an inexpensive product gives one plenty of information from which to decide whether to purchase it again.

Do Ads Create Desires?

One source of the hostility toward advertising is the notion that ads manipulate us as if we were puppets on strings. Some people believe that human beings are completely malleable—that we are clay that can be molded by psychological techniques, gimmicks, and so on. When somebody is charged with a crime, defense attorneys will often argue not that the accused didn't do it but that the accused couldn't help himself: If somebody cannot help doing what he/she does, he/she cannot be guilty. Nor can he/she be praised, however. And if that's the case, we're all just preprogrammed robots.

Yet, underlying the whole ethical framework of human life is our awareness that people ordinarily can choose. This would be evident even in someone's criticizing the claim just made: To criticize others is to assume that they could have done otherwise.

One famous critic of advertising is John Kenneth Galbraith, professor emeritus at Harvard University Department of Economics. He has been a widely known public figure, including an ambassador to India under John F. Kennedy's administration. As he put it, "An even more direct link between production and wants is provided by the institutions of modern advertising and salesmanship. These cannot be reconciled with the notion of independently determined desires, for their central function is to create desires—to bring into being wants that previously did not exist."[3]

This idea has shaped what many academicians think about advertising. They treat it as a weapon directed at people who are helpless to resist. But it isn't, and they aren't. Indeed, one of the reasons advertising has to be cleverly designed is that *people can ignore it*. They can walk away from commercials in a jiffy, even from the best of them. That's also why advertisers *target* their audience. They try to reach the folks who are already disposed to buy the kind of thing they have to sell.

In the real world as we normally perceive it, we can easily tell that advertising is not the cause of our desires. If we dislike sports, it doesn't matter how many commercials for surfboards, jerseys, and Monday night football that we see. They just bounce off us. We buy a book instead.

F. A. von Hayek argues as much when he points out that "Professor Galbraith's argument would be easily employed, without any change of the essential terms, to demonstrate the worthlessness of literature or any other form of art. Surely an individual's want for literature is not original with himself in the sense that he would experience it if literature were not produced."[4] Of course, any response to the things of the world requires that those things exist prior to our response to them! There is an objective reality out there, but that is no bar to free will!

Galbraith's attitude makes sense only if the whole of human action is a matter of stimulus provoking automatic response. But if that were so, no additional onus of culpability could be imputed to advertising and to the businesses that produce it. Advertising would be just as moral or nonmoral as any other activity we engage in.

Fortunately, the situation is otherwise. Far from regarding their prospects as sheep, most advertisers assume, at least implicitly, that the customer will do some serious examining to find out if their product or service really does suit his/her purposes.

The Benefits of Advertising

Advertising benefits both producers and consumers. It makes possible mutually beneficial exchanges that might not have taken place otherwise. This is true even though advertising annoys and irritates many who are faced with it, especially via the broadcast media.

What do advertisers accomplish for themselves when they successfully pitch a product? They will have found a way to make a living.[5] Consider the poor benighted telemarketer, calling you up in the middle of dinner with a proposal to switch your telephone service.

Should one hang up on the guy? Not necessarily, even when one isn't in the market for a new long-distance phone service. Consider that all these folks are trying to earn a living. Why not take a moment to say, "No, the service here is quite satisfactory. Thank you, and good-bye." Why not extend some courtesy, out of appreciation for what they are trying to do: earn a living? That is a bond between us all and deserves at least a modicum of respect.

In this age of broadcasting, advertisements are often presented to many millions more than are in the market for the product or service being promoted. As one views a television or listens to a radio program, an ad interrupts and this tends to annoy us (our annoyance is, incidentally, yet more evidence that advertisers cannot simply reconstitute our preferences at will). Most viewers would rather continue attending to the program without interruption The ads thwart this desire.

Occasionally, an ad strikes squarely at one's own needs and wants, demonstrating the benefits of advertising for consumers. So perhaps one can be tolerant of ads that miss the mark. (And are there no mute buttons?) In other contexts, ads are more narrowly cast and thus less annoying. Indeed, sometimes readers of specialized magazines will flip through looking only at the ads.

Advertising has additional benefits. Thanks to television ads, we don't have to pay for network television—and the cost of cable television is reduced. Without ads, we would not enjoy access to so much free information on the Internet. Internet access itself is now available at no charge, if one's willing to tolerate some pop-up ads. Advertising is thus one modern method for spreading the benefits of new products, services, and information from the few to the many.

Advertising and Prudence

Ideally, when both parties have done their best to learn what would be prudent for them to do, only then should they engage in trade.

Not everyone is always prudent, it's true. Some people just see ads and simply yield to the desire to get what is being offered; they buy on impulse. Impulse buying most closely resembles the phenomenon that Galbraith and others think advertising engenders all the time. But people who buy on impulse don't have to buy; they simply have chosen carelessly. (And even then, the impulse buyer's imprudent purchases are confined to the realm of his/her already chosen values and interests, be they clothing, lottery tickets, food, or books.)

Just as having the capacity to reason does not mean that one will always reason, so having the capacity to be prudent does not mean that one will always be prudent. Participants in the market can fail to be alert, to pay attention to their own responsibility in a trade. They may shirk that responsibility and then, afterwards, when they are suffering the losses, blame the other party, not themselves. But they are complicit for having neglected to pay sufficient attention to what was going down.

What's a Good Ad?

The primary purpose of an ad, and thus the responsibility of those who make them, is to call attention to a product or service so effectively that people will have difficulty overlooking or ignoring it. Is this morally proper and ethical? Ought business try to capture people's attention this way? Yes, and here is why: It's important for us to prosper and thus important for us to promote the services or wares that we have to offer for sale to earn our livelihood. If human life is a value, then advertising is a value, given its life-serving aims.

Advertising is self-responsible, not selfish in any cruel, nasty, or brutal sense of the word. People in business must make this effort to take care of themselves, to do justice to the prospect of succeeding and prospering in their lives. Moreover, everybody benefits—the customers, the people who own and run the businesses, and the employees whom businesses are able to hire when the advertising succeeds.

It should be noted, in conclusion, that mistaking advertising for an information dissemination rather than a promotional process has the consequences of blaming ads for not doing what they aren't meant to do. Ads only alert us to options and opportunities, they are not the guide to how we should spend our money. One philosopher we have already mentioned even blames ads for not telling the whole truth about products and services.[6] As if advertisers have taken the sort of oath witnesses do at a criminal trial—to tell the whole truth and nothing but the truth.

For witnesses, that is indeed the proper oath, since trials are procedures to learn the truth about guilt and innocence and in the absence of the whole truth and nothing but the truth, there would be a serious miscarriage of justice. This doesn't at all apply to ads. Their purpose is to attract attention to something a seller may be able to do for a potential customer. Ads are more like jewelry than like some hand tool—they function to put something in the best light! That is the point of jingles and celebrity endorsements.

Arguably, the critics of advertising as such—as distinct from those who criticize bad, deceptive, or offensive ads—have something against promoting goods and services to potential buyers, fearing, as Galbraith fears, that those encountering ads simply have no free and independent will to handle appeals made to them. We believe this is both mistaken and condescending.

Notes

1. Burton Leiser, "Deceptive Practices in Advertising," in *Ethical Theory and Business*, ed. Tom. L. Beauchamp and Norman E. Bowie (Englewood Cliffs, NJ: Prentice Hall, 1979).

2. Notice how all these elements show that ads are not mainly informative but promotional and must be judged accordingly.

3. John Kenneth Galbraith, "The Dependence Effect," in *Ethical Theory and Business*, ed. Tom. L. Beauchamp and Norman E. Bowie (Englewood Cliffs, NJ: Prentice Hall, 1983).

4. F. A. von Hayek, "The Non Sequitur of the Dependence Effect," in *Ethical Theory and Business*, ed. Tom L. Beauchamp and Norman E. Bowie (Englewood Cliffs, NJ: Prentice Hall, 1983).

5. A little compassion for junk ad mailers might be appropriate here, given what they are trying to do: make a living. They're calling out, "Hey! Here we are! Please consider us when you embark on trade."

6. See Leiser, "Deceptive Practices in Advertising."

~

CHAPTER SIX

Capitalism and Racial Justice

Ever since most Americans rejected slavery and segregation and repealed policies supporting them that were defended, indeed, imposed by their governments, there have been numerous efforts to set things right in the area of race relations. One example of a sound measure was the abolition of government-imposed segregation in the form of separate but (allegedly equal) public institutions throughout the nation. If, for example, the state is to educate our children, it has no business doing it in a way that serves up different goods on the basis of color. An example of a half-baked measure was forced integration, including legally mandated affirmative action and, in some cases, quotas in hiring and promotion. That is because it is wrong to impose racially based disadvantages on the grounds that in the past such disadvantages were imposed on members of a different race. Such an approach to justice, resting as it does on collective guilt ranging over generations, is exactly what the concept of procedural due process is supposed to replace.

A society that exhibits systematic mistreatment of certain identifiable groups whose members are not guilty of anything to deserve such mistreatment is one the legal system of which leaves much to be desired. We know well enough that slavery was unjust and permitted the infliction of great mistreatment and harm on millions of human beings. Most of all, we know that an adult human being isn't authorized to take over another's life without that person's consent.[1] We know, also, that state-fostered segregation made it more difficult for former slaves and those whose ancestors had been slaves to make the most of their lives. And there is still a considerable momentum of hard times for many members of the U.S. black community, in large part because human beings do not easily and rapidly overcome some of the pressures of their upbringing and community. The morale among blacks in the United States has been understandably low about their history since their ancestors were forcibly brought to this country. There is every reason, then, to work seriously for improvement, thereby making our society better not just politically but also as a community in which all human beings can live and flourish.

That said, it seems clear that mandated affirmative action—that is, applying special favorable terms of trade and of hiring and promoting to African Americans and other minorities—and similar state measures conflict with the basic principles of the free society, including freedom of trade in the market of goods, services, and labor. These general principles are the basic rights of individuals to life, liberty, and property. They rest on the idea that each individual is sovereign and may not be subjected to involuntary servitude.[2]

When applied throughout the community, these rights imply, among other things, freedom of trade or commerce. Such freedom means that as one engages in trade with others, no outsider, not even government, is justified in setting the terms of that exchange. So long as the right to liberty of all (including third) parties to do with themselves and their belongings is not violated, government may not force anyone to do what he/she refuses to. This is the right of free choice in human associations as applied to commerce.

How does this conflict with the current efforts to remedy the past failings of our society, namely, with affirmative action, integration, or quotas?

The usual defense of such programs is that certain groups in society have had enormous advantage by way of oppressing others, which gave members of those groups economic and bargaining advantages resulting in being able to set favorable terms of trade, so it is only just that the tables be turned for a while, until a level playing field has been achieved.[3] The idea does not heed the issue of individual rights but that of group advantages or disadvantages. As such, it conflicts with the theory of individual rights, especially the right to liberty and free trade.

Liberty versus Efforts at Decency

If the idea of individual rights to life, liberty, and property is sound, and if people in the marketplace don't want to practice even the sort of affirmative action that might be justified,[4] affirmative action on their own accord, then no official opposition to what they choose to do is justified. In short, banning irrational discrimination is unjustified in a free society. Instead, employers are owed protection of their freedom to do what they want, just as a newspaper is owed such protection, by way of the First Amendment, against any attack on it for saying unpopular, antisocial things.

Public policy and legal decisions in the United States are increasingly guided by the ideals of group integration and collective restitution—including affirmative action, hiring quotas, and even the idea of compensation to current members of the black population for what was done to their ancestors by those who enslaved them. So, government has been violating and undermining the right to liberty in the name of these objectives. If you do in fact own your home, you must be able to select to whom you will sell it—you must be the one who sets the terms of sale, otherwise your ownership rights are curtailed.[5] If you own your business, you must be the one to decide who will be hired to work for you, as well as promoted or fired—again, depending on the terms of the employment agreement. Those who own a hotel are not enjoying their right to liberty if government has legal power to tell them that they must rent their rooms to anyone who wants to rent them. Schools that must admit everyone who might wish to enroll are not free institutions but do the bidding of whoever imposes such a policy on them. And however much one might value the objectives of fairness and decency that are being pursued by such policies, there can be little doubt that when government forces people to stop being racists, this is a violation of individual rights.[6]

Legal mandates that dictate to producers that they must hire certain persons because this rectifies a social injustice are comparable to legally requiring consumers to patronize certain businesses whether they want to or not because, say, it is only fair.

Some people surely refuse to shop in certain stores for racist or bigoted reasons. They might, indeed, find what they want if they were to shop there but they irrationally choose not to do so. Consumers own their money or credit and, if they should not use it in certain ways that will promote some social ills, perhaps they should be forced to behave accordingly. Were government to force them to shop or eat or play in places they perhaps irrationally avoid, that would clearly violate their right to liberty.

Or consider the worker who refuses to apply for a job in a firm owned by Jews, blacks, or members of some other group he/she is prejudiced against. The worker has a property right to his/her skills and labor time, just as the owners of firms and shops have a property right to their wares and services, and they, too, will want to set the terms under which they will sell these. Suppose a worker were forced to apply for a job he/she does not wish to apply for based on a prejudice. Surely it would be coercive, a violation of the worker's right to freedom.

Now, if such hypothetical cases involve the violation of individual rights, so must the actual cases we know of, regardless of whether they are needed to achieve important social or political objectives.

The Failure of Government Regulation

It is hardly disputed that current public policies aiming to abolish racial and sexual discrimination do not work well. There are many local government regulations—building codes, zoning ordinances, and so on—that place limits on the way property may be used and business conducted. There is considerable legal precedence for government intervention in the private sector, so one cannot at this point object to racially motivated government regulation on the grounds of legal principle.

Yet, it is arguable that these are irrelevant in the present context since even when there was no national law against discrimination in market transactions and employment, these kinds of laws had been in place. Furthermore, arguably, in a society whose legal system consistently upholds negative individual rights—to life, liberty, and property—these local governmental measures would be illegal and in violation of these rights. Also, such restrictions on market transactions as might exist would emerge from contract, not from legislation or regulation. Providers of unsafe buildings and other facilities could be subject to legal action on the grounds of failing to offer their services or products in line with "reasonable person" standards.

Another problem with government-mandated affirmative action–type regulations is that there are numerous ways to evade compliance with them. A myriad of approaches can be taken to evade the kind of regulations that have made it public policy to implement general remedial measures to correct past injustices. For example, in higher education, the funds are simply not available to fully comply with legal mandates for a national search when a job is available, so the effort at affirmative action is not possible, albeit legally required. Thus, many institutions simply hire very late, when the law allows exceptions. Loopholes are exploited galore, not necessarily so as to succeed at discrimination but because taking the measures government has devised is too costly and cumbersome.

There is one serious complication about mandated affirmative action policies that needs to be faced. This is that many institutions of our society are heavily involved with the various levels of government. For example, many educational institutions, from elementary schools to colleges and universities are either operated by the state outright or receive extensive state support garnered from the taxpayers who have no opportunity to allocate these taxed resources in line with their own priorities and convictions. What about requiring affirmative action policies at such institutions?

If one imagines that state-run outfits are completely legitimate, no different, say, from a government printing office or courthouse, then one might argue that the mandating of affirmative action is but a feature of the management of these activities, some of which may benefit from affirmative action. So such a policy must be considered a feature of administering these state operations, to be decided on the basis of sound management principles. Is it sound management to mandate affirmative action at state-run institutions?

This cannot be decided without recourse to a detailed understanding of the concrete situation that prevails at a given institution. The same approach would have to hold true as does a private company that may elect to practice some form of affirmative action—for example, one owned by Polish descendants that practices preferential hiring and promotion policies regarding Polish Americans.[7]

Yet, so conceiving of all state-run institutions would be a mistake. Some of these ought, perhaps, not be part of the state at all—arguably a kind of separation of education, art, science, athletics, and the state, analogous to the separation of state and religion or the press, ought to apply in many cases. Exactly where the line should be drawn is a complicated issue that cannot be treated here. However, it is important to see that a problem arises about just which state functions are privatizable and which are essential. On that matter will depend, in part, what is to be decided about the application of the principles that should govern the administration and enforcement of laws.

In any case, the policy of racially preferred hiring, promotion, admission to schools, and so on is prima facie in violation of the principle that animated the enactment of the Fourteenth Amendment to the U.S. Constitution, namely, that the law must apply fairly and equally, without any discrimination, to all citizens. So there is no basis for implementing racially, ethnically, gender, or similarly based preferential treatment at state-run institutions. When everyone's life's work, from which taxes are taken, supports an institution, there exists no justified authorization for administering an institution based on preferences for some segment of the taxpaying public. Thus, some of what is said here about the way to deal with racism[8] in the marketplace will apply, as well, to what may need to be done with state-run enterprises.

Unintended Consequences of Forced Racial Decency

Perhaps the most damaging results of such racially motivated regulations of market behavior in the battle against racism is the fostering of righteous indignation that can disguise, especially from those who have them, racist feelings. Someone who is coerced into hiring, serving, or selling to blacks, women, or other minorities can rightfully be angry at the intrusive, dictatorial efforts that are ostensibly associated with helping members of these groups, even while they harbor vicious feelings toward those members. It is morally (and should be legally[9]) objectionable to be dealt with coercively—something admitted even by supporters when they claim that such measures can only be justified as correctives, a kind of retaliation, or a temporary necessary evil. So, those who must comply with such directives can divert their attention away from their racism, sexism, and bigotry and stand tall in support of a righteous cause.[10] Indeed, they can easily turn this into a kind of righteous resentment against members of the minorities, thus reaffirming their irrational attitudes by means of a kind of moral and psychological package deal.

Arguably, if affirmative action were the only route available to rectify past wrongs, it would have to be tolerated—after all, slavery and segregation are recent enough political evils that the demand for justice may be exerted on behalf of some people, however clumsily or imprecisely, if only to approximate the search for justice.[11]

Reconciling Liberty and Decency

Yet, what if there were ways to achieve both aims of preserving liberty and abating as well as rectifying racism? There are two possible ways of serving these objectives, namely, compensation and full disclosure.

Compensation for past injustices could be sought through the courts by those who were victimized, when it is demonstrable that certain specific persons have been the beneficiaries of slavery, segregation, or sexual discrimination. If no guilty party can be found or no one can be identified as benefiting from the harm done to those victimized, then no case could be made. If government is the culprit, some rectification—comparable to damage awards when the municipal police are found guilty of violating someone's civil rights—would be available. The hit-and-run approach to broad social "rectification" would not be permitted since collective guilt is not a valid concept and any policy assuming it would have to be invalidated.

As for fighting current discrimination, a different approach (that avoids the violation of individual rights to liberty) would be appropriate. The following will explain how this could work.

Full Disclosure versus Racism

When people own restaurants unburdened by either national or local legislation and regulation addressing the reparation of past injustices—they nevertheless open their establishments to the public; and when they announce employment opportunities they usually do so to the public at large. In a competitive, free market, opportunities at the workplace are usually announced as open to all in the qualified workforce; and houses are usually being marketed to those who are shopping for homes to purchase.

The examples could be multiplied endlessly: In all these cases, the common factor is the implicit claim made by those who are opening their hotels, restaurants, homes, or business to potential trading partners that anyone in the market may make an offer and be considered. A restaurant is open to people seeking to buy a meal, with some conventional requirements satisfied (such as, they are dressed decently, they behave in an orderly fashion, etc.). Thus, if no racial, sexual, ethnic, or similar criteria are specified as terms of trade, none need be considered by those attempting to do business. Entering a restaurant with sufficient funds to pay for the meal (and well-behaved enough not to constitute a nuisance) should suffice to be served a meal. If and when a proprietor tries to eject one for racial or ethnic reasons, that would constitute a breach of implied contract or fraud and failure to live up to the tacit terms of trade. All such conduct should be legally actionable in the courts of a free society.

This approach differs from legislation barring racism, sexism, and so on by making it entirely legal to discriminate provided one announces the policy up front. "Whites only," "women only," "blacks only," "Catholics only," "Baptists only," and the like could be made part of the advertisements for trade and there would be nothing anyone, including government, could legally object to.

At first blush, this may appear intolerable, yet in many areas of life various kinds of discrimination, more or less reasonable, are accepted—in church attendance, in hair salons, in some clubs (e.g., American Association for University Women, Parents without Partners, bowling leagues, bridge clubs, etc.), or other services aimed at only women, men, or some other specific group. Many of these organizations are formed around decent, legitimate activities. Yet, some may well involve activities in which at least some members of the organizations should not engage. And sometimes the organizations themselves could be considered irrational. Certain ideological, athletic, or religious groups, fraternities, associations, and the like may well have dubious reasons for their existence, but because of the principle of freedom of association they must be legally tolerated.

Moreover, in an unregulated marketplace it is no doubt possible to enter into contractual relationships that contain restrictive covenants, some of them beneficial, some indifferent to social values, and others in violation of decency and goodwill. But in the long run, such policies would undermine a merchant's market advantage—economists will point out the inefficiency of racism in the marketplace. Yet, this is no remedy against the indecency of such racism perpetrated on those individuals who experience it at the beginning of the process that will undermine a merchant's long-run market success. Once the merchant's racism, sexism, or bigotry is up front and openly stated, its potency seriously diminishes. This is especially true in a democratic enough society such as ours, in which government can muster a constituency for public policies that aim to further decency by way of legislation and regulation.

In any case, in a consistently free society, when policies of discrimination make clear sense, up-front announcements would find little opposition in the culture. But when they are irrational, unfair, or pointless, their presence would expose them to public view and invite peaceful measures of opposition, criticism, ridicule, rebuke, or ostracism.

No doubt, some pockets of discrimination would persist despite their openness to scrutiny. But that is undoubtedly true now, in addition to the widespread violation of individuals' right to liberty. So, the comparison to some ideal of perfect racial, ethnic, or sexual decency and harmony is unjustified.

The compensation and full disclosure approaches would be far superior to current policy. They would make possible remedies based on compensatory justice or rational terms of trade implicit in market exchanges.

These approaches would avoid the resentment now involved in all the affirmative action, reverse discrimination policies government has created and with which businesses only grudgingly comply. It would also ferret out those who have irrational attitudes, exposing them to direct criticism and making it impossible for them to invoke their more plausible objections to legally sanctioned but immoral coercion in their own defense.

All in all, these approaches seem justified on many fronts beyond our ability to explore here. But most important, they would avoid the current tragedy of public policies and legal mandates that constantly erode our basic right to individual liberty.[12]

Notes

1. There are occasions for this, as when someone goes under the knife in an operating room, leaving everything up to the surgeons.

2. A clear contrast to this view is that propounded by Karl Marx. In *Grundrisse*, he explicitly construes human beings to be parts of an organic body (or whole). See Karl Marx, *Grundrisse*, trans. Martin Nicolaus (New York: Vintage, 1973), 100. This, along with his use of the term "specie-being" and his claim that "The human essence is the true collectivity of man" leaves no serious doubt about Marx's anti-individualism. See also Karl Marx, "On the Jewish Question," David McLellan, ed. (London: Oxford University Press, 1977), pp. 39–62. For an alternative, see David L. Norton, *Personal Destinies: A Philosophy of Ethical Individualism* (Princeton, NJ: Princeton University Press, 1976); Tibor R. Machan, *Classical Individualism: The Supreme Importance of Each Human Being* (London: Routledge, 1998).

3. This policy of "turning the tables" is now widely accepted both in the culture and our legal system. For example, in the culture we have Black Television Network, Conference of Black Governors or Mayors, black student unions, and so on, all of which are accepted as legitimate when it is clear that if there were a White Television Network, Conference of White Governors or Mayors, and so on, this would be deemed racist!

4. Affirmative action is widely practiced by private individuals—old and successful Polish refugees often hire recent ones, Chinese or Italian proprietors or owners of business firms often go out of their way to lend a hand to recent immigrants. Moreover, there is much reverse affirmative action, as when Jews refuse to trade with Germans or with Arabs. Some of these are justified morally, some of them are not. Here, we do not judge individual cases, only to make note of the moral acceptability of some such cases.

5. Of course, if you merely put the home up for sale, with no prior notice of your preference for buyers with certain special traits and attributes, then you are deceiving the public and this could even be legally actionable: The "reasonable person" standard implies that anyone with the requisite money or credit is a qualified prospective buyer. More about this later in the present chapter.

6. There are some circumstances under which grouping blacks, women, Asians, or short people is justified, for example, in efforts to organize against attacks by racists or those with other unjust prejudices who exert power against these groups. If some powerful people are violating the individual rights of blacks, blacks have just cause to group themselves as blacks. But if this isn't the case, there is no inherent common political interest for blacks as blacks or women as women. What remains are certain concerns based on, say, race- or sex-based medical vulnerabilities, aesthetics, or fashion.

7. Arguably, some firms may initiate affirmative action when the law penalizes them for not doing so merely to fend off being forced to do so, but this need by no means be their motivation.

8. By "racism," we mean an attitude whereby someone takes another person to be morally and/or politically inferior or superior because of his/her membership in some racial group. This is distinct from the alleged racism of opposing public policies that many members of a racial group support or desire and from the alleged racism of disagreeing with the proposed public policies of those who believe that they are promoting racial justice by means of these policies. These latter need have nothing to do with racism, although in some cases they may be motivated by it.

Nor is it racism not to like, enjoy, or, alternatively, to give special preference to and gain enjoyment from the practices of members of a given culture on the grounds other than the race of those members. One may prefer the blues, even to the exclusion of alternative musical forms, usually sung by American blacks, without being a racist. One may not like rap music, performed mostly by blacks, without being a racist. These considerations may rest entirely on aesthetic preference or dislike, comfort or discomfort stemming from familiarity or the lack thereof.

Of course, "race" is itself a controversial concept, one that is difficult to employ when, for example, there are people of innumerable mixtures of colors, ethnic origins, and race within a given community. Since, however, the official policy of the United States depends on the concept of race, we will not bother to embark on a critical analysis of that concept in this discussion.

9. This brings up the matter of the relationship between morality and law, a topic legal and political theorists have debated for centuries. Our remark here implies, of course, that we hold that valid, proper laws ought to be in some accord with morality, although precisely how is a long story we cannot deal with here.

10. It is interesting to notice how such attitudes on the part of members of bizarre groups gain support from otherwise decent people. Consider the way the federal government lost the moral high ground against David Koresh when it perpetrated what appeared to many to be a ruthless attack on the cult. People who would probably never consider lending credibility to the Branch Davidians started to take the side of the cult because of such official abuse of power. Following the September 11, 2001, terrorist attacks in the United States, when the federal government began to ask for powers that appeared to most civil libertarians to cross the line and violate individual rights, many saw this as a manifestation of government's inclination to use even the most tragic events to gain more power. Such power grabbing led some to begin to focus not on the terrorists but on the threats of expanded state powers.

One can compare this to how government officials, such as the police, lose their moral standing when they carry out unnecessary force or engage in brutality, even if the target is guilty as charged. This kind of reversal of the moral dynamics of the situation is evident, also, in the misbegotten fight against racism that affirmative action represents.

11. Some, arguing from a purely utilitarian perspective, have held that the idea of any kind of rectification of the wrongs of slavery has to be moot, given that the offspring of slaves in the Unites States have been much better off than the offspring of those who were not enslaved and remained in Africa. This brings to light one of the problems many find with utilitarianism: the failure to consider rights violations and the undermining of the consent of individuals, a significant wrong that requires rectification even if the consequences are beneficial to the victim.

12. It is often argued against a position such as ours that it is too rigid or not pragmatic enough and that it sees matters in terms of general principles rather than on a more properly case-by-case basis. But nothing can be viewed case by case—there is always some principle that governs our assessment of cases. What some take to be rigid, even ideological thinking may in fact be the result of an integrated, consistent approach to personal conduct and to public policy.

CHAPTER SEVEN

~

Professional Responsibilities of Corporate Managers

We have touched on this subject—namely, what ethical principles ought to guide corporate managers—in the introduction to this book. It is perhaps the most widely discussed topic in the literature of business ethics. So, we should explore it in more detail.

In the field of business ethics, one account of the moral (sometimes referred to, question-beggingly, as the social) responsibility of corporations stands out as under extensive scrutiny if not relentless criticism. This is Milton Friedman's view to the effect that managers of corporations have the obligation to make a profit (within the framework of ordinary morality and the legal system), nothing else.[1]

Friedman's can be called a minimalist conception of corporate moral responsibility—the "bottom-line" theory. Do what you promised to do. But perhaps the promise should never have been made. Is this a problem? Friedman does not shed light on this. As do most economists, Friedman assumes that the pursuit of profit or, more generally, prosperity is morally unobjectionable.

Yet, as is clear from a great deal of criticism of capitalism and even of semi-capitalist American and other Western societies, this idea is highly controversial, especially as it applies to corporate business.[2] People frequently refer quite derisively to "commercialism," "materialism," and related ways of characterizing a sustained interest taken in living well and enjoying what can be bought in the marketplace. In contrast, vows of poverty, returning to a preindustrialized way of life, and the idea of small is beautiful tend to command a moral high ground, even if not widespread adherence, in many circles.

Is the libertarian, capitalist economic philosophy Friedman embraces compatible with the different, perhaps richer and deeper, conception of the moral responsibility of corporations? Let's examine a position that we call "classical individualism" and see whether it can address the issue of moral responsibility of corporations better than the position Friedman defends as well as positions that are out and out critical of the libertarian/capitalist framework of political economy.

Classical Individualism

Classical individualism may not fully accord with Friedman's minimalism but neither does it support the position advanced by those who wish to limit the freedom of action of corporations in the effort to further responsible corporate conduct. Classical individualism—or egoism—is the ethical view that everyone ought to benefit him/herself (though not exclusively) and that an objective human nature provides standards or guidelines as to what benefits someone.[3] Furthermore, it is by reference to such standards that private, professional, and political conduct ought to be carried out.

According to this form of individualism, contrary to Marx's claim that "the human essence is the true collectivity of man,"[4] the human essence is the true individuality of every human being without the implication, however, that the human individual is self-sufficient and capable of living a full life cut off from others.

How does this position differ from what is commonly referred to in ethics texts as "ethical egoism"? This latter position is that, as one business ethics text states, "all choices either do involve or should involve self-promotion as their sole objective. Thus a person's only goals and perhaps only moral duty is self-promotion; one owes no sacrifices and no obligations to others."[5] Classical egoism may be compatible with this statement but by spelling out the meaning of "self" in line with a robust, Aristotelian conception of human nature, classical egoism does not imply, for example, that "one owes . . . no obligations to others."

Since by nature we are social beings, our own fulfillment being possible only when we are involved with many other persons surrounding our lives, virtues such as generosity, liberality, and charity must be part of our character. And while a classical egoist does treat prudence as a moral virtue—unlike, say, do Beauchamp and Bowie who distinguish "moral rules from rules of prudence"[6]—the highest of the moral virtues is living rationally. This is identified by the fact that human beings are rational animals and depend for their self-development and self-fulfillment on the choice to use their minds and to focus on their lives conceptually and thoughtfully. In essence, then, the difference between classical and what might be called modern (neo-Hobbesian) egoism concerns the way the human self is understood within the two positions.[7]

Classical individualism is an ethics of self-development, self-perfection. It encompasses a greater role for individuality than do more familiar egoist or individualist views. It also leaves more room for sociability, recognizing the fact that a human individual is by its nature social as well as being a sovereign individual.

Accordingly, whereas it is often argued that an Aristotelian virtue ethics implies a communitarian theory of politics, classical individualism rejects this and favors a libertarian politics because it makes room for both individual development and broad social engagements.

In terms of classical individualism, the task of self-perfection must be chosen by the individual. Thus, the emphasis is on individual choice and responsibility, following the Kantian stress on the fact that "ought" implies "can." If someone or some group of persons ought to act in certain ways, this is of moral significance only if the option of not so acting is actual and not foreclosed (even by the punitive measures of the law). Therefore, morally significant conduct cannot be regimented or imposed by force.[8] That includes the choice of social engagement or community that human beings will have a chance of making throughout their lives. This is how classical individualism gives support to the libertarian, laissez-faire capitalist political economy.

Classical individualism provides such a libertarian polity with a distinctive rationale, different from the standard classical liberal or Homo economicus support. This last stresses the greater efficiency of free action for the purposes of securing public prosperity. Classical individualism stresses the need for liberty for one who is embarking on the morally good life to flourish as a human individual. This ethical stance has a good chance of being superior to others that tend to stress altruism as the sound ethics for human life.[9]

Classical Individualism and Corporate Responsibility

Since the central features of the free market system may be defended on the basis of this more robust individualism, Friedman's position on the social responsibility of corporations can now be amended without compromising his libertarianism, that is, his laissez-faire economics. Nevertheless, as will be evident presently, corporations can be seen to have a broader range of responsibilities than Friedman ascribes to them.

The essential task of businesses—firms, partnerships, companies, enterprises, and other establishments—needs to be defensible by reference to the general tenets of whatever turns out to be the ethical theory that is most successful, most suited to the task of guiding us most consistently, coherently, and completely in our conduct. Needless to note, it would be difficult to demonstrate here that classical individualism is this ethical theory. What can be achieved here is to show that classical individualism is a richer ethical framework from which to identify the ingredients of a system of general and professional ethics than that presupposed in Friedman's often discussed theory of the social responsibility of corporations.

We can define "professional ethics" as a code of conduct pertaining to a specialized field of activity—such as law, medicine, education, diplomacy, or business—justified in terms of a sound ethics.[10] By "business," we mean an organized human endeavor that has economic enhancement or prosperity or wealth as its dominant end. Businesses are profit-making institutions.[11] Whereas physicians heal, attorneys make a case before the law, and educators develop and impart knowledge, the business professional's central task is to increase wealth.[12]

Is Business Morally Legitimate?

Any profession, whether very generally conceived, such as medicine, or highly specialized, such as plastic surgery, can be subjected to ethical scrutiny. For example, pacifists argue that the military profession is morally misguided, if not outright vicious. Those convinced that Christian Scientism preaches the moral truth argue that physicians do the wrong thing. Most Roman Catholics argue that abortionists are morally corrupt. And there are utilitarians who condemn the use of animals for human purposes. Whether we judge from a narrow or broad moral perspective, we often hold professions up to such critical scrutiny. And even from a rather commonsense moral perspective, some professions seem to be at the brink of immorality. Espionage comes to mind here.

In commonsense morality or the ethics that tends to guide most people within a given culture and that requires philosophical assistance only when dilemmas arise, the profession of business may be viewed as based, ultimately, on the virtue of prudence. Prudence was identified at one time as the first of the cardinal virtues. It requires that we take conscientious care of ourselves.

It is a virtue to do so, whereas slothfulness, recklessness, carelessness, inattentiveness, and so on are all deemed moral failings.[13]

The fact that prudence is a virtue does not settle the matter of the moral basis of commerce. Two questions need to be addressed to ascertain whether that is so. For one, what exactly is the nature of the self to be taken care of? An idealist and even dualist idea of the self will lead us to understand by prudence a less emphasized prosperity in this life than would a naturalist conception. If human beings are essentially divided into two parts, one tied to this world the other reaching for a superior supernatural dimension, prudence will have different implications from a view that conceives of the self as part of the natural world alone.

The second question is whether we can rank the familiar moral virtues when they seem to be in conflict from the viewpoint of common sense.[14] Here is where we need an ethical theory that succeeds in placing our commonsense ideals and ethics in a coherent framework. Hard cases in ethics aren't decidable without a systematic moral viewpoint at hand. Classical individualism is a candidate for success at serving this purpose and one plus in its favor would be if it managed the hard cases well and could be applied readily within the fields of professional ethics such as business.

Classical Individualism and Business Ethics

Assuming for now that there is some promise in classical individualism, what are its implications for professional ethics and for business ethics in particular?

A significant part of what a person ought to do in life is to secure economic values and objectives that enable one to obtain worldly goods, pleasures, joys, delights, and so on. But in contrast with the individualism of many textbooks in ethics,[15] classical individualism aims to make oneself as good as the human individual one is, and *that involves many capacities to be realized outside economic ones*. While it is vital to serve one's economic or, more broadly, prudential goals, even these can extend far beyond the mere satisfaction of one's desires. Thus, given the classical individualist outlook, one's desires should be shaped by the vision one creates of oneself as the human being one can and would ideally or optimally become.

Professional versus Social Responsibilities

There are vital community and political dimensions of oneself that may require enhancement even in the course of conducting one's professional tasks. In the case of corporate business, for example, one may be morally responsible to reach not only one's economic objectives—which are moral—but also various objectives associated with being a member of one's community.

Professional ethics involves determining the responsibilities and restraints one needs to observe in the profession one has chosen to pursue. Of course, there are preprofessional ethics in terms of which one is to be guided in determining what one's profession will be. So it is assumed that the choice of profession is itself capable of being morally justified. Once so, then the question left is what that choice implies—mostly conscientiousness toward one's professional conduct—and toward whatever else is connected to the profession one has chosen.

Friedman's thesis was that no other moral claim may be made on those in corporate business than to fulfill their implied promise to their clients, namely, to secure for them the greatest possible economic benefits "while conforming to the basic rules of the society, both those embodied in law and in ethical custom."[16] This view is consistent with the radical individualist conception of the human being: Beyond the mere imperative of keeping a promise made in the service of one's self-interested goals, there is nothing more one ought to do in one's capacity as a business professional.

Critics rightly see this as an impoverished conception of what a human being ought to do in a professional role. Often, however, they go to the other extreme and argue that business should nearly be sacrificed for whatever alternative need is evident in the community.

The classical individualist position understands professional ethics to require that one's *dominant* yet not *exclusive* objective is the conscientious performance of one's professional tasks, to fulfill one's job description, as it were, and to carry out what one has embarked on in one's capacity as a professional. In business, this amounts to what Friedman believes is the exclusive or sole task of business, namely, the pursuit of profit. To the contrary, professional responsibilities are not the only ones a manager ought to carry out. Attending primarily to the bottom line is fully consistent with paying heed to other goals, including fulfilling parental duties, being a good friend, enhancing the quality of one's community, protecting the environment, and developing and maintaining sound political institutions.

First, one has obligations to achieve goals other than those one takes up professionally, and some of these take priority over one's job. Second, even in the course of fulfilling one's professional responsibilities, attention might have to be paid to goals that do not directly bear on profit maximization. Thus, the totality of one's moral tasks, including those arising from the fulfillment of professional tasks within the physical and political setting of one's place of work, oblige a business professional to go beyond what Friedman claims he/she ought to pay exclusive heed to.[17]

Ethics and Choice

There is a dimension to classical individualism that recalls a certain feature of deontological ethics. This is the importance of moral sovereignty, the role of the choices of the moral agent in the determination of conduct. This is where fundamental individuality or selfhood enters the moral situation by recognizing that it is the person who chooses morally significant conduct, not others for that person. Instead of atomistic individualism, this view embraces moral individualism, the view that the individuality of a human being is central and emerges through everyone's moral agency—that is, *in being the initiator of morally significant conduct.*

Accordingly, the scope of legally enforceable moral responsibility within the classical individualist ethics is the respect of others' moral agency, nothing more. This framework does not identify individuals as being naturally *connected* to society, in the fashion in which a team member is tied to the team or a business partner is tied to the partnership. Social ties in adulthood, even if they are essential and proper, must in classical individualism be left to choice, not imposed by law. And law enters only when citizens are intentionally or negligently caused by others to lose their sovereignty.

So, while the moral demands of classical individualism on those in various professions, including business, are greater than those advanced in Friedman's position, the political framework of business conduct implicit in this ethics is close to that advocated by Friedman. For example, although business ought to support the neighborhood so as to give it better quality, it may not be forced to do so.[18]

Basically, Friedman derives his "bottom-line" ethics from the promise managers make to shareholders or owners, while classical individualism derives its "bottom-line-plus" ethics from a broader moral framework. It is the neo-Aristotelian idea that everyone ought to live a reasonable life and this includes being considerate of one's own economic well-being. But there is more to living ethically than that. Moreover, sometimes promises must be broken, namely, when more important matters require one's attention.

The ethics of management aren't a set of categorical imperatives but contextually binding responsibilities. Classical individualism accounts for them better than what Friedman provides.

Notes

1. Milton Friedman, "The Social Responsibility of Business Is to Increase Its Profits," *New York Times Magazine*, 13 September 1970, 33. See also Milton Friedman, *Capitalism and Freedom* (Chicago: University of Chicago Press, 1961), 133–136. Friedman's essay is widely reprinted and also discussed in numerous collections of business ethics textbooks and journal articles. For some of the nuances of Friedman's position, see Thomas Carson, "Friedman's Theory of Corporate Social Responsibility," *Business and Professional Ethics Journal* 12 (spring 1993): 3–32. It is notable that Friedman is usually represented as holding the more radical view that business ought to aim solely at profit rather than the milder version in which the ethics of society ought also to be followed in the course of doing business. This is understandable, though, especially in light of the apparently cultural relativism implicit in Friedman's position. In an international and intercultural world of commerce, however, the prescription to strive for profit is far more direct and practicable than that requiring one to follow "law [and] ethical custom." In short, the only genuine ethical stance Friedman considers is that profit ought to be pursued, given that managers promised to do just that, although he makes allowances for circumstances.

2. John Kenneth Galbraith, *The Affluent Society* (Boston: Houghton Mifflin, 1958); Ralph Nader, Mark Green, and Joel Seligman, *Taming the Giant Corporations* (New York: Norton, 1976). For a different view, see Robert Hessen, *In Defense of the Corporation* (Stanford, CA: Hoover Institution Press, 1979).

3. The most developed version of this type of individualism is found in David L. Norton, *Personal Destinies: A Philosophy of Ethical Individualism* (Princeton, NJ: Princeton University Press, 1976). Earlier, Ayn Rand sketched a similar position in *The Virtue of Selfishness: A New Concept of Egoism* (New York: New American Library, 1966).

4. Karl Marx, *Selected Writings*, ed. David McClellan (London: Oxford University Press, 1977), 126.

5. Tom L. Beauchamp and Norman E. Bowie, eds., *Ethical Theory and Business* (Englewood Cliffs, NJ: Prentice Hall, 1983), 16.

6. Beauchamp and Bowie, *Ethical Theory and Business*, 2.

7. For a development of this distinction, see Tibor R. Machan, "A New Individualist Basis for the Free Market," *International Review of Economics and Ethics* 2 (1987): 27–39. As an additional indicator of the classical egoist position, consider Aristotle's remark, that "such a man (who 'at all events assigns to himself the things that are noblest and best, and gratifies the most authoritative element in himself and in all things obeys this') . . . is most of all a lover of self." See Aristotle, *Nicomachean*

Ethics, bk. 6, trans. W. D. Ross, in *A New Aristotle Reader*, ed. J. L. Ackrill (Princeton, NJ: Princeton University Press, 1987), 1168b28–33

8. This point raises the perennial issue of freedom of the will. The classical individualist position can draw on the work of, for example, Nobel laureate Roger W. Sperry, *Science and Moral Priority* (New York: Columbia University Press, 1983), who defends free will based on his scientific research and analysis. Sperry's technical paper "Changing Concepts of Consciousness and Free Will" is also a good case for the scientific legitimacy and naturalistic character of free will. See Roger W. Sperry, "Changing Concepts of Consciousness and Free Will," *Perspectives in Biology and Medicine* 9 (autumn 1976): 9–19. See also Tibor R. Machan, *The Pseudo-Science of B. F. Skinner* (New Rochelle, NY: Arlington House, 1974); Tibor R. Machan, *Initiative—Human Agency and Society* (Stanford, CA: Hoover Institution Press, 2000). For an argument showing this thesis to be true, see John Searle, *Rationality in Action* (Boston: MIT Press, 2001).

9. See chapter 3 of this text for our discussion of "selfishness."

10. This is developed further in the introduction to Tibor R. Machan, ed., *Commerce and Morality* (Lanham, MD: Rowman & Littlefield, 1988).

11. By "profit," we don't mean the technical term defined in tax law or even economics in general, but the familiar idea of prospering in one's ability to obtain goods and services for purchase in the marketplace. As such, profit is a kind of condition one has attained in which one has capacity to contribute financial support to one's chosen ends, some of which could mainly benefit others!

12. This is not the place to work out a full ethical system in which wealth pursuit can be seen as morally proper. Nevertheless, it should be hinted that such a system is person relative about the nature of the good and sees living economically, successfully, or prosperously as a goal that constitutes a significant aspect of the good life for any human moral agent. See Douglas J. Den Uyl, "Teleology and Agent-Centeredness," *The Monist* 75 (January 1992): 14–33. There is an ontological feature of a moral perspective that would be applicable to evaluating the various professions people embark on, namely, that there is no basis for precluding the possibility of free will in human living. Indeed, there is both philosophical and special scientific justification, beyond a reasonable doubt, to believe that human beings are facilitated to activate their mental functions, to initiate their own conduct, and to, thus, govern themselves.

13. See Douglas J. Den Uyl, *The Virtue of Prudence* (New York: Peter Lang, 1991).

14. This is akin to our not understanding the structure of the physical world from simply experiencing it by way of the normal use of our senses.

15. For a survey of these, see Tibor R. Machan, "Recent Work in Ethical Egoism," in *Recent Work in Philosophy*, ed. Kenneth J. Lucey and Tibor R. Machan (Totowa, NJ: Rowman and Allanheld, 1983), 185–202.

16. Friedman, "Social Responsibility of Business," 33.

17. This point is advanced by Fred D. Miller Jr. and John Ahrens "The Social Responsibility of Corporations," in *Commerce and Morality*, ed. Tibor R. Machan

(Lanham, MD: Rowman & Littlefield, 1988), 140–160. We call this the "bottom-line-plus" theory. It's worth noting that Carson faults Friedman for not including as a requirement the social or ethical responsibility of business to "warn the public about all serious hazards or dangers created by the firms which they represent." See Carson, "Friedman's Theory of Corporate Social Responsibility," 20. One might think that the current position also falls prey to this flaw. Yet arguably, neither Friedman nor we can be so faulted. Friedman is, after all, a defender of an individual rights–based free market economy, including privatization in all possible realms of production, trade, transportation, and so on. In such a system, exposing customers to known hazards and dangers that pose risks (beyond what is reasonable, that is, measurably above the normally prevailing hazards and dangers of their lives) without informing them about these risks constitutes legally actionable misrepresentation or deception. Product and service liability lawsuits are entirely consistent, indeed, native to, a bona fide free market system. A socialist system, for example, cannot make theoretical room for such an individual rights–based legal action. It is even doubtful that a government-regulated legal system can escape the force of the charge that in view of such regulation of business, liability action might have to be significantly circumscribed. Responsibility for hazards and dangers would, in such a system, be shared between the business and the regulatory agent (the public!) ultimately complicit in the hazardous or dangerous behavior. For more on this, see Tibor R. Machan, "Bhopal, Mexican Disasters: What a Difference Capitalism Can Make," in *Liberty and Culture: Essays on the Idea of a Free Society*, by Tibor R. Machan (Buffalo, NY: Prometheus, 1989), 180–181; Tibor R. Machan, "Corporate Commerce vs. Government Regulation: The State and Occupational Safety and Health," *Notre Dame Journal of Law, Ethics and Public Policy* 2 (1987): 791–823; see also Tibor R. Machan, *Private Rights and Public Illusions* (New Brunswick, NJ: Transaction, 1995). A very interesting argument favoring adjudication as a proper approach to solving problems now dealt with via government regulation is provided in J. C. Smith, "The Processes of Adjudication and Regulation: A Comparison," in *Rights and Regulation*, ed. M. Bruce Johnson and Tibor R. Machan (San Francisco: Pacific Institute for Public Policy Research, 1983), 71–96.

18. In *Individuals and Their Rights*, Machan explains in detail why the moral dimension of human nature requires the classical liberal political framework. See Tibor R. Machan, *Individuals and Their Rights* (La Salle, IL: Open Court, 1989). For a treatment of negative externalities such as air or water pollution, see Tibor R. Machan, "Pollution, Collectivism and Capitalism," *Journal des Economists et des Etudes Humaines* 2 (March 1991): 83–102. For more on our relationship to animals, see Tibor R. Machan, "Do Animals Have Rights?" *Public Affairs Quarterly* 5 (April 1991): 163–173. For an application of this framework to government regulation of business, see Machan, "Corporate Commerce"; Tibor R. Machan, "Should Business Be Regulated?" in *Just Business: New Introductory Essays in Business Ethics*, ed. Tom Regan (New York: Random House, 1983), 202–234. For more on environmental ethics in

general, see Tibor R. Machan, "Pollution and Political Theory," in *Earthbound: New Introductory Essays in Environmental Ethics*, ed. Tom Regan (New York: Random House, 1984), 74–106; Tibor R. Machan, "Environmentalism Humanized," *Public Affairs Quarterly* 7 (April 1993): 131–147. For a discussion of parental responsibilities, see Tibor R. Machan, "Between Parents and Children," *Journal of Social Philosophy* 23 (winter 1992): 16–22. For further discussion of the philosophy of the social sciences and the moral foundation of the free market system, see Tibor R. Machan, *Capitalism and Individualism: Reframing the Argument for the Free Society* (New York: St. Martin's, 1990).

CHAPTER EIGHT

~

What Is Morally Right
with Insider Trading?

Some Preliminaries

Although insider trading is something of a special topic in business, one reason it takes center stage in many business ethics discussions is that it is said to be quite unfair. And fairness has been a big issue in ethics ever since John Rawls advanced the view that justice consists of fairness. If Rawls is right, then anything unfair would be unjust. Insider trading certainly seems unfair to some people, so it would appear to be unjust. And since it is via the law that injustice is combated in civilized societies, it would then follow that the law should forbid insider trading.

In this chapter, we will explore what insider trading is, whether it is unfair, and whether, if so, it is really unjust.

Basic Moral Issues

Insider trading per se is obtaining information from nonpublic sources, such as private acquaintances, friends, and colleagues, and using it to one's financial advantage. As Vincent Barry explains, "Insider dealings refers to the ability of key employees to profit from knowledge or information that has not yet become public."[1] Sometimes, such a practice can be conducted fraudulently, as when one who has obtained the information has a fiduciary duty to share it with clients but fails to exercise it, or in some other criminal fashion, as when the information is itself stolen. These are not, however, features of insider trading as such, as understood in the context of the discussion of business ethics.

Never mind that in the enforcement of government regulations it is in fact fraud cited as making the conduct called "insider trading" illegal.[2] (Thus, the bulk of the relevant law does not concern itself so much with what many in the business ethics community worry about, namely, "justice as fairness," but with "justice as honoring of contracts or fiduciary duty.")

What makes business ethics discussions of insider trading distinctive is that the information on which such trade is based is not known to others within the interested trading community aside from the insider. Insider trading turns on something other than so-called public knowledge by giving the trader an advantage over the rest of the market participants who are on the outside.

This common view of insider trading presented in business ethics discussions should be examined more closely. It may be one's achievement or good fortune to learn of opportunities ahead of others and this may not be morally wrong but quite industrious. Acting on such information may be prudent and exhibiting good business acumen whenever it does not involve the violation of others' rights. The conventional view rests on the belief that others have a right to one's revealing to them information one has honestly obtained *ahead of them*. But there is no sound general moral principle that requires this. Quite the contrary, morality may require one to act promptly, ahead of everyone else, so as to make headway financially.

We often make morally unobjectionable use of special information for our own benefit, though others might also benefit were it available to them, such as when we are first to learn of the presence of a potential dating partner, a good buy on a used car, or a house coming up for sale in a highly preferred neighborhood. To take advantage of such special opportunities is a sign of good judgment, not of unfairness or deception.

Those who object to insider trading confuse the marketplace with a game in which rules are established with the special purpose of giving everyone an even chance—for example, in golf, where handicaps are assigned, or when in professional football the lowest-ranked team gets first choice in the player drafts. The market is more akin to life itself where different persons enter with different assets and liabilities, talents, looks, genetic makeup, and economic and climactic circumstances—and they must do their best with what they have. In life, apart from the occasional generosity or charity of others, all one has is a fighting chance. Children of musically proficient parents will likely benefit "unfairly" in obtaining musical opportunities. Those born in Bombay, to poor parents, will likely face harder times than those born in Beverly Hills to movie star parents. These are simple facts of life evident to everyone.

No general moral requirement exists for strangers to even this out, only to abstain from imposing obstacles on others and from violating their rights to liberty. The marketplace, too, is a setting wherein different persons face different circumstances. People do not have a natural obligation to perform involuntary service to strangers. In competing freely with others for opportunities that the market provides, one is treating other agents with the respect they deserve as potential partners in the marketplace.

Exceptions exist, of course, as when one trades with friends or family, which may raise some moral complications. But the norm is people interacting to find opportunities for trade, nothing more. Other human relationships may be involved, of course, but we can keep the commercial ones distinct enough to understand the ethics that ought to govern us as we embark on trade.

It should be noted that there is a distinctively utilitarian defense of insider trading advanced, for example, by Henry G. Manne.[3] Utilitarians defend insider trading because it contributes to the overall efficiency of market transactions. They argue that those trading from the inside send signals to others whose reactions then help propel the market to its new level of efficiency.

There may be merit in this line of defense, although it comes perilously close to arguing that the end justifies the means. Unless the actions of the individuals who engage in insider trading can themselves be shown to be justified, such arguments are without force. One can show benefits to society at large based on theft, even murder, yet these are by no means justified because of the benefits.

Moreover, this defense fails to consider the issue of justice as fairness. While on the whole insider trading may indeed improve the efficiency of the stock market, as Manne argues, what of those left out of the loop, those who are left uninformed? Utilitarianism will not suffice to show that no injustice has befallen such market agents. Of concern in business ethics here is whether practicing insider trading and acting on inside information is morally proper, not whether it may have overall beneficial results.[4]

Business Ethics and Insider Trading

In fact, however, the concept "insider trading" employed in business ethics discussions has a broader meaning: It includes anyone's ability to make deals based on not yet publicized knowledge of business opportunities. Insider trading as such, apart from what it may be related to in some cases (such as fraud or the violation of fiduciary duty), involves making financial investments on the basis of knowledge others do not have and may not be able to obtain in ordinary ways. Person A knows the president of a firm who (perhaps by talking loosely) tells him/her that the firm is thinking of expanding one of its divisions or has struck oil in a new field, so A buys a block of stock in anticipation of the increase of value once the deal is done or the knowledge becomes public. Person A is neither deceiving nor defrauding anyone. He/she is not taking anything from others that he/she wasn't freely given. Regardless, Person A is acting on special "insider" information.

Now, it is conventional wisdom to treat this version of insider trading as morally wrong because it supposedly affects others adversely by being unfair. As John Hetherington puts it, "What causes injury or loss to outsiders is not what the insider knew or did, rather it is what they themselves [the outsiders] did not know. It is their own lack of knowledge which exposes them to risk of loss or denies them an opportunity to make a profit."[5] Because these others do not know what the insider knows, they are harmed since they are not able to make use of opportunities that are in fact available and knowable to others.

But what kind of causation fails to make a difference when it does not exist? If someone's knowing about a good deal has no impact on what another does, it cannot be said that this *caused* harm to another. Certainly, had the other known what the insider knew, he/she could have acted differently. By not acting differently, he/she could easily have failed to reap advantages the insider did reap. But nothing here shows that the insider *caused* any harm, only that he/she had a better set of opportunities. Unless we assume that valuable information known by one person ought morally—and perhaps legally—be distributed to all interested parties—something that would beg the most important question—there is no moral fault involved in insider trading nor any causation of harm.[6]

Because of the widespread but mistaken view that insider trading is morally wrong, it is conventional wisdom to support its legal prohibition. Of course, even if morally wrong, it may not follow that it should be legally prohibited. But there is reason to think that the moral objections are wrongheaded. Thus, we may suspect that the opposition to insider trading is more likely the result of widespread, strong *prejudice against gaining economic prosperity without sharing it*. Clearly, there is considerable thinking in our era to the effect that a level playing field is morally mandatory in the marketplace.[7]

Why Insider Trading Is Right

Certainly, one is at an advantage when possessing information others lack. Nearly everyone in the marketplace is in that position to some degree. One might even wish to call this "unfair" in the sense in which any kind of good fortune may be to some people's but not to others' advantage. But the concept of fairness does not apply in this context, though many believe otherwise. For someone to act fairly requires some prior obligation to distribute burdens or benefits among a given number of people in some suitable proportion or in line with certain specified procedures. To act fairly is not a primary moral duty—it depends on prior obligations such as paying attention to all the students in *one's own* class or feeding all of *one's own* children equally well. And fairness can occur even in morally corrupt circumstances—for example, thieves can fairly distribute their loot. Only when one ought to treat others alike does fairness count for something morally important.

Applying this to insider trading, if one has a prior obligation (say, a fiduciary duty) to share information with others, then what makes one's dealings objectionable is not that the information is "from the inside" but that it is *owed to others*. Only in such cases is fairness obligatory, as a matter of one's professional relationship to others, established by the promise made or contract one has entered into prior to the ensuing duty to be fair. Only then can one cause injury by refusing to do what one has agreed to do, namely, to divulge information prior to using it for oneself. Accordingly, Hetherington's objection to insider trading lacks moral force. He should have objected to the breaching of fiduciary duty, which may occur on occasion by means of failing to divulge information (possibly gained "from the inside") that has been— perhaps even contractually—promised to a client. Furthermore, if one has stolen the information—that is, spied, bribed for, or extorted it—again the moral deficiency comes not from its being inside information but from its having been ill-gotten.

What if the information were obtained accidentally? One overhears some people talking within earshot in the lavatory or at a bar after they've had too much to drink and have loose tongues. Is it ethically wrong to make use of this? Here again the issue concerns what one owes others. Does one have a natural obligation to share one's good fortune with other people?

In emergency situations, when others are in dire need or have met with some natural disaster, virtues such as generosity and charity are usually binding on those who are able to assist. Yet, these are not obligations in the sense of something the law must enforce. Indeed, enforcing generosity or charity is impossible—the moral significance of a virtue is destroyed if it is practiced at the point of a gun! Furthermore, in the context of the normal hustle and bustle of life, no such virtues are called for toward strangers, only toward those one is related to by prior commitments, intimacy, and love. Instead, in the ordinary course of life one ought to strive to live successfully, to prosper, and to make headway with one's legitimate projects, not embark on the tasks of emergency crews during an earthquake.

From the viewpoint of commonsense ethics, the idea that there is something morally amiss with insider trading has little to support it. One clearly has no moral, let alone legal, obligation to share information with strangers that may benefit one in other familiar circumstances.

Imagine, for example, that an appealing eligible single woman whom several eligible men would like to meet moves into a neighborhood. Suppose that one of these men obtains (insider) information about her arrival before others and approaches her before others learn that she will be part of the community. Given that the prospect of successful romance is more important to most people than the prospect of successful investment, has he done wrong? Suppose, again, that one learns of a very good violin teacher who is moving to one's town and is first in line to take lessons from him/her. Is this doing something morally wrong? Nothing supports such a view that would, in any case, condemn most people since trying to be first in line, so to speak, is something most of us do, especially in the marketplace.

Of course, were one in no great hurry to find a mate and had a friend who is, one might generously tell him about the impending arrival of the lady. This would be generous but not obligatory. Similarly, if one had a friend with ambitions to study the violin, one might share the news of the opportunity for taking lessons from a new master in town. To deliberately withhold such information from one's friends in these cases would most likely be blameworthy. But one owes no such favors to strangers.[8]

There are professions wherein a version of insider trading is, in fact, highly prized. Consider newscasting. When a reporter scoops the competition, no one considers this legally actionable, nor, indeed, morally insidious. On the contrary, it is a mark of professional excellence. Why doesn't this apply to insider trading?

The reason these situations, as distinct from insider trading, do not invite widespread moral rebuke is that we tend to consider objectives such as finding the right mate or learning a musical instrument something benign and morally untainted. When it comes to making economic or financial gains, in many quarters there is an initial moral discomfort about it. The shadow of greed looms very large and tends even to overwhelm prudence.

Why Insider Trading Seems Wrong

Indeed, the intellectual source of moral disdain for insider trading is the more general disdain for economic or commercial self-enhancement, at least among moral philosophers and others in the humanities. There seems to be no end to how fiercely commercial success is demeaned among many of those who preach and reflect on morality. But this attitude is utterly misguided.

Becoming prosperous can be a means toward the attainment of numerous worthy goals and should, thus, itself be respected. Moreover, not only the pursuit of riches, but also any other goal can be taken *to a fault*. An artist can be overly ambitious about being an artist and, thereby, neglect family, friends, and polity. Parents can be doting. Even truth can be pursued fanatically. The chances for corruption through the pursuit of economic advantage are no greater than through other pursuits. The disdainful attitude toward commercial professionals is entirely unjustified and deserves as much study as prejudices toward racial, religious, or ethnic groups.

What about the fact that we encourage fairness in athletic competition, such as imposing handicaps in golf and horse racing? Or the way baseball and football leagues utilize the player draft to even out the advantages of teams. Don't we find fairness heavily stressed even in the allocation of chores in families and fraternities, not to mention teams? Shouldn't this apply to business as well?

Bad Analogies

These examples are misleading. It isn't fairness per se that's stressed in golf and horse racing; what appears as such is actually an effort to foster games and races that capture and keep the interest of spectators. The same holds for the policy on player drafts. If a team wins repeatedly, interest will begin to wane and the sport will lose its fans. In these cases, fairness serves as a means to an end, not as an end in itself and not as a matter of what is right.

As to families, there exists a prior obligation to share burdens and benefits among the members, if not equally then at least proportionately. Parents have invited their children into the family, as it were, and when benefits (or burdens) are reaped, all those invited should share them.

Among people who are not in such relationships no fairness principle operates. No doubt, sometimes we make a mistake and transfer the attitudes we have acquired for how to handle matters in the family to other areas of our lives, but that is an illogical extrapolation. And this is evident enough by considering that if one is born with musical talent or good genes, it is not one's duty to make sure that people born to families without them somehow share one's advantages. Nor is one doing the right thing in imposing one's burdens on members of families who do not suffer as one does. That sort of policy would generate envy and resentment, not moral decency.

The Moral Merit of Insider Trading

Accordingly, seeking to benefit through ingenuity and shrewdness is good business, and good business is as important a professional trait as good medicine, good law, good education, and so on. Professional ethics, in turn, cannot condemn that which is in accord with ethics in general, such as fortitude and prudence. Competence and skill, even excellence, at managing the material progress one might be able to make in life ought not to be treated as less important than competence and skill at managing artistic, scientific, educational, or other types of endeavors.

Insider trading is held to be morally suspect because many regard fairness, equality, and a level playing field the most important criteria for a morally decent marketplace. But those are actually not what counts most for the morality of trade. That place is occupied by the respect for individual rights. Within the framework of such respect, insider trading is entirely unobjectionable. In addition, it can be perfectly and ethically commendable to act based on such information: It is a matter of prudence and commercial savvy, both of which should be encouraged from those who work for a living.

Notes

1. Vincent Barry, *Moral Issues in Business* (Belmont, CA: Wadsworth, 1983), 242.

2. Rule 106-5 of Securities Exchange Act of 1934. See also *SEC v. Texas Gulf Sulpher* (1968); *United States v. Chiarella* (1980); *United States v. Newman* (1981). Both definitions and sanctions vary somewhat from state to state and case to case. *Black's Law Dictionary* states that "Insider trading . . . refers to transactions in shares of publicly held corporations by persons with insider or advance information on which the trading is based. Usually the trader himself is an insider with an employment or other relation of trust and confidence with the corporation." See *Black's Law Dictionary* (St. Paul, MN: West, 1991), 547. Pub. L. 100-704, Sec. 7, Nov. 19, 1988, 102 Stat. 4682, provides that there be a study and investigation of, among other things, "impediments to the fairness and orderliness of the securities markets." While the language of securities law does mention the fairness that is most often the concern of those discussing insider trading in the field of business ethics, it seems that the main focus of the law and the regulatory bodies is on fine tuning and enforcing it has to do with fraudulent trading in insider information or its misuse by those who have fiduciary duties not to disclose and use it until it is made available to the general trading public.

3. Henry G. Manne, *Insider Trading and the Stock Market* (New York: Free Press, 1966); Henry G. Manne, "What Kind of Controls on Insider Trading Do We Need?" in *The Attack on Corporate America*, ed. M. Bruce Johnson (New York: McGraw Hill, 1978), 119–125.

4. Of course, some claim morality is precisely about producing overall beneficial results. But this leaves out certain crucial factors, including whether those not part

of the group that is benefited may have just claims of having been wronged. Indeed arguably, utilitarianism fails largely on the grounds of its insufficient attention to the moral issue of individual rights.

5. John A. C. Hetherington, "Corporate Social Responsibility, Stockholders, and the Law," *Journal of Contemporary Business* (winter 1993): 51; quoted in Barry, *Moral Issues in Business*, 242–243. One feature of the business ethics discussions of insider trading and other normative topics is that there is little attention paid to the distinction between ethics and public policy. Thus, even if there were something ethically objectionable about some business practice, this does not ipso facto render it illegal or subject to government regulation. An analogy might help here: When we discuss journalistic ethics, it is clear enough that journalists may engage in unethical behavior that should not be made illegal. This same distinction is not generally observed when it comes to the profession of business. For an exception, see Tibor R. Machan, ed., *Commerce and Morality* (Lanham, MD: Rowman & Littlefield, 1988), especially "Ethics and its Uses." For a business ethics perspective hospitable to viewing business as a morally honorable profession, see Tibor R. Machan, "Professional Responsibilities of Corporate Managers," *Business and Professional Ethics Journal* 13 (fall 1994), on which chapter 5 of this book is based.

6. If someone does not do what he/she ought to do, the causation involved may be the kind that consists in taking away a supporting feature of an action. Someone who steals a part of a car engine causes it to fail to operate properly by removing what such operation needs. That is how stealing can cause the ensuing harm. Fraud produces harm similarly: something one owns, namely, what another has legally committed to one, is in fact withheld. But without such commitment, nor even a moral duty to provide, no causation of the lack of desired advantage can be identified. For more on this, see Eric Mack, "Bad Samaritarianism and the Causation of Harm," *Philosophy and Public Affairs* 9 (summer 1980).

7. The most prominent is, of course, John Rawls, *A Theory of Justice* (Cambridge, MA: Harvard University Press, 1971). One main problem in Rawls's defense of "justice as fairness" is that Rawls believes that no one can deserve his/her advantages or assets in life—it's all a matter of luck. As he puts it, "No one deserves his greater natural capacity nor merits a more favorable starting point in society." The reason? Because even a person's character (i.e., the virtues he/she practices that may provide him/her with ways of getting ahead of others) "depends in large part upon fortunate family and social circumstances for which he can claim no credit" (104). If one rejects this deterministic account of virtues, then a trader's prudence cannot be discounted as one assesses whether he/she deserves to gain from how trade is conducted.

8. The position that in the best of all societies all have in mind only the public interest or we all love one another as intimates is not just an impossible but a dreadful dream. Most people have the emotional capacity to love and the time to be involved with just a few others. The love distributed throughout humanity would have to be meager and ineffectual.

CHAPTER NINE

~

Fundamental Environmentalism

Business versus the Environment?

It is now nearly conventional wisdom to think that business conflicts with efforts to be environmentally responsible. Yet, there is also much evidence that the opposite of a business society—one in which the right to private property is denied and most resources are owned in common—engenders a most damaging phenomenon with drastic results for the environment, namely, the tragedy of the commons. This is the condition we discussed in chapter 2, wherein people who own resources in common and make use of them without constraints posed by the property rights of others are thus depleting the resources irreparably.

In this chapter, we look at some of the most basic elements of environmentalism that do not conflict with business and are, indeed, supported by it.

Some Philosophical Issues of Environmentalism

Perhaps the most problematic aspect of a philosophical reflection on environmental issues is that two incommensurable approaches to the world meet head-on here. On the one hand, ecology is a natural science and the developments on Earth bearing on it are often deemed to be a matter of ineluctable laws. Whether some forest is sturdy or vulnerable is, thus, not a matter of human choice but how life evolved here on Earth. On the other hand, we repeatedly raise questions about how we ought to act vis-à-vis the world ecology—release or not release various chemicals, clear-cut forests, engage in strip mining, preserve some animal species, and so on.

Yet, if the former point holds and evolutionary forces drive Earth's ecological system—including human interaction within that system—then there is no room for free choice in how we comport ourselves regarding the environment. If, however, we ought to do one thing but not another with respect to the environment, then the development of nature is not driven exclusively by impersonal evolutionary forces—human will or choice has a role as well. Putting it differently, either the environment is a deterministic system, including what we do in it, or some ways the environment evolves depend on what we choose to do.

Unfortunately, little attention is paid to these more metaethical issues in environmental literature. Thus, confusion reigns about just what we face and what if anything we can do about it. This discussion will accept the idea that environmentalism must pay attention to some metaphysical–ethical features of human life and to a need for metaenvironmentalism. Accordingly, it can be argued that the normative presuppositions of the field are serious and roughly right: We *can* do something about how we interact with the environment. In particular, it will be shown that a certain ethical–political controversy has direct bearing on environmental matters.

To put it briefly first, if human life is lived most successfully in collectivist terms—groups, nations, ethical clans, tribes, and so on—then the management of the environment via collective action (via state or government policies) would likely be the right approach. But if human life is lived more successfully in individualist terms—so that among the things crucial to take into consideration in leading such a life are not just some general or universal features of human nature but also *who* we are, the individual, idiosyncratic aspects of our nature—a privatized approach to environmental management makes better sense. (For example, this may well address the tragedy of the commons more successfully.)

So we cannot ignore the issue of just what human nature is as we consider what kind of environmental approach needs to be taken to deal with that part of human life optimally. And when explored, these issues are closely connected to broader metaphysical issues about causality, free will, individuality, and so on.

The Problem of Norms

Environmental concerns center on how human beings ought to act. Clearly, no one is hoping to advise birds or fish how they ought to act—the idea is absurd on its face because we deem animals and plants, apart from human beings, incapable of choosing how they will behave, let alone being capable of changing their minds as to their habits and patterns of behavior. The concern with the environment aims to advise human beings about what is sound behavior and policy concerning various issues such as conservation, wildlife preservation, endangered species, the ozone layer, the rain forests, and so on. Those who study environmental issues want to arrive at an understanding of what human beings ought to do and hope to influence us to do the right thing.

Yet, there are problems surrounding this understanding of environmental concerns or intentions, especially from the perspective of the scientific aspect of environmentalism. For centuries, since at least the time of Thomas Hobbes in philosophy and Galileo in science, the notion that human beings can choose how they act has been in serious dispute. Indeed, this has always been a focus of controversy among philosophers and others interested in the nature of human life. Hobbes spent his life disputing the idea of free will, claiming that a proper understanding of the laws of nature renders the idea nonsense. Freedom is to be understood not as the human capacity to take the initiative or to cause things to happen in the world, but as the absence of intrusiveness on one's behavior from other persons—political freedom, in other words. Today, there are numerous champions of just this view: No such idea as free will is compatible with what science tells us about ourselves, except insofar as we mean by it that people aren't being made to do what they do but do it without interference. Any other notion of free will flies in the face of the findings of the natural and social sciences that tell us that there are in our case, as in the case of any other beings in the universe, laws of nature that govern how we behave. (The most explicit, no holds barred, advocate of this view was B. F. Skinner.)

If this view is correct, then there is a serious problem about any talk of how human beings ought to act, since, as Kant has taught us, the concept "ought" implies the concept "can." Morality and law, generally, assume human initiative, free will, and individual agency and nothing in good science contradicts this assumption.

The normative aspects of environmentalism assume that we are, indeed, free to choose some of what we do on our own initiative. That is what is clearly implicit in admonishing people—in government, business, their personal lives, and so on—to do the right thing environmentally. Blaming a firm for polluting the environment makes no sense if that is what had to happen, just as it makes no sense to blame a meteor that hits a farmhouse or a tornado that demolishes a trailer park. The underlying view of human nature of normative environmentalism is that in the case of human beings, some attribute exists that makes it possible to make free choices that are open to critical assessment. We ought to save fuel, reduce CFC production, stop rain forest destruction, decrease air pollution, and so on. That is the broad message of much environmental work and it assumes that we are free to make choices as to how we act.

This view of human nature assumes, among other things, that normal people can of their own initiative start to do some things or, alternatively, fail to start to do them. Such is suggested by the ordinary expression that "damn it, I didn't think" when a mistake has been made. Indeed, in most cases it is with abstract (though not necessarily *self-conscious*) thinking or the lack thereof that most human actions get started. This seems to make sense because what distinguishes us from other living beings is our capacity to think, to reason, to form abstract ideas, and be guided by them.[1]

Even this is not enough to get to the bottom of the story. Something about reality in general is part of it, as well, in particular the issue of causality—what kinds of causes exist? If the only kind is efficient causes—the sort we illustrate so clearly with the behavior of balls being moved around on a pool table, one hitting the other and making it move, and so on and so on—that would pretty much rule out self-causation, self-determination, and free will. On this view, we are simply moved by forces to behave in various ways.

But if there can be causes other than the efficient, event-resulting-in-other-event type—say, if some things can cause events to occur without their having to be caused to do this—then we have room for the kind of action assumed to take place in human life that is open to moral and political assessment.[2] Then what we do is really our doing it, so when one blames us for having done something, that blame is meaningful, on target, and true.

It should be noted here that several philosophers have held that a determinist—at least a soft-determinist—view makes room for morality conceived as a kind of encouragement–discouragement system for controlling or influencing human conduct. Yet, it is difficult to see how that could work all the way through to the end. Even to advise that we ought to hold that viewpoint assumes that we are free to hold another, something that is not compatible with either hard or soft-determinism. Indeed, if our conduct is but a link in a chain of events linked by efficient causal relations, the only picture that makes sense is the one expressed in the song "Que sera, sera" or "What will be, will be." Accordingly, we can apply this view to environmental issues: whatever will happen will happen and we aren't in the position to alter it. Human conduct is different only in complexity from the behavior of plants and other animals—what they will do they will do, and there is no point in urging them to do something else.[3]

Room for Ethics

Let us assume, however, that this idea of nature, whereby everything is part of an interconnected system of inevitable events, is mistaken. Certainly, there are serious difficulties with it. Much of what we find normal and customary in human life does not square with that picture. For example, we distinguish between prejudice and objective judgment in the context of scientific and judicial work, but such a distinction does not make sense if our minds are determined to see things in certain ways and we have no self-control over whether and how they work.

It is not our intention to explore the problems of determinism here. Suffice it to note that there is another way of understanding human conduct, namely, as caused by the individual agent. Within certain limits, everyone not crucially incapacitated—with brain damage or the like—can take the initiative to act and is responsible for the quality of the action that he/she chose to take. The details are not important here. Let us just note that it will require a conception of nature wherein different kinds of causes are evident. So the cause of the ball moving on the pool table is different in type from the cause that produces Mozart's music, Shakespeare's dramas, a U.S. president's foreign policy decisions, or a mother's treatment of her child. Purposive or teleological causation, for example, would be as much a part of nature as would mechanical or efficient causation and occasional random behavior (say, at the subatomic levels).[4]

What follows from this is merely the possibility that some essential human conduct is caused by the human being whose conduct it is. Now we can talk about whether human beings have done the right thing vis-à-vis the environment. Have they disposed of their wastes responsibly? Have they cleared forests wisely? Have they built their dwellings prudently? Have they exploited resources with care and caution?

These and many related questions would be meaningful if people can make significant choices regarding what they do. And if so, they can lead to the discussion of past, present, and future human actions and policies that have a bearing on environmental issues.

Another matter would have to be cleared up as well before this approach could become legitimated. Some standard of right versus wrong human conduct would also have to be available in order for such a question to be raised meaningfully. There is no point to asking whether we have done right by the environment if "right" and "wrong" aren't objectively distinguishable. If environmental activists are no more than a lobby group for state-funded outdoor health clubs or wildlife preserves, with no reason that can be given why their goals have merit, the entire environmental movement would be a fraud. And even though for some people that may well be the end of the story, many others would consider their claims and urgings to be better founded than to rest merely on their likes and dislikes.

Why the Antimarket Stance Is Environmentally Wrong

At this point, we should sketch a defense of an essentially individualist–capitalist environmentalism. On the basis of a sensible metaphysics and metaethics, the most theoretically satisfying environmental ethics and politics would be one where privatization of all environmentally significant realms would be advisable. While sounding perhaps incredible, there is good reason for this belief.

First, none of anyone's bona fide, reasonable environmental worry justifies distrusting the "free market," as opposed to some scientific bureaucracy that is to do the monitoring, regulating, and containing that so many champions of environmental regimentation are calling for. Put plainly, if men and women acting in the marketplace and guided by the rule of law based on their natural individual rights to life, liberty, and property were incapable of standing up to ecological challenges, there is absolutely no reason to believe that those could be met better by some new statist means.[5]

Second, why should ecologically minded bureaucrats be better motivated, more competent, and more virtuous than those motivated by a concern for the hungry, the unjustly treated, the poor, the aesthetically deprived, and the uneducated masses of the world? There is no reason to attribute to any ecological politburo or central committee nobler characteristics than to the rest of those who have made various failed attempts at coercing people into good—that is, prosperous, generous, prudent, courageous, wise, moderate, and other kinds of virtuous—behavior. In short, if free men and women will not manage the ecology, neither will anyone else. But there is much more to be said than this.

More optimism is warranted about the prospects of managing environmental problems in a legal framework of individual liberty than is expressed by most environmentalists. This results, first, from examining the sources of our ecological troubles. Given, especially, the fact of collectivism's far greater mismanagement of the environment than that of the mixed economies we recklessly label individualist or capitalist, there is already some suggestion implicit here about what the problem comes to, namely, too little individualism. What many in the environmental movement fail to realize or reveal—for it is no secret and takes no genius to discern—is that the environmental problems that can be clearly identified rather than merely speculated about are due to the tragedy of the commons, not to the privatization of resources and the implementation of the principles that prohibit dumping and other kinds of trespassing. With more attention to protecting individual rights to life, liberty, and property, there would be fewer human-created ecological problems.

Third, the positive case for a free market environmentalism is better than many believe. Let's put the case in its most general terms first.[6]

An Individualist Environmentalism

The natural individual rights approach to political decision making rests on the realization that it is the nature of human beings to be essentially individual. This can be put, alternatively, by saying that the individual rights approach is most natural—that is, it most readily accommodates human nature and, therefore, the natural ecology. If there is a crisis here, it amounts to the history of human action that has been out of line with ecological well-being, health, and flourishing. But how do we know what kinds of human action might have been more or less conducive to ecological well-being? We need to know about human nature—what it is that human beings are and what this implies for their conduct within the natural world. If, as the natural rights tradition has intimated, human beings are individuals with basic rights to life, liberty, and property, that also means that this is how they are best fitted within the natural world.

The market is, after all, merely the result of the implementation of the principle of private property rights. As noted, Aristotle and others have discovered that such an arrangement of a community, into individual realms of authority, tends in the main to facilitate responsible conduct. There can, of course, be exceptions—irrationality is not preventable even by the establishment of the most natural and useful organizational social principles. Even at great cost to themselves, people will sometimes misbehave.

Yet, it makes good sense that when this cost does not affect individual agents or affects them so remotely that the connection between their actions and the consequences that follow is very difficult to observe, confusion and mismanagement are more likely. And what is a human-created ecological crisis but the macroresult of such individual confusion and mismanagement—individual persons dumping their potentially harmful waste onto the lives of others, apparently without cost.

Clearly, the ecological realms most affected adversely by human agency are public realms—the air mass, lakes, oceans, many parks and beaches, and, of course, the treasuries of democratic states (for what is deficit spending but a tragedy of the commons?), and so on. The ultimate harm, of course, befalls individual human beings and other living things on which human life often depends or from which it gains great benefit and satisfaction. Yet, the injury does not occur in a way that is judicially manageable—namely, where victim and culprit can be linked and the crime may be dealt with.

We have already noted that the idea of individual moral responsibility is indispensable to a normative environmentalism. To even implore others to do the right thing assumes they have a free choice to make. To criticize them assumes they could have done otherwise and should, on their own initiative, have done the right thing.

But if human beings do not have a realm of personal authority, a sphere of jurisdiction within which their judgments guide their conduct, the preconditions for responsible action are missing or seriously undermined. Collective responsibility encounters the tragedy of the commons—individuals can submerge their obligations within the group and no one need face, let alone admit, moral guilt for wrongdoing.

This holds especially for conduct affecting the environment. Of course, securing realms of individual responsibility will not guarantee the optimal outcome because people can misbehave even without any incentives to doing so. Yet, the pressure to do the right thing is greater when one must carry the burden of having done the wrong, so there is a greater likelihood of a well-managed realm where privatization prevails.

The Practice of Individualist Environmentalism

The practical implications of this position are many and current public policy is far from following them. The main policy implied is that discernible, determinate realms now under public supervision should be transferred to the private sector. That will provide the greatest systematic assurance for their optimum care. (Now and then, of course, public sentiment might secure reasonable public care, as well, but that approach is subject to systematic volatility.)

Private property rights need to be firmly established, secured, and protected within the legal system. Trespassing on private property will have to be promptly and justly punished. There must be no toleration of uninternalized negative externalities—that is, bad and costly but avoidable side effects—however much clamoring for them on the grounds of special privilege exists in the political arena.

In the few spheres where it is technically impossible to discern distinct domains, instead of reliance on bans on trespassing, personal injury laws will have to be strictly applied. To pollute the air mass, for example, constitutes injury to innocent third parties and must, therefore, not be tolerated on the grounds of some kind of social cost-benefit accounting. Individuals matter most, not their aggregates.

With this approach we could make significant improvements on the environment and encourage balance of the ecosystem. Some transitional problems will, of course, have to be faced. Some past collectivization and the resulting tragedies of the commons cannot be undone. But, to use a cliché, it is better late than never. As Terry Anderson and Donald Leal put the point: "People are beginning to realize that markets can be a powerful force in the environmental movement. Market-based incentives have become a common approach in both the private and public sectors. Corporations are searching for ways to increase profits in environmentally friendly ways. Policymakers are facing the reality that a cleaner environment comes at an increasingly higher cost."[7]

There is evidence for this all around us but, perhaps, most clearly in what Soviet-style socialist central planning has done to the environment in eastern Europe versus the comparatively less harmful results arising from the far more capitalist, free market, private property–based system of the West. The point here is to suggest that such an approach (resting as it does on the political and legal implications of classical individualism[8]) is more consistent with the nature of reality and better grounded metaphysically and scientifically. And that should be the central concern of environmentalists—to urge the adjustment of human choices, actions, and institutions to the nature of our world.

Notes

1. That there are many unconscious, maybe even subconscious motivations is not of relevance—the point is that even those can only be properly addressed if we think about them. Psychologists may insist that much of our lives are governed by such unconscious or subconscious motives, yet they also want to bring them to our conscious awareness so we can deal with them properly.

2. For more on this, see Robert Kane, The Significance of Free Will (London: Oxford University Press, 1998). For a thorough discussion of the idea of human agency—the capacity to act on one's own—see Edward Pols, Mind Regained (Ithaca, NY: Cornell University Press, 1998).

3. For more information on this, see Tibor R. Machan, "Applied Ethics and Free Will," Journal of Applied Philosophy 10 (1993): 59–72.

4. Pols, Mind Regained. For a discussion of why human reasoning is fundamentally different from that of even the most developed nonhuman animals, see John Searle, Rationality in Action (Boston: MIT Press, 2001).

5. For more on this, see Tibor R. Machan, "Pollution and Political Theory," in *Earthbound: New Introductory Essays in Environmental Ethics*, ed. Tom Regan (New York: Random House, 1984).

6. See Terry L. Anderson and Donald R. Lea, *Enviro-Capitalists: Doing Good While Doing Well* (Lanham, MD: Rowman & Littlefield, 1998).

7. Terry L. Anderson and Donald R. Leal, "Nature's Entrepreneurs," *The Freeman* 48 (November 1998): 647.

8. For more on this, see Tibor R. Machan, *Classical Individualism: The Supreme Importance of Each Human Being* (London: Routledge, 1998).

CHAPTER TEN

~

Bribes and Kickbacks

Primary Fault

Is there not something terribly wrong about paying off officials to escape various regulations that lawmakers of some region impose on the people in business?

To answer this question, one must first consider what are the proper standards for laws about doing business. Such an ethical issue can be raised about any law, including those that bear on doing business. After all, the laws that are enacted, even in democratic societies, can be awful, stupid, and even out and out morally despicable. Slavery, segregation, and other less drastic but still unjust measures have all been part of the history of the United States, one of the most democratic societies in human history. Some of these laws have had a very serious impact on commerce, often in ways that are morally repugnant.[1]

Once this initial issue is explored, we can ask whether paying off bureaucrats is always wrong, but not whether it is illegal—by definition it is illegal to fail to go by the law. But it may not always be immoral.

Bribes and kickbacks are often blamed on people in business. This is curious. Business people lack the power of the law, the most awesome power in society, that would enable them to impose a bribe or a scheme of kickbacks on public officials. One may "buy" other people's misconduct only if those others are willing to sell their integrity. But when one has the law on one's side, one can forcibly subdue people, including subvert one's relationship to them by abdicating one's official role and selling illegitimate services instead.

151

When people in business want to accomplish something they deem proper, they often need to first overcome the hurdle of government bureaucracies. Bureaucrats are often convinced that they are acting in the public interest, which can render their will intransigent. Only great benefits will make them yield their opposition to something professionals in business want to have achieved. So, people in business are often tempted to pay out what bureaucrats demand, hoping that this will make it possible for them to get on with the job of doing business. From this arises the phenomenon of bribes and kickbacks: "If you let me get on with my job without my having to jump through your innumerable loops, I will pay for it, albeit grudgingly."

The cost of doing business is often great but people in business are willing to pay it because if they do not, delays and other obstacles impose even higher costs on them.

How to Do Business Anywhere?

Like anything else, business is supposed to be done without violating the rights of people. It's based on voluntary exchange, not on coercion. We may not build on your property without your permission. We may not trade in slave labor. We may not engage in fraudulent trade, whereby what we promise to provide to you doesn't match what we actually provide to you. And so on. The crux of doing business is that no force or fraud is involved, period, at least among free and responsible adult human beings. Not only is doing business this way very productive, it is also morally right.

Many believe that businesses must be regulated to constrain their submitting to various temptations. So, they have succeeded in setting up regulatory agencies to tame the beast, as it were. However, no one is clear just how the regulators should be contained when they are tempted, how to tame the tamers.

Let's use a very good model we have in our society, journalism, the conduct of which may not be regulated. Unlike any other profession, journalists are unencumbered by law enforcers until they actually do something wrong to someone. In short, prior restraint is prohibited when it comes to dealing with the press. That is the meaning of the free press.

Discrimination against Other Professionals

This isn't how people in the business world are treated. No, they are dealt with paternalistically—their conduct is supervised by government's various regulatory agencies. They are legally required to meet various municipal, county, state, and federal standards. They may be inspected by bureaucrats and if found not to be in compliance they may be fined and even jailed.

This, in part, has led to their efforts, at times, to circumvent what they see as obstacles to getting on with business. Their actions are, of course, illegal. But are they necessarily unethical and morally wrong? In countries where laws are mostly reflections of a dictator's or single "party's" rule that can be more or less arbitrary and unrelated to considerations of justice, bribing an official can mean the difference between life and death. A public official can arbitrarily delay one's transportation of perishable goods so that everything is lost in the process, leaving a merchant bankrupt. Less dramatically, it can make the difference between living in relative peace and prosperity versus struggling against great odds. Such an official can withhold a license to do business and thus make it nearly impossible for a qualified professional to carry forth with the task of earning a living.

When this occurs, there is clearly nothing wrong with a business professional resorting to bribery. The people to be blamed are the leaders and bureaucrats themselves because they literally have made unjust laws that make bribes and kickbacks a way of life. They are, thus, effectively in violation of the job description of political or legal authorities. People in business could be and most often are doing the right thing to try to circumvent evidently unjust laws and regulations.

Law Breaking and Ethics

This, of course, involves them in law breaking. But it is not always morally objectionable to break laws. The laws of tyrannical societies are often thoroughly corrupt and we even make heroes of dissidents who break them. Ordinary folks would never have been able to survive in Nazi Germany and Soviet Russia without breaking and circumventing many laws. This is true even in many democratic societies, given that there are some terribly stupid laws, ones completely obsolete and on the books in nearly all communities. Also, whether laws are binding on us depends on how they are made, even apart from their content. A tyrant may impose a rule that makes sense but since his authority is bogus, the rule is not binding.

Generally, if laws and regulations are made with the consent of those governed by them, then violating the laws is a betrayal of one's word, a breaking of a promise, as it were. It is akin to breaking terms of a contract one has voluntarily and freely signed. That is morally objectionable and should be legally opposed and punished.

What if one voted against a law and it passed anyway? What if the regulatory bodies standing in the path of doing business effectively are created via the democratic process?

Arguably, democratic creation of public bodies suggests that these bodies are quite legitimate, so violating their edicts is morally wrong. But that assumes that the democratic process may achieve anything and everything. That is false. Some things should be beyond the reach even of the majority of the people and their representatives. The U.S. Constitution gives recognition to this by placing journalists and religious organizations out of reach of majority opinion and political control. The exceptions to this occur only where violations of the criminal law are at issue.

Limits on Democracy

So what are the proper limits on the democratic process? The plain answer is "Anything that's wrong for individuals to do." Just as a lynch mob is wrong, even if it's made up of the majority, so any democratic accomplishment that violates basic tenets of morality is wrong.

This suggests that however democratic some policies may be, they could also be morally wrong, which would justify circumventing them. The only objectionable element of this would be that law in general could be undermined.

Accordingly, it is good form in relatively free, democratic countries to attempt to change laws via the political process, not unilaterally. This isn't so much a matter of ethics or morality as of political realism. Without majority support, laws cannot be changed except by force of arms. Democracy is a force needed to establish and maintain laws—it doesn't make laws right. Those, in turn, who want to change the laws of a largely democratic society are realistically though not necessarily rightfully compelled to go through the same process that has led to the laws that they oppose, even if their opposition is completely justified.

So what is wrong with bribes and kickbacks in a largely democratic political order? It is that they undermine the integrity of the legal process, not that they are necessarily unethical or immoral. They circumvent the only effective means for both enacting and abolishing laws. Such circumvention may well be realistically justified in all other systems—especially when they are matters of life and death—except in those wherein it is possible to change the law via essentially peaceful democratic politics. This is not because all peaceful actions are just but because they are less unjust than ones achieved through coercion and violence.

Note

1. It may be appropriate here to mention that we are using moral terms in cognitive ways and we do not accept any version of relativism concerning basic moral principles. This is a big topic, but just to fend off some of those who might be easily tempted to be relativist on the grounds that there exists considerable variety and diversity of moral opinions, it bears noting that advocates of relativism are, in a way, contradicting themselves by insisting that we all ought to treat different moral opinions as having merit. This is, in other words, their own nonrelative moral absolute. For some nuances of the relativist position about truth, see Robert Nozick, *Invariances* (Cambridge, MA: Harvard University Press, 2001).

CHAPTER ELEVEN

~

Why Globalization Is Good

Let us start by asking why we should even bother about the ethics of global-ization—or, indeed, the ethics of any institution or public policy.

The term "globalization" was coined fairly recently, although the actual process has been under way for quite some time.[1] In mainstream discussions, including many academic books, it refers to a grab bag of policy ideas for re-moving impediments to trade around the globe and thus increasing interna-tional labor and capital flow. But in practical usage, the term also refers to various policies the World Bank and the International Monetary Fund link to their support of developing countries.

Growing globalization has, however, characterized economic and political life for several centuries now, ever since the first world-girdling trade routes emerged out of the ashes of the Middle Ages. At its heart, it has to do with the increasing ease with which a person in one part of the world can engage in mutually beneficial exchange with a person in another part of the world. We talk about it now because it's been going so much faster these last few decades. Every big advance affecting transportation or communication—telephones, airplanes, television, computers, and now the Internet—has served to shrink the world further.

The alleged bane of globalization has ended up in the crosshairs of more than one aspiring politician as well as some academics concerned with inter-national trade.[2] Economic democrat consumer activist Ralph Nader does not speak well of the process. Neither does populist Ross Perot, who thinks it could drain the United States of all its jobs (Mexico will get them all). Nor

157

does former Republican presidential candidate Pat Buchanan believe that properly conceived conservatism supports globalization.

Furthermore, the riots and vandalism at the 1999 meeting of the World Trade Organization (WTO) in Seattle, and then at its 2000 meeting in Prague, the Czech Republic, as well as those at the July 2001 Group of 8 (G-8) meetings in Genoa, Italy—not to mention some of the underlying hatred that brought about September 11, 2001, and the cheers heard from many around the globe when it happened[3]—showed that many people around the world are critical of, indeed, despise, globalization.

Given all this antagonism, it's important to tackle the ethics of the matter. It is not enough to show that globalization reaps economic advantages for most of those who are affected by it. The more vital question is: Is globalization in accord with certain basic values and moral standards of human life and should we, therefore, support it? Or do the many critics have a decisive point against it?

What does it mean to say that an action is ethical? Presumably, it must have some good and worthy purpose, a beneficial end that can be achieved without violating any of the basic principles that define proper conduct. A morally worthy public policy or institution must be in accord with principles of the good or properly lived human life.

Ethics assumes that there are at least some basic principles that apply to us as human beings any time and everywhere. They are valid because they derive from human nature itself, which is the same in every time and place despite the effects on human behavior of differing circumstances and cultural sensibilities and values. Even members of a society that denigrates reason and burns so-called witches at the stake must act on the basis of reason to some extent if they are to survive at all. And we are justified in saying that they are wrong, would be better off if they acted on reason all the time, and did not burn innocent people at the stake. The perpetrators are in fact morally wrong and culpable.

Or, to take a more familiar example, consider that wherever there are parents, there is a principle that ought to govern their behavior. If they fail to obey or live by that principle then they are in default of their obligation. They are engaging in parental malpractice. As parents, we take an oath of office: "I shall bring up these kids so that they are able to cope with the world around them." This obligation goes with being a parent. Now, that's a universal principle, even though many people don't observe it. But we criticize them if they fail to observe it and in so criticizing, we concede the existence and force of that universal principle. And it is reasonable for us to do so.

We all know about human rights organizations, like Amnesty International, that investigate various societies around the world and judge them on the basis of whether and how much they violate fundamental human rights. If the violations are large and chronic, the governments of such societies are deemed to be corrupt because they breach basic aspects of human morality. However, if these societies do abide by the principles of basic human rights, then at least in that respect they're morally and politically acceptable. The yardsticks being applied are identical in each case: human life has value, freedom has value, it is wrong to muzzle dissenters, it is wrong to torture and murder innocent people, and so on.[4]

So, whether one lives in Mongolia or in Tahiti, is a man or a woman, fifteen or eighty-five, the resident of a primitive society or an industrial one, there are some things we ought to do and other things we ought not to do. This does not mean that ethical principles cannot be deployed differently, just as engineering principles may be, depending on circumstances. Bringing up children in one society will involve certain specifics that don't exist in another society. In the twenty-first century, in Orange County, California, parents don't need to give children heavy overcoats in winter. It's not that cold. But in Alaska if parents fail to give their kids coats, and have the means, they are probably guilty of child neglect. The same with honesty. We ought to be honest, but being honest on our cell phones versus in person versus on the Internet will vary. The expectations of others are different and the needs for privacy are different in the different contexts. So there can be many variations permissible within the framework of an overarching ethical standard. The specifics vary, but the broad principle remains the same.

These are just a few examples. Obviously, most of the standard moral rules we hold ourselves responsible to follow—for example, to tell the truth, to treat others with some measure of decency and justice, to be loyal to one's friends, and so forth—share this feature of being applicable to all human beings. So we have at least a plausible if not decisive case for the validity of certain basic moral principles that cut across cultures and ages.

One more point must be made before we proceed to the issue at hand: the moral realm and the legal realm are not coextensive. Laws are an application of moral principles, setting forth rules and limits for social behavior. But they are not moral principles as such. Not all that is immoral should be illegal. Nor is everything illegal also immoral. Indeed, only in a totalitarian society do the rulers attempt to proscribe or prescribe every possible kind of human act. In free societies, citizens are free to choose wrongly as well as rightly; that is what it means to *have* the choice. But when unethical conduct also intrudes on another, forcibly violating that other's basic rights, then the law should protect him/her against such violations. The whole point of law is to protect rights so people can act morally on behalf of themselves and those about which they care.

Now, we are ready to consider the questions: Is globalization objectionable from the moral point of view? Is there something so wrong with globalization that not only should we avoid it ourselves, but we should ban it altogether, on principle?

It's likely that the animus against globalization is really just a new form of the antagonism for commerce as such. The fact that the person with whom one is trading is farther away than one's next-door neighbor does not alter the fundamental economic (and moral) character of the transaction. The question we need to confront first, then, is whether it is a basic human need—hence, moral—for us to engage in at least some measure of commerce. If so, then the economic–moral principles underlying globalization are not culturally specific and optional, but universal and necessary expressions of the needs of human communities as such. For example, that everyone has the right to strive for economic well-being and that men and women may not be prevented from trading are principles affirmed by globalization. If these are indeed general governing principles of human commercial life, then globalization is no more a form of cultural imperialism than was the movement to abolish slavery.

Now, to ask what are the ethics of globalization really amounts to asking whether some bona fide ethical standard justifies this policy, this newly christened institution. In order to find out, we have to know a little about globalization.

The term "global" means, of course, the applicability of something everywhere on the globe. To globalize something is to implement it throughout the world. But what is it that we're exporting throughout the globe?

It's not dancing, poetry, soccer, badminton, e-mail, or matzo ball soup (although instances of these may and do end up in regions far from the point of origin as a result of globalization). The issue is whether to globalize certain economic policies and institutions. So, our question is whether the exportation of these policies and institutions throughout the world is something good and worthy of our approval.

What are the institutions and policies that characterize globalization? And why, if we recognize that cultures have distinctive, properly unique elements, might their economic institutions need, nevertheless, to conform to something basic and common among human societies?

This is really not very mysterious. What's being globalized is free trade and those standards of law and governance that are hospitable to free trade. What's being thwarted and shunted aside—to the extent globalization does take place—are those elements of any society that run counter to these policies. The country of Bhutan was once so fearful of outside influence that it actually banned television, a ban that was lifted only in mid-1999, about the time the country's first Internet service provider came on-line. The leaders there have come to realize that in order to advance economically and to take advantage of what globalization has to offer, they must rescind policies that were probably at one time advocated vehemently. They've had to become more hospitable to markets and entrepreneurship. That will be true wherever globalization takes hold.

For example, globalization tends to promote the idea that society ought to respect contracts, that is, voluntary agreements that are signed and backed up by the law. Globalization advances these ideas for the entire world, not just for certain select societies, because without protection of contract and property rights there cannot be trade at all. If one doesn't own something, one cannot agree to sell it; and if those who would buy it don't own anything, they cannot agree to buy anything.

The right to private property may be suspended or set aside among members of a family or religious community where charitable work, giving, and sharing will accomplish sufficient levels of economic prosperity for all. But this kind of small-scale communal arrangement is only suited to people who have a common history and purpose and are willing and able to sustain the unity of purpose. It presupposes a familial or tribal context in which everybody knows everybody else. (But even in a small community, one can make the case that the introduction of economic incentives will serve to increase the goods available to all, as the Pilgrims, for example, discovered.) In larger societies, communal strictures cannot function and they discourage economic life altogether. If there is anything that explains the failure and fall of Soviet-style socialism, it is this attempt to export the principles of small-scale communalism to the entire country. Where globalization integrates and facilitates economic life, socialism gives it the noose.

Economic exchange is impossible without ownership, and it's next to impossible on a sustained basis without the legally enforceable agreements that are contracts. One cannot plan long-range that way. People in societies without the institution of contract must act for the short run, unable to plan ahead and to rely on what we might call economic trust. Sure, in most societies lacking the protection of private property rights and contracts it is possible to at least *make* an agreement. But agreements are less reliable and trustworthy absent the instrument for *securing* the agreement: the contract. If the other party defaults, there's no way to take an action against him/her short of force.

Economic arrangements occur among people who don't know one another and cannot rely on their intimate knowledge of one another. Among friends, a promise is usually enough. If you have good friends and you shake hands and say, "Yes, I will pay you back what I owe you," you don't need a contract. But if you don't know the people or if you're dealing with your grocery store, your bank, and so on, a handshake just won't do. Long-term trust requires a more formal arrangement. So, people without the availability of contracts don't make long-term economic arrangements. They don't invest in the elaborate projects like bridge building or large-scale manufacturing—the kind of projects that really give heft and sinew to an economy—because tomorrow morning or three days from now the government or some extortionist group might swoop in to destroy what they've built for some capricious purpose of their own. Maybe they don't like somebody's politics or religion, it's the wrong family, they don't have the proper ratio of ethnic characteristics, and so forth. In societies where long-term agreements are insecure, the odds of long-run economic investment are long at best.

Globalization spreads the institutions that secure economic stability. Where people can make formal agreements—subcontracts, long-range contracts, employment contracts, and so on, so that they can count on each other's promises—long-range economic investment and development are possible. Globalization is in part about exporting contracts and ownership rights. Societies that lack these are not hospitable to trade, investment, and development. As a consequence, they cannot make headway against poverty and destitution.

So, globalization, at its best, is about fostering certain kinds of institutional safeguards that are the hallmark of economically prosperous societies. These safeguards give people the capacity to trust one another over the long haul. They allow people to expect that they'll be able to hang on to things they make—a shop, a firm, or a company—without the government and others coming in and capriciously grabbing what they've earned. Globalization has come, so they will build.

Sounds Good So Far, So What's the Problem?

One of the complaints against globalization is that it is disruptive. It can threaten, even destroy, certain elements of a culture—just as capitalism itself always has. The economist Josef Schumpeter famously described capitalism as a process of "creative destruction," and it is certainly true that capitalism shakes things up. If all persons are protected in their liberty to enter into a contract, age-old social hierarchies may be disrupted. If one is an untouchable in India, for example, and not allowed to do certain things, instituting contractual relationships will definitely rock the boat. Suddenly, today, one is free to agree to do what was, yesterday, banned. Today, you're touching people around the globe.

Or consider a peasant in a monarchy who invents something, gets rich, and no longer has to till his little plot of land. Such a person now represents the incipient demise of standard cultural patterns that so many people venerate.

Such rocking of the social boat is the very thing Marx saw as one of the better results of capitalism. But while the changes benefit those now able to improve their lives, they can be very disconcerting for others. Consider a society in which women suffer second-class status and must always ask a man's permission to do anything. Suppose she can now enter into contracts and even acquire property, on her own, without asking anybody. That's liberating for her but very grating for those who regard these traditional roles as sacrosanct. On the traditionalist view, women ought to stick to rearing children, scrubbing floors, attending church socials, and leaving business to men.

Granted, there is value in steadiness and stability. Traditions persist for a reason. The traditional and familiar can be comforting. Even if a change is justified in principle, people are not always ready, let alone willing, to embrace it. It's understandable for there to be cultural resistance to potentially revolutionary policies brought about by globalization. Many people feel threatened by much of what requires them to change their routines.

What we now need to ask, then, is: Are traditions worth preserving just because they are traditions? Should traditions be immune to ethical evaluation? Is there some overriding ethical standard to do this?

Everything human beings do is subject to ethical evaluation, so long as human life is a value and living it well is a value. The overriding standard is precisely the most basic social requirement of human nature, namely, individual sovereignty.

Consider that in some places in the world slavery still exists, as it has for centuries. In these societies, certain people are declared unworthy of leading their own lives in accordance with their own judgment. From early on in their lives, they are allowed to exert no will of their own. They belong to others to be done with as these others see fit. Is that acceptable from an ethical perspective, just because it is consistent with the established tradition of that society? That assumes all traditions to be benign, and surely we know better.[5]

When abolitionists began to crusade against slavery, they were not intimidated by the fear that they might disturb tradition. That was their goal. They rightly believed that they had a better understanding of human nature than did the slaveholders. They believed that it was the slaveholders and their systems that did violence to humanity, not those who proposed to abolish it. They wanted to overthrow the tradition. They saw the tradition as unworthy and wrong.

The impetus to globalize rests on the same ultimate principle as abolitionism: the sanctity of each individual life. Globalizers want to introduce patterns of economic life that make all parties equal players, in the sense of having the equal right to engage in a contractual relationship—whether they're men or women, black or white, short or tall, American or Thai. This idea is upsetting to some people, but it is more in accord with our fundamental humanity than the encrusted traditions opposed to it.

Another criticism of globalization is that the principles it embodies are appropriate only for societies at an advanced stage of development. Developing societies, by contrast, are supposedly not ready for a system that protects free trade, freedom of contract, the right to private property, and similar elements of a free and open marketplace. Presumably, the inhabitants of these societies require leadership from an educated elite group to set priorities for them and to steer clear of the kind of "anarchy" in commercial life that is evident in more advanced cultures.[6] Undeveloped societies cannot afford squandering their resources on productivity that does not address their dire needs. They shouldn't be spending their time growing the Internet when they could be improving rice-paddy irrigation.

This is the argument, for example, of political leaders in the People's Republic of China, who defend their top-down management of society. While leaders have realized the value of a decentralized economy, China is still centrally coordinated, supervised, and, in places, collectivized. All of this is defended by some on the grounds that such measures are right for China—or Cuba, North Korea, or Iraq—and Westerners should mind their own business. Of course, the bosses of authoritarian or totalitarian regimes are prickly not only about globalization, but also about any suggestion at all that they apply the principles of human rights to the legal orders of their society.

Such complaints don't carry much weight, however, unless the repressive practices are morally superior to the alternative offered by globalization. But there can be no moral justification for employing slave labor, forbidding employment to members of certain ethnic groups, or preventing people from moving from one job to another. If monopolies granted by governments are threatened by competition from others, domestic or foreign, that again is no warrant for prohibiting some people from doing what they have a natural right to do.

In general, there is something suspicious when political leaders and bureaucrats complain about globalization. The experience of an editor of the *New Republic* is revealing. He had attended a conference on economic matters in Japan—not exactly an underdeveloped country—and spoken with Japanese officials who made no bones about their distaste for "the Americans," so pushy and arrogant in wishing to impose on everyone the American way of life. In particular, the Japanese officials didn't like the near laissez-faire economic system Americans tended to champion, at least in principle. And that is exactly what one hears repeatedly from critics of globalization, that allowing it is tantamount to caving in to U.S. cultural and political imperialism! So freedom really is slavery, after all.

The charge would be amusing if such blatant special pleading had not succeeded as much as it has in besmirching globalization. Here we have a case of folks desperately trying to hang on to their vested interests at the expense of the millions who would benefit from the freeing up of economic institutions—millions who need jobs, markets, and opportunities to get ahead in life. And yet, somehow, their rhetorical backing and filling is taken seriously. The movement toward free trade liberates people everywhere, at times slowly and with short-term hardships, yet steadily in the direction of controlling their own economic affairs.

Globalization does threaten imperialistic officials who want to keep "their subjects" in line by taxing semiprivate enterprises to the bone and even confiscating, at the government's whim, entire business establishments, farms, plants, and other productive endeavors.

The purported domestic price paid by the developed countries is another source of objections to globalization. Pop critics like Nader and Buchanan, as well as their more careful academic associates, claim globalization exploits lower-paid workers abroad to undermine the wage-earning capacity of workers in their own developed societies (though benefiting domestic consumers, they fail to add, *including those very wage earners*). This competitive pressure is possible in part because globalization encourages some child labor in poor societies; child labor is of course widely frowned on and forbidden in the United States. And maybe there are other labor, environmental, and workplace standards imposed in the United States and other developed countries that are absent or less enforced in the country of one's competitor.

But such arguments implicitly dismiss the right of competitors to enter the market fair and square. Nobody is entitled to immunity from economic change. Once customers discover that the same products and services are available from abroad at lower prices, their choice to purchase these should determine what prices get paid and who is to receive them. In a free economic system, no producer can enjoy a guaranteed right to have customers purchase his/her offerings. Such involuntary consumer servitude is the hallmark of communism, not capitalism.

What we are talking about here is not so much differing cultural patterns as differing economic conditions. Human beings don't all happen to be in the same position economically and therefore cannot demand the same returns for their economic efforts as people elsewhere. Factors affecting entire societies can range from the climactic, which cannot easily be helped, to the political, which are often defended tooth and nail by ruling elites. (Variations in economic conditions exist, of course, even within the same country, based on such differences as age, talent, willingness to take part in economic striving, good or bad luck, and so forth.)

In most countries, the negative political ingredients in the mix are far from accidental. One reason people in Southeast Asia cannot command the level of wages of people in Detroit is that for a very long time they've suffered the impact of bad economic ideas that discourage development. The same is true of the Middle Eastern countries where certain tenets of Islam (regarding inheritance) have not permitted the development of capitalization. In many places there's no contract, no private property, and thus economic stagnation. Workers never earn more than subsistence-level income. People don't develop skills and don't invest in technological improvements.

If this is their chosen way of life, nothing about globalization prevents their pursuing it. However, if there is interest in economic development, then globalization will help with that, but it will also challenge some of these ideas as they shape a country's laws and public policy.

So, there are political and cultural reasons why many people throughout the world have fewer economic opportunities than those who live in Houston, Manchester, or Auckland. As a result, they're willing to work for less to get themselves out of their dire straits.

But one needn't do much globetrotting to appreciate how economic power can vary according to underlying factors. If a person is untrained and inexperienced, his/her bargaining power with a prospective employer is not as great as that of someone with thirty years of experience and highly developed and renewed skills. Even in a developed society, labor is more easily replaced, hence less economically valuable, in some workplaces than in others. Employees at McDonald's face the unpleasant reality that they can be easily replaced with others who at a certain age are also willing to work there. McDonald's doesn't require many skills as long as one is willing to wear that funny hat and not spill hot coffee on customers. Still, if an employee is very competent and reliable, a good manager will value that employee more than one less competent and reliable. No matter how low on the totem pole you are when you start out, there is always an opportunity to improve your economic power and marketability, if the market you're dealing with is a free one.

This reality doesn't upset most people because they see reasons for it— they have the local knowledge required to understand why older, more educated, and more experienced folks get better pay, better perks, and higher rank. They realize that people at the beginning of their career and with few skills will have greater hardship than those who have "paid their dues."

By the same token, different cultures in different regions of the globe have had different rates of development. So when their populations enter the global marketplace, those at a relative disadvantage cannot command the same returns on their skills and time as do others from the more advanced regions. At the same time, that lower cost lures investment from those who do have investment dollars to spend, thus improving the economic prospects of those who are behind in the game. Slinging burgers at McDonald's is not the most fulfilling endeavor but it's better than not to be working anywhere at all—and it is a stepping-stone to better things. Likewise, the first hints of globalization in developing countries are a stepping-stone to better things for the struggling people there.

Developing countries don't have to be just like developed ones in order for the two to trade, something to keep in mind when issues like child labor come up. Child labor is illegal in the United States because we have a fairly wealthy society in which children don't have to be relied on to help pay the bills. The United States can afford to ban child labor. But in most developing societies, every little bit matters, including sometimes a child's labor. If we start cutting off trade with these people on the grounds that we dislike this or that about the way they do things, we will lose economic opportunities and cheaper prices on this end, true enough. But it is the citizens of the poorer countries, struggling to advance, who will suffer the most, not we. Is a poor family in an undeveloped country better off if it is unable to feed its children at all, so long as none of them has to work?

Globalization involves mutual trade for mutual benefit, with participants living on opposite sides of the globe. Trade has made it possible for us to emerge from the caves. The fantasy world imagined by those who disdain free trade depicts those seeking to make a good living, with decent pay so as to provide for family and loved ones, as unscrupulous robber barons who live off the unrequited labor of others. But that is an economic (and moral) myth. And wherever this view is seriously enacted as public policy, ruin follows.

International markets increase options and resources for everyone involved. If we care about improving the lot of the world's most disadvantaged populations, we should help them to become as rich as possible, help expand their opportunities, and help them grow. Globalize, globalize!

So, there are many good reasons why globalization should be affirmed, not rejected. Nevertheless, some complaints against globalization, loosely understood, do hit the mark.

Suppose a company sets up a branch in a country whose government secures for it conscripted labor, as has happened in China for quite a long time. The laborers are not free, have no legal right to unionize, no right to bargain, and indeed have none of their rights protected at all. They are simply commandeered to work for some enterprise. Could it be justified?

No. There is no justification for relying on conscripted labor at any point in trade relationships. Involuntary servitude is a fundamental violation of human rights, as is outright slavery. That is elementary humanistic ethics. Just as tradition as such is not an all-conquering rubric, neither is globalization. Both must comport with the basic ethical requirements of human life.

Some of the issues that can arise are not so easily parsed, however. Suppose you take a branch of your firm to a country that has lax environmental standards—in effect, there is no strict protection of private property, personal integrity, and liberty there. Accordingly, the law allows dumping waste throughout the neighborhood and the affected region. The firm generates pollution that measurably damages persons and property, and there are no laws to protect the victims.[7]

This issue cannot be addressed briefly because in order to achieve economic development in some societies the value of a clean environment may need to be compromised to an extent for the sake of accelerated productivity and how to balance these values is quite complicated. Yet, there is a general standard by which to look at the problem. When doing business abroad, it is vital that one does not coercively impose costs on people who have not agreed to accept those costs. In other words, one does not trespass on other people's lives or property in order to reduce production costs and thus the cost of the product being sold.

It's sometimes very difficult to apply this standard because in many countries there is a deliberate public policy of allowing such dumping so as to attract industry and thus boost economic development. Moreover, every business owes it to its owners to take advantage of cost-reduction opportunities. Yet, as a matter of business ethics, no business has the right to intrude on others for the sake of advancing its own projects. And pollution clearly does involve dumping on those whose cooperation may not have been voluntarily obtained.

So it's up to the globalizing businesses themselves to treat the rights of others with respect, even if a particular host country does not absolutely mandate that they do so. And if they fail to respect rights, folks in the home country are certainly justified in protesting.

Unfortunately, some activists raise so much ruckus about even the obvious benefits of globalization that they lose credibility when it comes to any truly legitimate complaints. Their arguments, when they bother to provide some, are often as indiscriminately vandalistic as their actions, and often there is also a certain disingenuousness to them.

Consider the people who protested in Seattle, Prague, and Genoa at the recent WTO and G-8 meetings. Most insisted that we shouldn't exploit the people around the world who are so vulnerable (and who, presumably, cannot see that when they benefit from access to global markets, they are worse off than when they starve!). That was about the extent of their rhetoric. Behind the rhetoric and rioting, however, often lay another agenda about who should reap the economic benefits of markets. There is much similarity between antiglobalization and protectionism along these lines—both wish to preserve a status quo that benefits a few at the expense of many.

Many of the protesters—and their leaders, especially—have managed to secure for themselves fairly nice wages in Western societies. (Certainly, they have managed, somewhat mysteriously, to obtain support for their rather extensive travels to the places where the media would pay them ample heed.) If you globalize economic competition, those now peacefully enjoying high capitalism-produced wages may face some serious competition. They want to be protected against this and seek to ban from the market the hordes of low-paid workers who may start accumulating capital on their own. There's reason to be more than a bit skeptical about this antiglobalist mission that pretends to be concerned only with how to avoid exploiting people. Very often, it has to do with reserving the benefits of market transactions for oneself alone, an ethically problematic stance to say the least.

True, globalization can be destructive to certain established cultural and economic patterns. But the threat to these patterns is often either merely apparent or, taken all in all, a positive boon. The fact is, no one has a right to keep others from competing, so long as they gain customers fair and square. Even child labor, if it does not on the whole harm children, is better than dooming families to starvation.

The kinds of problems that attend globalization are just the kind that have attended civilized life throughout the ages and are no excuse for shutting the process down. Globalization—the market—helps people to survive, flourish, and prosper. The fact is, human survival, flourishing, and prosperity are *good*.

So globalization is good. Additionally, since globalization increases the interdependence and interconnectedness of peoples of the world, its continued development increases the chances for world peace. This may prove to be the greatest historical irony of all.

Notes

1. Arguably, the message of Adam Smith's *Inquiry into the Nature and Causes of the Wealth of Nations* (New York: Modern Library Edition, 1927) was that countries would benefit immensely from the removal of trade barriers in all goods and services, the central theme of what is now referred to as globalization. Indeed, much of developmental economic theory, advanced by such economists as Sir Peter Bauer of the United Kingdom, has stressed this throughout recent decades.

2. Some prominent books include Robert Gilpin, *The Challenge of Global Capitalism: The World Economy in the 21st Century* (Princeton, NJ: Princeton University Press, 2000); Robert Gilpin, *Global Political Economy: Understanding the International Economic Order* (Princeton, NJ: Princeton University Press, 2001). Gilpin both analyzes and largely supports globalization. See also Gary Burtless et al., *Globaphobia: Confronting Fears about Open Trade* (Washington, DC: Brookings Institution, 1998). For a very critical discussion, see Richard Falk, *Predatory Globalization* (Oxford: Polity, 2000).

3. The September 11, 2001, terrorist attacks involved the expression of hatred toward globalization, given that globalization is a central element of international capitalism.

4. For a very insightful discussion of this topic, with special reference to the alleged difference between Western and Asian values, see Amartya Sen, "Human Rights and Asian Values," in *Business Ethics in the Global Market*, ed. Tibor R. Machan (Stanford, CA: Hoover Institution Press, 1999), 37–62.

5. We come face to face here with a trendy modern philosophical topic, namely, can one ever escape one's tradition or culture, can one be objective about anything at all? The main theme of Richard Rorty's work has been to deny that we cannot "climb out of our minds" or find "a skyhook—something which might lift us out of our beliefs." See Richard Rorty, *Objectivity, Relativism, and Truth* (Cambridge: Cambridge University Press, 1991), 7. Yet, this very claim assumes the opposite—that he can do so and, after his investigations, conclude that we cannot! See Tibor R. Machan, "Some Reflections on Richard Rorty's Philosophy," *Metaphilosophy* 24 (January–April 1993): 123–135.

6. This very notion annoys some people but in their annoyance they reveal that they, too, believe themselves to be more "advanced"—read: tolerant and accepting—

than those they chide for being arrogant and chauvinistic. The bottom line is that such rankings cannot be escaped, only done well or badly.

7. We are not alluding to the muddled idea of some country lacking precautionary policies, prior restraint, or what has been dubbed policies of "preventive justice." See Tibor R. Machan, *Private Rights and Public Illusions* (New Brunswick, NJ: Transaction, 1995). For a detailed discussion of the relationship between justice and government regulation, see M. Bruce Johnson and Tibor R. Machan, eds., *Rights and Regulation* (Cambridge, MA: Ballinger, 1983).

Epilogue

After eleven chapters of exploration, it may sound odd to say that we've merely scratched the surface, but that is in fact the case. We've examined a sampling of issues in business ethics, and even those we have only touched on. Two things must be said, which, we hope, have become evident to the readers of this book.

First, ethical issues, both professional and personal, presuppose some matters in the more basic branches of philosophy, namely, metaphysics and epistemology. This may strike some as highly contentious but the point is rather plain: For there to be principles to guide us as we conduct ourselves in various areas of our lives, there must be something permanent and stable on which they are based. And we need to be able to know they are to learn of those principles rather than merely invent them as we like. Ethics would be bogus, hardly binding on us, if it all rested on nothing more than the quicksand of our current feelings or sentiments.

Of course, various areas of philosophy are not neatly separated, they overlap and intertwine, such that problems in one area invite and sometimes necessitate investigation into another area. Still, the primary question of ethics—how ought I live my life?—presupposes that we have answers to something more fundamental: What kind of being am I? What is my nature? It also assumes we can reasonably and reliably come to know the answer to such a question.

We have tried in this book to pay heed to that question without straying far from our primary concern: business ethics. Clearly, however, the questions of professional ethics do not stand alone, and we cannot have confidence in answers for which we have no basis in a stable enough reality.

None of this means, of course, that one must be a moral philosopher or have a grasp of moral theory in order to be moral or act ethically in a profession. After all, there were morally good and bad people long before there was moral philosophy, just as moving objects in the world had mass, force, and velocity before there was the discipline of physics. The purpose of theory is to enlighten us and explain in general and abstract terms the world that we experience in particular and concretely.

Second, our treatment of business ethics has been unabashedly friendly. This may strike some readers as unusual, perhaps even untoward, for a textbook. While it is unusual, it isn't because competing texts are objective and balanced in their treatment, but just the opposite, as we have found. Much of what comes out of the academy, both in print and at the podium, is negative, or grudgingly neutral, at best, with respect to commerce.[1]

Our view is that this negativism is misguided, ungrounded, and ultimately unjust. One reason for this, we believe, is that much is quite troublesome with current thinking about professional ethics and ethics in general. The prominent moral teachings of our time are topsy-turvy. Perhaps the best statement of this fact came from Adam Smith, who is known primarily as the founder of scientific economics but was in his own eyes and by his university appointments essentially a moral philosopher. Here, in a famous passage that we have seen before, but bears repeating, is the gist of our problem with contemporary thinking on morality:

> In the ancient philosophy, the perfection of virtue was represented as necessarily productive to the person who possessed it, of the most perfect happiness in this life. In the modern philosophy, it was frequently represented as almost always inconsistent with any degree of happiness in this life, and heaven was to be earned by penance and mortification, not by the liberal, generous, and spirited conduct of a man. By far the most important of all the different branches of philosophy became in this manner by far the most corrupted.[2]

It has, sadly, not strayed from that course. Moral teaching for the last several centuries has been predominantly of the self-sacrificial variety: those who strive to live well aren't morally worthy and those who strive to make others live well are. Moreover, much of theology and even some social science claims that people are innately selfish and that this is the source of immorality. And if this is so, if selfishness is hardwired into everyone, then of course it makes no sense to bother learning and teaching how to care for oneself and do well at living. That is why in so many discussions of ethics or morality we see that prudential conduct is *contrasted* with ethical conduct. In fact, however, prudence is itself one of the important moral virtues.

Furthermore, how to live well is not hardwired into us. Common sense alone can reveal this: Consider how many millions of people act recklessly and ruin their lives routinely. Living well is a skill that must be taught, not an automatic response.

Another reason that unselfishness appears to be the height of especially professional—including business—ethics is that professionals often take an oath to help others who seek them out. That makes it look as if it is this alone that morally justifies the profession.

But professionals devote themselves as they do largely because it is rewarding and fulfilling in itself to them. Indeed, nearly all parents urge their children, and teachers their students, to find work that is self-fulfilling, not a constant drudgery or chore. It is hardly surprising that the helping professions are very satisfying (we are, after all, social beings), but that is not the beginning and end of morality.

Modern ethics tells us mainly that it's good only if it hurts and is done for others. Not just that self-indulgent conduct is unethical, but more strongly, that living one's life by following one's inclinations can neither promote one's life nor that of other people. We are told that morality requires that others, not ourselves, be the primary focus of our efforts. And yet, as we have argued, it is the business of ethics to guide one to the true, actual, serious enhancement of oneself, the life one leads, which in most cases includes the well-being of many others. A self-enhancing moral code leaves sufficient room for generosity, kindness, and compassion, without being self-sacrificing and self-denying.

It is especially pointless to talk about business ethics if one regards the pursuit of profit—which is the economist's term for prosperity—as morally suspicious and efforts at economic success as essentially underhanded. That simply means business people will see themselves as morally second rate, and some may then tend to disregard ethics altogether.[3] Disaster waits along such a route. However, if it is clear that business is truly a professional calling that requires success within certain limits, just as all life does, business ethics can make clear sense.

Unless moral education changes toward teaching people to be ethical because that is how happiness is achieved in life, and away from the view that morality requires self-sacrifice, many will indeed take the downward path. We naturally desire our own happiness. So, if one has been convinced that cheating, lying, and stealing are the road to happiness, while honesty, justice, prudence, generosity, and the like make one a loser, the call to goodness will be weak and why, indeed, be moral? Such seems to be the prevailing view.

We have argued that it shouldn't be this way. Ethics is a discipline that's supposed to help us live well and flourish. When we are generous or charitable toward others, such actions should be seen as enriching our own lives in the process. The morally virtuous life should be seen as beneficial to those who live it. Such was the wisdom of Socrates, and of the ancients generally.

Once morality is recognized as life enhancing, it should not be difficult to champion it among our professionals. A culture that makes morality constantly painful, however, cannot expect morality to be well received.

We think it fitting to close our examination of business ethics with a summing up, a bringing together the major ideas that have motivated and, we hope, given life and substance to this work. And so, we'll conclude with what by now should be familiar, a series of reminders. If it is, and if the reader is inclined to agree, then our objectives will have been met and our efforts rewarded. Here, in a nutshell, is our message.

First, there is a very general cultural prejudice against commerce, despite its obvious value to us all. This prejudice has a number of sources, including suspicion of the so-called profit motive, the popularity of altruism, and the prevailing tendency to view capitalism as somehow inherently immoral. This prejudice refuses to see commerce as a noble enterprise, thinking of it as something of a necessary evil, at best an awkward step in the direction of what many consider a truly moral ideal, the common ownership of all goods. The dramatic collapse of communism and the slow but clear rise in the standard of living for more and more people, which includes increased education in economics and the role of economics in history, count against this prejudice.

Second, the view of human nature typically assumed by economic study, namely, Hobbes's view of man as desire-gratifier, though serving certain scholarly purposes well, is basically misguided and contributes to the prejudice against commerce just noted. This overly narrow, hedonistic view of human behavior puts human beings in the marketplace as in mortal combat, ready to kill or be killed, economically speaking. Without factoring in human intelligence, moral considerations, and many extrahedonist purposes, which are in fact a part of daily life, including commercial life, understanding human beings is impossible.

Third, the choices that people make in the commercial aspect of their lives are part of a more comprehensive plan, namely, to realize as complete and flourishing a life as possible. Conversely, though business is a profession, everyone, including nonprofessionals, engages in business to some degree as part of a larger effort to realize a complete and flourishing life. So, the ethics of business is everyone's business.

Fourth, human beings, by and large, recognize and admire the basic moral virtues of honesty, courage, generosity, compassion, self-reliance, and so on and recognize and detest the opposing vices of dishonesty, cowardice, stinginess, malice, dependency, and the like. This recognition extends into commercial life, such that a merchant does well to protect his/her reputation for honest dealings.

Any moral theory that fails to accommodate these facts is bound to collide, either with the demands of actual ordinary life, where theories are tested, or with itself, as it tries to meet the demands of consistency. Morality and moral theories arise because human beings can suffer harm and can bring harm to themselves and others. Among the purposes of morality is the reduction of human suffering through the guidance of rules, principles, and practices. Thus, a moral theory, if followed, ought to reduce human suffering. A corollary of this is that morality ought to enhance human relationships and social cohesion. Additionally, since human beings come into conflict, morality ought to provide ways of resolving conflicts of interest justly. Within a just society, human flourishing and happiness are possible. These purposes or functions of morality, then, can provide criteria for assessing moral theories. The major moral theories do not meet these criteria equally well: much of the literature of contemporary moral research involves debate and discussion about which moral theory best serves the purposes of morality. Given the pervasiveness of commerce in contemporary human life, and the significant role that commerce plays in the pursuit of happiness, any moral theory worthy of rational embrace must offer guidance for conducting ourselves in our business endeavors. We have argued that classical egoism, or moral individualism, provides such guidance and is particularly well suited to capitalism and the doctrine of natural rights to life, liberty, and property, which we take to be the underpinnings of a free society.

Here is a final thought: Moral theories have emerged from moral philosophy as systematic attempts to explain the experience, phenomena, and facts of the moral dimension of life. That theories in any given discipline compete tends often to obscure the agreements that exist. This is especially true with moral theories, almost all of which agree, for instance, that there are virtues and vices, that human beings make choices for which they can be held accountable, that there are standards of accountability, and so on. The theories typically conflict not in whether, say courage or generosity are virtues, or whether the welfare of others is morally significant, but, for example, in whether and how the virtues and vices are to be ranked, or whether the welfare of others or of self should have priority in moral deliberation. Since philosophy is characteristically argumentative, one finds in the literature and hallways of philosophy a focus on the points of disagreement, and this tends to give the impression that nothing is settled, that there are no shared values or principles or common ground.

Such is not the case, as nearly every philosopher will attest. From this, a student or layperson giving serious thought to moral issues ought to take hope, rather than despair. The ongoing debate in moral philosophy is itself testament to the shared conviction among the disputants that the exchange of ideas, debate, deliberation, and inquiry are necessary and fruitful for the moral life—otherwise, there would be no point in arguing for one's view. At very least, it is agreed on all sides that the application of reason to moral questions can yield insight, perspective, and clarity, which are the conditions for genuine solutions.

A related point here is that since moral theory arises in response to the actual experience of human beings, moral philosophy must ultimately begin and end with common human experience. And so a moral theory must be in accord with at least the most general and fundamental facts of human experience. In this light, business ethics can be established, on commonsense grounds, as a legitimate discipline. Consider the indisputable fact that human beings have, very naturally, in all regions, and in every era dating back to prehistoric times, engaged in trade, the most fundamental act of commerce. Trade, in turn, presupposes ownership of goods or services to be traded. Trading, selling, or transferring that which one owns makes sense only on the assumption that human beings have interests to be served, purposes to be satisfied, and goals to be realized.

The realization of one's goals requires, at various times and to varying degrees, the exercise of one or another of the commonly recognized virtues, such as honesty, courage, temperance, patience, and generosity. Among the goals that human beings share commonly is the goal of continued economic strength sufficient to meet, at the very least, the practical needs of life. Realizing this goal requires that one chooses to think and act intelligently, thoughtfully, and seriously about ends, means, and some very practical and sometimes mundane matters, and that one remain poised and mentally attuned to situations, events, and conditions that can affect one's economic life. Admittedly, practical matters are not as lofty as, say, struggling with a moral dilemma or finding the courage to surmount a great loss. But attending thoughtfully to the health and management of one's economic life is inseparable from one's general obligation to live a morally good life, which includes taking care of oneself, which means acting prudently, rather than being dependent on others or acting recklessly and inattentively to one's well-being. And so it is a serious moral requirement for a serious moral goal. It is, in fact, a virtue, one highly regarded by ancient philosophers, but barely recognized in modern life: the moral virtue of prudence. The proper exercise of prudence is impossible in the absence of the other virtues, and the rational demand of consistency requires that all of the virtues be integrated. This means that the truly prudent life would also exhibit courage, honesty, commitment, patience, and the like.

In the course of life, and in the effort to live life prudently, one is faced with issues, challenges, and conflicts that raise the question: What ought I do? There is no escaping this question. In the life of business and commerce, and in the practical world of acquiring and spending, we must engage in moral deliberation, choice, and action. Business ethics is the discipline that guides us on our way and shows us how to conduct ourselves in the marketplace with integrity and dignity.

In conclusion, we would like to make just some brief remarks about perhaps one of the most widely discussed cases in contemporary corporate history, the demise of Enron, the giant energy company. We will not discuss the cumbersome details of the fiasco because most of it is irrelevant to business ethics as such. It is legal malfeasance that finally brought the company to its knees, although some of this malfeasance was probably the consequence of questionable ethics.

What we want to discuss with reference to the Enron case is just how common it is for critics of business—for example, Ralph Nader and Kenneth J. Galbraith—to lament the incredible power of multinational corporations. Some have made a career of promoting the line that nearly everything bad in the world comes from massive corporate power.

Yet we often witness the demise of huge corporations. In the later twentieth and early twenty-first centuries, the most visible of such cases was the demise of Enron. But there were, and continue to occur, others as well—Montgomery Ward, K-Mart, Global Crossing, and WorldCom. Oddly, it is in connection with the collapse of the bigger of these, Enron and WorldCom, that many seem to be outraged.

What is remarkable, though, is that if corporations had all the power their critics ascribe to them, none—certainly not the biggest ones—would go under. They'd manipulate, coerce, and otherwise control the market so that they would be winners, never losers. They would use the power they are criticized for to make themselves invincible.

Yet, after the fall of numerous big companies, including a huge one such as Enron, one does not read recantations from critics concerning the almighty power of business corporations. Hundreds and more of these big firms have bitten the dust over the last several centuries, showing clearly that far from being invincible, business corporations are subject to all of the mishaps, foibles, malpractices, and calamities that plague the lives of human beings. No wonder. They are, after all, human organizations and will show both the powers and weaknesses that we human beings are capable of.

However, myths often manage to survive contrary to the facts that should have spelled their extinction. The reason for the constant bad mouthing of corporations isn't that they are as powerful, invincible, and capable of massive manipulation and coercion as the critics allege. We believe the major reason for the critic's ire is that business corporations are in it for the money. When one is in it for the money, one cannot do right, as some prominent voices would have it, no matter what. Whether a big commercial company succeeds or fails, for those like Nader it is guilty of something.[4]

It isn't simply that, as in all human affairs, there are no guarantees that one will succeed and so one needs to be prepared for big companies going belly up just as one needs to be prepared for them flourishing and prospering. No, for many critics and, yes, antagonists of corporate commerce when companies succeed, they must have done something wrong—exploited workers, ripped off customers, polluted the environment, what have you. And when they fail, then, too, they—which is to say, their managers, executives, and owners—must have done something wrong, such as miscalculated, kept doctored records, and most of all hoodwinked their shareholders and, especially, their customers.

In reality, though, corporate commerce exhibits all of the ups and downs and mediocrities of human life. Contrary to what some argue, the economic or commercial dimensions of human life are not radically different from the artistic, scientific, educational, or athletic. They are all, essentially, peaceful but can become corrupted to be aggressive and vile, too.

The same is the case with corporate commerce, and Enron's fall, whatever the details, should be no cause for a great deal of handwringing about how supposedly the free market, private sector, or capitalism just doesn't manage to live up to standards of morality. As if the government's remedies could withstand all ethical scrutiny.

But then, arguably, the flap is not about Enron. No, it amounts to some people eagerly using the highly visible and very likely quite shady Enron case as another nail in the coffin of capitalism. It isn't enough that too many people across the globe are hostile toward capitalism, so much so that their anger can issue in merciless and wild terrorism. The desire for controlling the economic affairs of human beings is so attractive to some they welcome any chance to give this a better chance, never mind that the fiasco has nothing at all to do with the failure of bona fide market processes.

Too many intellectuals and pundits seem to want to add fuel to the fire and denounce capitalism at every turn. When a big company fails, that's cause for cheer to them because it superficially makes it seem irrefutable that the marketplace is full of hazards. But since nothing is immune to hazards in life, the real issue is a comparative one: Is a free, capitalist commercial society of general benefit to members of the society in which it reigns, as compared to the planned, regulated, and otherwise regimented economy the critics tend to favor.

We think it can be shown, both by careful analysis and through the evidence of history, that when it comes to the securing of the important human values, a legal order hospitable to uncompromised free trade succeeds better than the live alternatives proposed.

Notes

1. For a survey of some of the relevant literature, see Tibor R. Machan and Douglas J. Den Uyl, "Recent Work in Business Ethics," *American Philosophical Quarterly* 24 (April 1987): 107–124.

2. Adam Smith, *Inquiry into the Nature and Causes of the Wealth of Nations* (New York: Modern Library Edition, 1927), 726.

3. It is notorious how often people in business proclaim that their main goal is service to others, something that's transparently disingenuous and fools no one. It does, however, indict their own sincerity and self-understanding.

4. For more on this, see James E. Chesher and Tibor R. Machan, *The Business of Commerce: Examining an Honorable Profession* (Stanford, CA: Hoover Institution Press, 2000).

APPENDIX A

~

Moral and Political Theories in Brief

Moral Theories in Brief

Most competing moralities offer answers to the main ethical question: How should I, a person, live my life? We will examine some of these by first outlining their idea of what is the highest good or the main goal to strive for in human life. We will deal only with those ethical positions that provide an argument in support of their answer to the basic ethical question. Others reject the very idea of arguing for such an answer and offer the vehicles of revelation, special intuition, mystical insight, and the like as means for obtaining answers to moral questions. We will touch on some of these later in this appendix.

Remember, however, that such theories are rarely embraced reflectively by ordinary folks. They may think of them when faced with unusual and difficult problems about, say, abortion or assisted suicide, but rarely in connection with normal, daily ethical problems such as how to deal with one's teenage daughter or what to do when a boss is being arbitrary. Ethical theories are what philosophers work out to make sense of the beliefs and actions of people who may not have thought deeply about these matters.

Hedonism

Most of us have heard of people who believe that the proper goal for us all is the pursuit of maximum pleasure. Sometimes, such people have in mind increasing the existence of pleasure as such (measured either by reference to degrees of intensity or amounts). Sometimes, not all pleasure, including

182

those of nonhuman animals, but only the pleasure of human beings in toto is viewed as the proper goal. For others, the pleasure of the individual actor or agent is the only relevant goal to be pursued.

What we are discussing here is an ethical, not a psychological position. Sometimes, it is held that everyone is always pursuing pleasure, whatever else one is doing. This is called psychological, not ethical, hedonism.

Ethical hedonism holds that *we ought to act so as to secure the maximum amount of pleasure* for ourselves, *for the individual who acts*. First, however, a few comments should be offered about the version of hedonism that proclaims *the maximum amount of pleasure* for humanity *as the proper moral goal for everyone*.

According to the form of hedonism that declares the maximum possible amount of pleasure as the proper moral goal everyone should pursue, pleasure is a good in itself. It is not the pleasure of some individual person but pleasure as such that is considered good. (This is often referred to as the view that pleasure has intrinsic value, independent of its value to someone or something.) That pleasure is good in itself seems to be evident: if one feels good, that is what pleasure amounts to, plain and simple. Now the goodness of good feelings is clearly self-evident. We are just the sort of beings who welcome pleasure and resist pain, at least under normal circumstances. Therefore, the theory that pleasure itself is intrinsically good has considerable appeal on the basis of our experiences with pleasure and pain.

It is not so evident that we should increase the amount of pleasure—regardless of whose pleasure is involved—just because it is normally preferable to pain. It may be possible, however, to calculate whether our actions will increase the amount of pleasure for us and those near us, so that we can identify principles of conduct that will accomplish this limited goal. Yet, calculation of the amount of pleasure versus pain in the world is not possible for any one person; therefore, one cannot learn the answer to the ethical question: How should I act? Thus, it is probably impossible to tell whether one's increase of one's own pleasure is an overall increase of pleasure, especially if it may also produce some pain. Remember that one of the requirements of an ethical theory is that the moral goal(s) specified must be reachable.

The best we might do in defense of this form of hedonism is to consider that it may evolve into a different form, one we will consider next. On the one hand, it seems possible that the very idea of the maximum amount of pleasure is confused; thus, it would seem best to abandon it and consider the type of hedonism that deals with increasing individual pleasures. On the other hand, it is also clear that something like the idea of maximum pleasure or "welfare," understood to indicate the satisfaction of desires, governs much *social* or *public* policy. When social planners allocate the resources put at their disposal, they often think in terms of whether a certain distribution scheme is more or less likely to increase the satisfaction of existing human desires in the community. This will be dealt with in more detail in the next section on utilitarianism.

More traditional is the hedonism in terms of which one ought to act so as to attain the greatest amount of *one's own pleasure*. Hedonism considers pleasure to be measurable. Both the intensity and the quantity of pleasure are open to determination. Some hedonists make a very sharp distinction between the finer pleasures possible to human beings and the simple pleasures other animals can experience. Others see no basis for that distinction and believe simply that each and every person has as his/her proper goal in life the accumulation of as many pleasurable experiences as possible. In turn, the principles of conduct we should all invoke in making decisions about what we should do are those most likely to lead to the attainment of that goal.

Notice that this doctrine has the correct form of a moral point of view. We are to do something we are capable of doing (in this case to choose to increase our pleasurable experiences) and we are to live by principles that we can identify. This does not yet show that the doctrine is correct, only that it can be a candidate for the best moral position for human beings. It appears to be a plausible answer to the ethical question: How should I live as a human being? Jeremy Bentham is perhaps the best known exponent of ethical hedonism.

Criticisms and Answers
There are some difficulties we should point out, however. These challenge the view that hedonism is the best answer to the moral question. We can raise some of these challenges and postpone for later whether they are decisive.[1]

An internal problem of hedonism is that by pursuing pleasure, we often find ourselves undecided about what to do. Many pleasures are of equal force. Going to the movies, staying home to watch television, having dinner with friends, reading a magazine article, or playing some basketball could each be equally pleasurable. To decide which should be done may require a standard apart from maximizing pleasure.

Even if this could be handled by, say, flipping a coin, by pursuing our personal pleasures we frequently find ourselves in conflict with what other people want to do. If someone would be pleased to have my company but I would not be pleased at having his/hers, one of us would then have to give up on pursuing pleasure. Thus, the goal of pleasure is often inapplicable to everyone involved because not everyone can pursue it, in which case one may question whether hedonism is a bona fide ethical theory. One cannot be required to do what is impossible to do for all ethical agents. A basic moral principle has to be universalizable. And in the community of others it would appear to be impossible for all people to pursue pleasure—some would have to abandon this objective on at least some occasions. A moral position that results in frequent conflicts between people is impossible to generalize for everyone.

Finally, as a criticism of one form of hedonism, it is very likely that physical pleasures are not the only ones we are capable of feeling. Human beings have a more complex emotional makeup than other (even "higher") animal forms. This is due, probably, to our advanced form of consciousness and our sensitivity to factors other than the physical. The restriction of pleasures to physical ones because these are more likely to be measurable could be artificial.

Also, we may find it possible, eventually, to measure at least the intensity of other experiences. Then they could become possible goals to be pursued. However, these more complex varieties of pleasure, such as feelings of emotional satisfaction, are products of learning and opportunity; they are not inherent in human nature. These complex pleasures or satisfactions are thus not universalizable. Not all people could refer to them and the possibility of conflict within oneself and among different people increases considerably when they are taken as goals that we all should pursue.

The hedonist will have replies to these objections, of course. The merits of these replies will not be discussed—readers will benefit from trying to assess for themselves whether they have any. For example, concerning pleasures of equal force the hedonist could argue that under such circumstances a flip of a coin is as good a device for deciding as any other. As for the conflicts between the pleasures of different people, which may cancel each other out and effectively render the pursuit of pleasure impossible for all concerned, the hedonist could claim that limitations on what people can do will exist no matter what their proper goal is. One must simply realize this and calculate the maximum attainable pleasure accordingly. Concerning more complex pleasures, the hedonist may admit that they are more difficult to calculate but urge that we do the best we can with what we know. Hedonists may reply to those who deny the possibility of universal pleasures (because of different education and circumstances generating different pleasures) by the following: Pleasures may come in many forms but they are all pleasures and can be measured as such. It is one's duty to increase the amount of one's pleasure no matter what kind of pleasure it is. The objection is irrelevant.

The idea that it is our moral responsibility to seek pleasure for ourselves is not widely proclaimed except perhaps in *Playboy* and similar magazines. Yet, in ordinary life most people do seek out many pleasures. Spectator sports, parties, vacations, eating, drinking, and, for most of us, sexual experiences are widely pursued. Some people pursue these pleasures diligently, some even systematically. Often, we view such conduct as the result of inner drives we do not really choose at all. In that case, the conduct would have no moral significance, since choice must be possible for morality to even enter the picture. But for some of us the pursuit of pleasure is indeed a serious undertaking, something to be learned and cultivated, not at all inborn. The idea that experiencing the maximum possible amount of pleasure could be the moral goal all human beings should strive for is not obviously absurd. Certainly, some very prominent philosophers (e.g., Bentham) have argued with great complexity and ingenuity for just this position. One who is concerned about what is good and what human beings ought to do will benefit from a close examination of these ideas, however unpopular they might be within our culture.

Utilitarianism

It will be evident in this section that utilitarianism is related to hedonism. From the name of this doctrine it appears that utilitarians emphasize what is useful. But this is just an appearance; the doctrine does not advocate that the good is that which is useful. Instead, the substance of the theory is that *the good is the greatest happiness of the greatest number of whatever can be happy*. The philosopher and political economist John Stuart Mill is most notably associated with ethical utilitarianism even though quite a few others, such as Henry Sidgwick, also espouse the position. (Quite a few social theorists, especially in the field of political economy, would classify themselves as utilitarians. But they are not thereby embracing an ethical or moral viewpoint instead of a more descriptive analytical framework involving considerations of what people actually desire, as distinct from what they should or ought to desire.)

Happiness in utilitarianism is not the same thing as pleasure, although it is related to pleasure. It would be more accurate to consider this view as the contention that the greatest welfare (well-being)—or even simply satisfaction—of the greatest number of human beings is the good, and that we should do that which helps to achieve this condition.

Before we can examine the arguments for and against utilitarianism, we have to get a reasonably clear idea of what welfare is supposed to be within utilitarian theory. What is welfare?

Among most of the several versions of utilitarian theory, welfare is closely tied to the achievement of desired goals and the satisfaction of preferences, wants, and wishes. Whenever someone has his/her desires satisfied, we can justifiably hold that that person is well off and that the person's welfare has been attained, or so utilitarians would maintain.

Utilitarians do realize that some desires cancel out others, lead to conflict, and may even be self-destructive or destructive of society. Some qualifications are needed to make this a plausible theory. Some theorists hold that desires or preferences that limit the realization of the preferences of others do not count as significant in understanding welfare and what we should do to achieve it. Others make welfare depend on what are healthful or natural desires or preferences.

Utilitarian welfare or happiness is frequently identified with physical and psychological well-being (as these are characterized by the medical and psychological scientists of a community), instead of being left to subjective determination of desires, preferences, and so on. Frequently, the health and the economic well-being of (the members of) a community are picked as manifestations of such a goal. (In political theory, this view emerges in the doctrine of the welfare state.)

With these initial points in mind, we can now ask why the good should be thought of as that which fits the utilitarian definition. Why is the greatest happiness of the greatest number the proper goal we should all strive for?

Utilitarianism, like many other ethical theories, is tied to broader philosophical positions. One crucial philosophical underpinning of utilitarian ethics is that the good must be identifiable by means of direct observation. Otherwise, it would not be possible to know what is good, that is, what human beings are supposed to achieve. If we cannot know what is good—and thus have no way of learning how to achieve it—then it could not make realistic sense to hold ourselves and others responsible for achieving it. If only the perceivable, sensible things in the world can be known, and if there is a good we should strive for, it must be perceivable.

Historically, the epistemological base of utilitarian ethics is that we can know only that which we can identify by using the senses and can measure so as to make sure it exists. There is ample plausibility to this view of human knowledge to accept it as a background for the sake of understanding the case for utilitarianism.

Given this point about identifying the good, the best candidate for what is the good or most desirable thing in human life is the combination of physical and mental well-being. The latter is difficult to identify, but the former would appear knowable, so utilitarians usually focus on physical welfare, which consists in having the basic human needs and wants satisfied. These needs include food, shelter, medical care, and protection from the elements and from disasters. Most obvious is the need for a certain degree of economic well-being—that is, the capacity to obtain from various sources in nature and in society what one requires for a decent level of subsistence. The material conditions needed to maintain one's physical health and safety and the requirements to sustain these are clearly identifiable as good for us.

Learning about mental well-being is not so easy. In utilitarian theory, this problem is usually handled by leaving the matter to subjective understanding. In other words, the psychic welfare is best left to the individual for judgment, except in some drastic cases where psychological distress is clearly evident to observers.

To summarize, utilitarian ethical theory is the view that the good is a state of physical and psychological well-being, the former identifiable publicly, the latter left to each person to judge privately. Right conduct maximizes the amount of what is good in the world, that is, increases to the fullest possible degree the physical and psychological well-being of people. The basis of this view is that it can be meaningfully implemented and it conforms to the requirements of a sound theory of knowledge.

Act and rule utilitarianism are two forms of utilitarianism that are generally considered in ethical discussions. Act utilitarianism is the position that on each separate occasion when one decides to do something, one must figure out what is going to contribute most to the greatest happiness of the greatest number and act accordingly. Rule utilitarianism is the position that a set of principles needs to be identified and applied to decision making. The consistent application of this set of principles will produce the greatest happiness of the greatest number. Rule utilitarianism tends to be favored over act utilitarianism, since the task with which act utilitarianism faces us seems ponderous, tedious, and time consuming. One's life would get incredibly bogged down with such an impossible task.

Criticisms and Answers
Utilitarianism is not without its problems. One criticism is that utilitarianism is unworkable. It is impossible to know whether or not some action does in fact manage to contribute to the overall well-being of the membership of a human community, and it is even more difficult to know whether it contributes to humanity in its entirety. If it is impossible to guide one's conduct by reference to whether maximum happiness is being promoted, then the theory fails to provide meaningful, implementable guidelines to conduct. Any ethical theory unable to provide such guidelines is unsuccessful.

Another criticism is that people could act in accordance with utilitarian ethics and have obviously nonutilitarian motives. An individual could contribute to the welfare of millions simply to achieve a good reputation, with no thought of the greatest happiness. Another could mistakenly believe that some act will benefit humanity, whereas it actually has adverse consequences. ("I meant well" is a frequent comment of those who are responsible for disaster, and sometimes it is quite true. Also, "He helped the poor a great deal, but he did it to satisfy his need for recognition" is a true description of some philanthropists.)

A further objection to utilitarianism is that it requires a centrally organized, dictatorial state. In order to satisfy the greatest welfare of the greatest number, a vast quantity of information is required, far more than any individual can obtain. Everyone's needs and the total resources of the community must be known in order to learn what actions would maximize the benefit to be reaped from these resources.

But all this knowledge would be useless if whoever had it could not control the distribution of resources to those who would get the most benefit from them. (The utilitarian theory of justice is therefore often called distributive justice.) But all of this would require that select experts of a community—or, on a large scale, a fully centralized state—shoulder the ethical responsibilities that each person is supposed to fulfill in the role of a moral agent.

Such an arrangement would be moral paternalism, critics have argued. The responsibility for attaining the proper goals of human conduct would be taken away from individuals and political leaders would be the sole moral decision makers. This would make utilitarianism something other than an ethical theory, which requires human self-responsibility.

Finally, utilitarianism appears to violate certain commonsense ethical precepts. It is argued that by its tenets it would often be morally correct to lie, cheat, or even murder to facilitate the goal of the greatest happiness of the greatest number of people. Some persons achieve psychic well-being by being lied to (about their actions, health, looks, achievements, and so on). Promises might have to be broken in terms of utilitarian ethics, because keeping them would not contribute to the "greater good." For example, one could perhaps enhance the public welfare by violating a person's last will and testament or by reneging on promises made to those with no power to enforce their fulfillment. These and similar loopholes render utilitarianism suspect. Our commonsense ethical precepts may not be a sufficient ethical doctrine, but we should beware of theories that violate them wholesale.

Now we can consider what utilitarians might say in response to these critical comments.

As to the unworkability of utilitarian ethics, it may be possible within util-itarianism to identify general principles. In terms of these, one could work to advance the overall happiness of humanity without even knowing how a par-ticular act contributes to it specifically. This form of the doctrine is called rule utilitarianism and it is contrasted with act utilitarianism, which is widely admitted to be unworkable. If we were able to identify some general princi-ples or rules of conduct that would aid us in supporting the utilitarian goal, then it would no longer be impossible to pursue that goal. For example, on the political level, by way of laws and policies, it is generally thought that fol-lowing a certain course of conduct enhances the national welfare, even the welfare of the entire globe. In personal, individual conduct as well, one might follow the principle: Whenever possible, pay heed to what people around you need. One's actions would thus be geared toward the general utilitarian goal everyone ought to pursue.

Concerning the problem that some people could further the good without intending it as their goal, one may view this as doing the right thing for the wrong reasons. The crucial fact is, according to utilitarianism, that actions are right because they contribute to the goal of the greatest happiness of the great-est number, not because they enhance the actor's reputation. Someone who acts from the wrong motives (i.e., wanting to be well thought of) may not be praiseworthy for his/her acts; however, it is another thing to deny the right-ness of what he/she does. In this case, we might recall the saying that hypocrisy is the compliment vice pays to virtue—so that even those with du-bious motives are drawn to do what is right in order to achieve their goals with some measure of respectability. The occasional misuses of a good tool do not make the tool bad; that people can do what is right by utilitarian standards, without meaning to, does not invalidate those standards. As for those who in-tend to further the utilitarian good but fail, perhaps they ought to have paid greater heed to the means of achieving their goal. Meaning well is not enough. One needs to make sure that everything required for success is being done. So "I meant well" is not an excuse, although it points out that one did not do so badly as one could have (by not even trying but intending the op-posite perhaps). (Even on a commonsense level, we suspect that "I meant well" is often an excuse for negligence, not testimony of serious intent.)

It can also be contested that utilitarianism requires a centrally organized so-ciety. Let's recall that each person is the best judge of his/her psychic well-being. There is a great deal of psychic well-being involved even in what ap-pears to be plain physical well-being. So decisions as to what will produce one's happiness would to a large extent have to be one's own. In turn, a utilitarian society would more likely be individualist than collectivist. Many utilitarians argue that it is impossible to engage in interpersonal utility comparisons—that one simply cannot weigh and compare the respective importance of different people's preferences, desires, and welfare, whether physical or psychic. Thus, the only way to secure the greatest happiness of the greatest number is by giving up on central economic planning and moral paternalism in general. Letting everyone engage in the pursuit of individual, personal happiness is the best road to the greatest happiness of the greatest number. (In this way, utilitarianism might change into a form of egoism, a position we will look at shortly.) From this perspective, one could also accept that the distribution of wealth for purposes of achieving the utilitarian goal is best performed in a free market economy. In such a system, if no one is permitted to use force or fraud on another, then desires, needs, and preferences can be satisfied in voluntary cooperation and competition. Since individuals tend to know best what is going to produce their well-being or happiness, this arrangement—and not a centrally organized society that requires massive amounts of knowledge about millions of diverse individuals—is best for purposes of living life in terms of utilitarian ethics.

Finally, a utilitarian could respond that the commonsense ethical precepts may not be sound, anyway; therefore, seeking mainly to adjust to them in a comprehensive ethical system could be a bad idea from the start. Even if these precepts do contain a kind of practical wisdom acquired in the evolution of human existence, it may not be true that they are contradicted by utilitarian ethics. Cases might be imagined in which utilitarian conduct would violate these precepts. It does not follow that realistically this would occur. It is quite likely, also, that if these precepts express practical wisdom, they are the general rules utilitarians believe will promote the greatest happiness of the greatest number. Being honest, keeping one's promises, and even abiding by someone's last will and testament could be useful habits by which to promote the utilitarian goal. Honesty, justice, integrity, and other virtues of wide acceptance would then be thought of as the correct means of achieving what utilitarianism holds to be the good we should all aim for.

Some features of utilitarianism will be touched on again later when we turn to political philosophy. For now, this brief discussion should suffice to acquaint readers with one of the prominent and philosophically significant ethical theories. Among Anglo-American philosophers, it is perhaps the most widely discussed and respected ethical position today.

Altruism
Altruism is undoubtedly the most widely advocated, defended, and proclaimed moral position within human history and within our culture as well.

"'Altruism' [is] *assuming* a duty to relieve the distress and promote the happiness of our fellows. . . . Altruism is to . . . maintain quite simply that a man may and should discount altogether his own pleasure or happiness as such when he is deciding what course of action to pursue."[2] Among the many philosophically discussed moral positions, this one has achieved the distinction of gaining prominence within the language of nonphilosophers. Most people have heard that altruism is the moral code by which we should live our lives. The idea is now virtually synonymous with being morally good. The term "altruism" was coined by August Comte, a French philosopher and sociologist. Its substance, though, is advanced by many moral philosophers, most recently Thomas Nagel.

Although the term "altruism" was coined in recent times, its basic idea is quite old. This is that the moral goal of every human being should be the well-being or good of others. Service to other people alone, or to humanity in general, is the altruistic moral goal and all the more specific principles of morality (or human virtues) must be geared to the achievement of this goal. The standard of morality consists in whatever others need for their well-being. (Here, too, some people believe that altruistic behavior is automatic, especially among some species of animals, but that is not an ethical view because it denies that we choose how we act. Among these are some sociobiologists who think that human behavior can be explained by the principles of our communal biological makeup. Ethics, however, is not concerned with explaining[3] but with guiding human behavior.)

The argument for altruism comes mainly from the belief that unless people take their prime moral responsibility to be doing good for others, they would conduct themselves ruthlessly and cruelly toward their fellow human beings. Altruism holds that it is a very probable, if not inherent, inclination of people to take advantage of others whenever the opportunity arises. In a way, altruism takes as given the evil or moral inferiority of selfish pursuits, considering these as leading to conflict among human beings unless restrained by morality, that is, the *obligation* to serve others, to help them, and to love them. Here, the doctrine of Christian charity, as proposed by St. Augustine, if divorced from the goal of gaining everlasting salvation, is close to altruism. Altruism views human nature as basically antisocial, with human behavior tending toward hurting others when this would satisfy one's pleasures and desires.[4]

Altruism considers it a central feature of morality to steer human beings away from inborn desires or inclinations for self-gratification, self-serving conduct, pride, vanity, and conceit. What human beings require for themselves is well enough provided for by these instinctual drives. To remove humans from the realm of the jungle, the sphere of the beast—like existence—to a higher, civilized, peaceful, and cooperative stage, a morality is required to provide for suitable motivation. Our natural motives are selfish; this we share with other animals. Our human motives, cultivated by a recognition of the quarrelsome, hostile tendencies in us, should direct us toward the well-being and benefit of our fellow human beings.

Once it is accepted that motivation toward self-satisfaction is part of our natural, even instinctive constitution and inclination, it is a logical consequence that any viable moral position must direct us toward something outside ourselves and away from self-service. This is because, as we pointed out earlier, moral goals must be something we can choose to pursue. Moral principles must be chosen. Altruism directs us toward the goal of benefiting others, society, or humanity (there are variations on this within altruistic positions). That is a goal we can choose; it is not automatic or innate. Also, we all can choose it, at least on first view. Therefore, it is a generalizable goal, one that can serve as the proper goal for human beings as such. Without the universal moral responsibility to pursue this goal, we would have no motivation to practice the virtues that can produce a peaceful, productive, and just society. Why would we be honest, fair, and the like? Why would we pay our debts, keep our promises, respect others' property, fight for the security of the community, and defend liberty? Guided by the motive for sheer self-satisfaction, as we are by our animal nature or instincts anyway, why should we not cheat, lie, steal, murder, and neglect the welfare of others or our community? According to the altruist position, no reason exists for abstaining from such conduct unless the duty to serve others is accepted as binding on all.

Criticisms and Answers

There are objections to altruism, despite its great prominence. First, it could well be false that people have inborn motives or drives causing them to serve their own well-being and take advantage of others when possible. We need morality to learn how to live well. Therefore, if morality applies to us, we do not have self-evident knowledge of what is to our or anyone else's benefit. We might, however, be able to discover our own best interest more readily than that of others.

Second, it is not obviously true that we are geared by nature toward harming others whenever the chance arises. It is quite likely that all of us have the *capacity* for destructive action, yet this does not mean that we are tending toward it. If human nature did contain these basic drives, it is doubtful that ethical positions advanced by philosophers and others could escape the influence. It would be very likely that altruism itself reflects these harmful drives or tendencies.

It seems also that many people who have chosen to pursue their self-interest and self-satisfaction have not found that doing harm to others helped them to achieve these; to the contrary, many selfish people, concerned with doing what is best for themselves, engage in very productive and widely beneficial endeavors. Thus, it is very likely untrue, even at a cursory glance, that selfish motivation must lead to taking advantage of others. Altruism assumes that it is in our selfish interest, more often than not, to hurt other people, to treat them unfairly, and to lie, cheat, and be unjust. This assumption conceives of human nature as benefiting from doing harm to others. This idea is not at all self-evident, especially without the assumption about the basically beastly or hostile innate drives of human beings. This idea of human nature, as tending toward mutual antagonism among people, appears to involve a view of nature in general as productive of freak entities, beings with mutually incompatible tendencies. (It is true that both theology and psychology have given us theories proclaiming just this kind of inner tension within human nature.)

Finally, altruism is not so evidently practicable as it appears on first inspection. Doing good for others requires that we learn what that good is. Yet, others may not accept this judgment; they may be mistaken not to, but to do good for them will require acting against their own judgment. This could very likely result in open conflict—and the evidence from meddling mothers, meddling friends, meddling governments, and so forth, all supported by reference to good intentions, seems to bear out this prospect. A related problem is that if people in general do look out for their own interests as a matter of innate motivation, then the need or responsibility to do them good and to serve others' interests (which they are already doing by nature) would be superfluous.

The altruist's answer to these critical points would consist, more than likely, of the following: History bears out the point about man's destructive nature. Some people may escape the force of this even without adopting the altruist position, but this is only by chance. Any sustained participation in social life requires altruism. The notion that people would themselves benefit from treating others fairly, speaking truly, respecting each others' needs and wants, and even helping each other out is perhaps correct for some occasions. But in times of danger or scarcity, people would most likely resort to anything if they were not bound by the moral duty to serve others first. Certainly, morality may not be needed under normal, uncomplicated circumstances. But when difficult decisions must be made, we can live right only by choosing the principles that do not come naturally and that do not simply accommodate our inclinations.

As a second reply, it is not at all odd for human nature to be somewhat freakish. Human beings are unique in nature; no other living creatures seem to have managed to create so much misery for themselves—so much internal conflict, agony, and tragedy. Human beings are neurotic, psychotic, nervous, guilt-ridden, awkward, frightened, and similarly plagued animals. In light of this peculiarity of the human species, it is not unreasonable that human conduct should be constrained by responsibilities directing people away from themselves and toward others. Left without such guidance, human beings would have disappeared as a species long ago.

When we come to the difficulty of practicing altruism, the only response to be made is that care must be taken to make certain that what we do for others is for their good. Once this is accomplished, we can justify acting against others' mistaken judgment. After all, is it not better to help others even though they disagree than to tolerate their acting contrary to what is good for them by rejecting our help? What would millions of people do without the help offered by laws that prohibit self-destructive conduct? Even if those who are being helped do not know it, their being helped is still a fact—and that is what is important, not what they believe.

As to why we ought to help others even though they are driven to help themselves, the answer could be that by removing ourselves from our own drives we can be more objective, accurate, and successful in helping people in general, thus securing some measure of peace. In those cases where others are being helped, arbitrary feelings can be put aside in favor of careful judgment.

Egoism
We have devoted an entire chapter to egoism already, so what follows is much briefer and merely a reminder.

Pseudoegoisms
Egoism has several versions. One famous variety of egoism is definitely not a possible ethical position, the view that everyone always does what is in his/her interest. This view, called psychological egoism, lacks a crucial feature of any possible ethics: the freedom to pursue or refrain from pursuing the right course of conduct. So, it is obvious that psychological egoism is not a possible ethics, since there is no mention of what should or ought to be done, only of what is being done.

Another often-discussed version of egoism that fails to qualify as a possible moral position is subjectivist egoism. According to the subjective egoist, only his/her unique best interest has merit. This fails because morality must by its nature be a universalizable system. It cannot be something that applies to only one unique person or group of human beings.

Ethical Egoism (or Individualism)
The form of egoism that can be a bona fide moral position is one that avoids the problems cited earlier. The basic statement of this position is that each person should live so as to achieve his/her rational self-interest. People will not automatically do what is in their rational self-interest, so it's for them to decide. Furthermore, such a standard of conduct can be universalized and used to guide everyone, supposedly because people's rational self-interest is *whatever suits them as human beings and as the individuals they happen to be*, the knowledge of which is available to anyone who cares to consider the issue. This view is proposed most notably by the novelist Ayn Rand and some of her students.

Finally, the goal, one's happiness, should be sharply distinguished from pleasure, fun, or thrills. Happiness, in this context, is rather *a positive or joyful attitude about how well one is doing in one's life as a person.*[5] This is because human beings, as reflective, self-conscious creatures, can benefit from doing what suits them, and knowing that they have been the cause of this benefit is a source of immense joy. This is similar to what some psychologists describe as having self-esteem.[6]

Criticisms and Answers
The critics have much to say about egoism. They condemn it for its allegedly naive view of human nature—the idea that we are born without destructive impulses and that we should simply go about achieving our natural goals. They say that egoism leads to self-centeredness, egotism, the ruthless pursuit of gain, wealth, and power, prompted by the complex and often destructive motives that lie deep within us.

On a more formal point, egoism as a moral theory is thought to disallow universal implementation. When conflicts between the interests of human beings emerge, egoism appears to send people on a warpath because it lacks a coordinating principle that goes beyond the self-interests of the people in conflict. This criticism amounts to charging egoism with generating contradictory plans of action: people both should and should not do certain things. Any ethical position found in this dilemma has to fail because it leads to the view that what one should do *cannot* be done!

A further objection is that all the talk about happiness is too vague. What, exactly, should we pursue? What is this happiness anyway? By saying that it is the awareness of ourselves as being successful at living as people—that is, rationally—this position prejudges that rational living will lead to something we ought to achieve. But is it not possible that something else besides this "happiness"—which seems very self-indulgent anyway—is worth pursuing? Could there not be far more important goals (e.g., political liberty, social justice, or being a productive member of society) that overshadow happiness?

Finally, it does not even appear likely that rationality can produce happiness for a person. On the one hand, many rational, scholarly, and artistic achievers such as scientists, lawyers, and writers have been notably unhappy. On the other hand, some of the most irrational, whimsical, and haphazard people retire in luxury to Miami Beach to live out their lives in full bliss.

The egoist of the sort we have been considering will have responses to these objections. Again, the reader will have to assess both the objections and the answers.

In response to the charge that he/she is naive about human nature, the egoist could reply that he/she is concerned only with the essentials. What the critic sees as naiveté is in reality an exclusive focusing on the morally relevant aspect of every person, the capacity to freely choose to think. The misery, neurosis, cruelty, and self-destruction that characterize some human life are explainable often in terms of people's refusal to think through the requirements of their lives and their willingness to meddle in the lives of others (always for others' good). Were people to stick to doing good for themselves, much of the disarray would disappear. Moreover, such factors do not prove inherent conflict in human nature. As long as we can find some well-integrated people who live with peace of mind and are happy, this possibility is established for all human life.

The case about conflicts of interest, usually a conflict of desires and wishes, begs an important question, the egoist would say. If rationality is the first principle or virtue of egoism, then the appropriate course is to deal with the question: What should we do when our desires conflict with others' desires? We should not assume that a conflict precludes resolution.

In general, egoism holds that each person should pursue his/her own self-interest: happiness or success in life; furthermore, the common factor for all human beings by which this goal is attainable is thinking rationally. Self-interest, so understood, cannot be viewed as presenting necessary conflicts among individuals. Conflicts between desires, wishes, and wants can be resolved by careful thought, which is in everyone's best interest. Only in periods of inattentiveness or irrationality—when one is impulsive and refuses to think matters through carefully—will conflicts be unresolved or resolved badly.

The difficulty of *defining* happiness is not a problem of ethics but of epistemology. This difficulty faces any complex system of ideas. It is enough to note, according to the egoist, that being happy does seem to be different from being satisfied, pleased, contented, thrilled, or fun-filled—it is the realization (and its corresponding feeling) of having carried on well in life and of having lived as a human being lives best.

Egoists grant that rational conduct will not *guarantee* a long and happy life; accidents can happen. Rather, a rational life makes reaching success more likely than does any alternative. What is crucial to ethical egoism is that by living rationally each person would very likely be happier, and certainly savor a better self-concept, than by living irrationally.

Duty Theory

According to Immanuel Kant (1724–1804), there is nothing good-in-itself, nothing good without qualification, except a good will. For Kant, the essence of morality is in having a good will. He defines "will" as the capacity to act according to principles—in other words, the ability to choose for reasons, with purpose, according to principles that one recognizes as rationally compelling, rather than acting from impulse, whim, desire, or inclination. The exercise of will is thus a distinctively rational activity and as such separates us from the rest of the animal kingdom (though not from other possible rational creatures: angels, for example, whom Kant characterized as having "holy" wills, that is, wills that recognize the good and function accordingly without a sense of duty or obligation. Holy wills do not have to resist the temptations of impulse, desire, or inclination that flesh is heir to).

A good will, says Kant, is one that recognizes and responds to a duty to act in a certain way. If I act for purely selfish reasons, to avoid unpleasant consequences, or for reasons other than from a sense of duty, then I am not acting morally. For Kant, then, one's motive or intention, one's reasons for acting, are what give moral significance to the action. Motive is decisive in moral evaluation. If, for example, Jones and Smith are each asked to assist in a charitable project and each agrees, but Jones does so in order to impress people while Smith does so from a sense of duty, Kant would say that only Smith's action was morally worthy. Thus, moral worth resides not in consequences, nor even in the action itself—after all, both Jones and Smith did (functionally/behaviorally) the same thing and their actions had the same (beneficial) result. Moral worth resides in the will/motive of the agent of action.

For Kant, the paradigm example of a true moral action is when the agent acts against an inclination or would have preferred to do otherwise or would have gained personally from doing otherwise, but acts as he/she does out of a sense of duty and respect for the moral law. That one is often called on to do one's duty despite the consequences of doing so, as Kant argues, makes his/hers a nonconsequentialist moral theory. For Kant, consequences are irrelevant to the question of what makes an action morally worthy.

How does one know what one's duty is? Kant offers a principle called the categorical imperative: Act only on a rule or maxim that could be made into a universal law binding on all rational creatures. In other words, the morally correct action is one that is universalizable, one that the agent could will that anyone and everyone would do if faced with the same decision. If the rule governing one's action is not universalizable, or if attempting to universalize it leads to a contradiction or is otherwise self-defeating or irrational, then one's duty lies elsewhere. What Kant means here is that morality is both a rational and a universally binding dimension of life—the imperative, duty, or obligation to do good is categorical, not conditional, and allows for no exceptions. Thus, if it is the case that I ought to do X, then it must be the case that anyone else in relevantly similar circumstances ought also to do X. In general, there is no compelling reason why any particular person should be an exception to a moral imperative.

To illustrate how the categorical imperative works, Kant offers the example of making a promise. If I make a promise knowing that I will break it if it suits me to do so, I am in effect saying, "It's okay for me to break a promise when I feel like it." Now, suppose that we try to universalize this kind of acting and thinking. Put in another and more familiar way: What if everyone did as I'm doing here? What if everyone acted according to the same rule? This is what Kant means by the categorical imperative: Can I will that the maxim of my action become a universal law binding on all persons? Can it be imperative for everyone and always?

Suppose the words "I promise X" were universally understood to mean, "I will do X unless I don't feel like doing X." If promising didn't have the force of keeping one's promise under pain of blame, shame, or guilt, then promising would be empty, would lose its point and meaning, and would altogether vanish. Furthermore, if it were understood that everyone ought to make false promises under duress or when it's convenient, then the person I am promising to, knowing this, would likely not take my promise seriously. The result is that in such a world, one where the maxim that one ought to falsely promise were a universal law, I would be unable to falsely promise! So, the very thing I intended to do by falsely promising, that is, getting another to take my word seriously, would be impossible if I attempted to universalize my action, if everyone did as I did. My action would have contradicted itself and thus its maxim cannot serve as a moral imperative.

According to Kant's analysis, it is immoral to make a promise I cannot keep because it is impossible to universalize that action. I cannot consistently will others to adopt this policy. In the end, for Kant, immoral action is irrational; it is a violation of the logical principle of consistency or noncontradiction. Immoral actions always involve a double standard on this view: one for the agent, and another for the rest of humanity. Kant's moral philosophy should be seen as an insistence that morality is a rational activity, subject to rational review according to the principles of logic. His categorical imperative is simply a method of determining whether an action meets the most basic requirement of logic and noncontradiction. Logical consistency does not in itself make for morality, but morality ought to be logically consistent. Kant attempts to demonstrate that there is a necessary connection between action, will, and rationality in the moral dimension. Thus, for Kant, the ground of morality is essentially a formal matter, a matter of logic, rather than an empirical matter, a matter of fact.

Divine Command Theory
According to this moral view, action is right which conforms to the will of God. What God wills is revealed in one or another of the sacred texts and is often most clearly or most certainly known by particular authorities: priests, ministers, rabbis, prophets, holy persons, and theologians. On this view, neither the motives of the agent nor the consequences of the action, nor anything inherent in the action are morally significant or relevant to answering the question: Is the action right or wrong? What is of paramount and decisive importance is whether the action conforms to God's will or commands. A classic and clear example of acting from the divine command position comes from the Old Testament in the story of Abraham, who was commanded by an angel of God to slay Isaac, Abraham's beloved son. Abraham was willing to do this, despite his deepest desire and inclination otherwise, and despite the evident consequence of losing his son, because it was God's command and will (or so Abraham believed).

Swiss theologian Emil Brunner expresses the essence of Divine Command Theory when he defines the Good as "simply and solely the will of God." According to Brunner, "There is no Good save obedient behavior, save the obedient will. But this obedience is rendered not to a law or a principle which can be known beforehand, but only to the free, sovereign will of God. The Good consists in always doing what God wills at any particular moment."

Intuitionism
This is a theory about how we come to learn what is right and wrong, not so much about what is right and wrong. According to intuitionism, we have a

moral faculty that, when properly functioning, informs us of the right action and makes clear what is good. We simply "see" or we "just know" what is right and what is good for us. An intuitionist might argue, for example, that what makes stealing wrong is not a certain consequence, the law prohibits it, God prohibits it, or because it isn't universalizable—it's simply wrong, in itself, and on its face.

On this view, there is a self-evident nature to certain acts. Murder, rape, assault, and theft do not await consequences, authoritative judgment, or analysis to be shown to be wrong; for the intuitionist, there is no need to demonstrate that these acts are wrong or to explain what makes them wrong, as though explanation were necessary. If someone doesn't see that such actions are wrong, he/she would not likely understand the explanation or be led to that understanding by some analysis. Such persons, the intuitionist might claim, are the unfortunate victims of improper education, which somehow distorts or thwarts the natural moral sense. This of course does not mean that for the intuitionist there is never a need for moral deliberation, analysis, or reflection. Indeed, some situations are complex and require thought and analysis. What one does in complex situations is, essentially, to compare and contrast that particular case with a paradigm case that it most resembles and let one's intuition lead the way. According to the intuitionist, that there are complex situations or borderline cases should not blind us to the fact that there are clear and certain cases of right and wrong—clear and certain on their face. These clear cases provide models and standards against which less immediately clear cases should be measured.

William D. Ross (1877–1971), one of the great twentieth-century intuitionists, argues that we have certain self-evident duties that he calls prima facie duties—duties that have immediate appeal to our moral conscience, but that are not in themselves absolute. That is, in general we have these duties, but in particular, which duty prevails will depend on the particulars of the situation.

Ross offers something of a balance between Kant's rigid absolutism and utilitarianism's insistent consequentialism. Ross agrees with Kant that morality should not be identified with consequences, but he disagrees with the inflexibility of Kant's rule-governed theory. According to Ross, the prima facie duties recognized as duties by all normal human beings are:

1. Fidelity, to keep our promises
2. Reparation, to make up for any wrongs we have done
3. Gratitude for the kindness of others
4. Beneficence, of promoting goodness and helping others
5. Self-improvement

6. Justice, to distribute goods equitably and according to merit and desert
7. Nonmaleficence, refraining from injuring others; preventing injury

According to Ross, morality consists in making decisions that fulfill these duties whenever they arise. He also recognizes that these duties will, on occasion, conflict. In such cases, he reasons that we should follow two rules: (1) obey the duty that, under the actual circumstances, is most compelling and (2) always do that which has the greatest prima facie rightness over prima facie wrongness. It would seem to follow from this that the duty of nonmaleficence would generally take precedence over the other duties.

On analysis, it emerges that Ross's theory rests on intuition—that is, he can offer no reasons to support the claim that these are indeed universal duties belonging to all persons, nor can he offer a reasoned way of determining which duty is more compelling. Some critics charge Ross's theory with this weakness. Ross states: "To me it seems as self-evident as anything could be, that to make a promise, for instance, is to create a moral claim on us in some-one else. Many readers will perhaps say that they do not know this to be true. If so I certainly cannot prove it to them. I can only ask them to reflect again, in the hope that they will ultimately agree that they also know it to be true."[7]

According to Ross, and to intuitionists generally, right and wrong do not depend on the good or bad resulting from actions, but instead are determined by our fulfilling or failing to fulfill certain duties that we all have or assume to have as persons because of the special relationships we have with others. For example, in making a promise to someone (a special relationship being established thereby), I have created a duty or obligation on myself to keep that promise and have established for the other person a certain right of expectation that the promise be kept. Since it is wrong to violate one's duty, and since a promise creates a duty, breaking a promise is wrong.

Natural Law Theory
In this case, too, the emphasis is on how we learn of right and wrong, good and evil. This moral view holds that one can derive proper human behavior by understanding human nature. Thus, both Aristotle (384–322 B.C.) and Hobbes (1588–1679), though quite different in their moral views, can be seen as natural law theorists in so far as they ground their respective views of ethics in human nature. The question, of course, is: What is human nature? Since Aristotle and Hobbes disagree on the answer, their moral philosophies also differ. (This illustrates the significance of one's most fundamental beliefs.) That said, natural law theorists generally agree that nature consists of a plurality of kinds of things that comprise an orderly system and that an understanding of the

natures of things in nature—of what they consist, how and why they interact, what function they serve in the scheme of themes, what is required for their existence, what brings about changes in them, and so on—will yield answers to how human beings fit into this system and what conduct by human beings is most fitting, given the system of nature as we understand it.

From this perspective, what can be determined as natural for human beings is thought to be the best ground for how human beings ought to live and choose to behave. Put simply, nature is our best guide. Now, clearly, given the survival imperative, it behooves us to learn what nature requires. But beyond this there is more for human beings, since we are more than merely physical beings responsive to environment. We are intelligent beings capable of choosing from among alternatives and fully aware of this capability. Such is our nature.

Now, one school of natural law is theologically based, holding that nature is the product of God, an omniscient and omnibenevolent being. This being so, nature is basically good, and so acting in accord with nature would be acting in accord with God. A famous proponent of theistic natural law thinking is St. Thomas Aquinas (1225–1274), the Catholic philosopher (heavily indebted to Aristotle) who argues that following the dictates of nature is our best bet for living a long, full, and happy natural life. Here, he says, Aristotle had it right—we are by nature intelligent animals, and so we should live our lives intelligently, that is, according to what we have learned about what is naturally good for us. This would include not only naturally nourishing food, rest, and shelter, but practices and conduct that would yield healthy relationships, rewarding labor, and fulfilling lives. Our conduct should reflect our understanding of our nature and our place in the scheme of things.

This is where nontheistic natural law ethics departs, for Thomes Aquinas holds that nature alone, though good and vast, is incapable of bringing us more than a satisfying natural life, and our natures yearn for more: we desire immortality, which transcends nature. Our deepest and highest needs, Thomas reasons, could be realized only by the supernatural. He thus adds to the natural, pagan virtues of courage, temperance, wisdom, and justice, the theological virtues of faith, hope, and charity. The former can provide us with a good and fulfilling natural life, but only the latter will guarantee the supernatural life that we desire.

Less ambitious are the nontheistic natural law theories. One of the most influential of them has been that of John Locke (1632–1704), an Enlightenment philosopher whose impact on modern political thought can hardly be exaggerated. Basically, Locke argues that human nature, our natural intelligence, ability to choose, and the requirement of intelligent choice for surviving at all, let alone for living well, implies that each human being is not only responsible for his/her own life, but is also entitled to live that life as he/she chooses. Put another way, since by nature we must reason our way through life, must live by our wits and labor, we should be free to do so, which means that others ought not interfere in our efforts to live a life. This is known as the doctrine of natural rights, which later served as a foundation of the U.S. Declaration of Independence and the U.S. Constitution. According to this view, our social and political relationships should be guided by and grounded in respect for individual rights to life, liberty, and property, as these rights are the preconditions for living at all, much less well, and, above all, morally. A life not fashioned by my own efforts is not my life and can hardly qualify as a worthy one, a life fit for a human being. If I ought to live my own life, as surely each of us believes that this is so of him/herself, then I must be free to do so, and it would be wrong for others to thwart such a noble effort. In short, I have—each individual has—a right to pursue happiness.

One can readily see that a system of rules, laws, and practices can be derived from this fundamental claim about the nature of the human condition, and much of social and political contemporary philosophical debate turns on whether Locke's view is correct, and if so, which rules, laws, and practices are consistent with it.

A contrasting nontheistic natural law perspective is offered by Hobbes, who argues that human beings in the state of nature are driven, like other animals, by the law of survival and see one another as dangerous competitors for the goods and necessities of life. We are thus always at the ready for battle, and in this "natural" condition of war, life is "solitary, poor, nasty, short, and brutish." However, unlike the other animals, we are able to reason and to come to the realization that, if we wish to survive, let alone live well, the intelligent thing to do would be to make peace with one another. This peace would depend on our mutual agreement to refrain from exercising our natural right to do whatever we feel like doing to survive, behavior that puts us in mutual fear of one another. Such a peace is possible only if there were something that we fear more than each other, that would keep us from breaking our agreement or "contract." This greater power Hobbes refers to as the sovereign or state. Once created, the sovereign would have power over us all and would provide the stability and peace necessary for civilized living and all of the amenities that civilization provides.

Virtue Ethics
In recent years, there has been increased interest in the philosophy of Aristotle. One result of this is the emergence of a view called virtue ethics, which

considers morality in terms of human character and moral psychology. The central question of virtue ethics is not "What is right action?" or "How should I choose?" but rather "What kind of person should I be?" Aristotle describes excellence at being a person in terms very much like we would describe a skill, something that has to be learned by practice and training until it becomes a part of oneself, or, as Aristotle puts it, "second nature." The excellences consist of the virtues: courage, prudence, wisdom, temperance, generosity, patience, perseverance, and so on, for each of the many kinds of challenges that one faces in living a human life. To meet these challenges requires the appropriately spirited action, the expressions of which are the virtues. For Aristotle, the prime virtue is rationality, since, though we may have a virtuous character, the variety of possible situations in which we find ourselves often requires our assessing a situation to determine the appropriate response, as well as its measure. Thus, what may be courageous in one circumstance may well be foolhardy or cowardly in another.

An interesting feature of virtue ethics is that though our upbringing may have been lacking in some respects such that as adults our characters are wanting, it is still within our power, having recognized the shortcoming, to make an effort to improve. This being so, though we may not be initially responsible for weakness of character, once it is recognized we are responsible for its continuance, for just as virtue is a habit, so too is vice, and habits can be broken just as they are formed, incrementally, one step at a time.

Ethics of Care
Just as virtue ethics has received attention in recent years, not coincidentally, a new moral perspective—called the ethics of care—stressing the emotions has also emerged. This moral perspective arose in part from the intellectual dispute concerning moral development between two psychologists: Lawrence Kohlberg and Carol Gilligan. Kohlberg had conceived a hierarchical system of stages of moral development, beginning with the first stage where right and wrong are equated with rewards and punishment (with authority figures such as parents identified as the source of morality) and ending with the highest stage, which involves moral deliberation according to abstract principles applied impartially (with moral authority residing in the reasoned autonomy of each individual). From his studies, Kohlberg drew several controversial conclusions, including the claim that females in general tend to reach a lower level of moral development than do males. This sparked a heated response, especially from feminist philosophers, but most poignantly from Gilligan, Kohlberg's colleague in psychology who challenged not only the construction of the studies themselves, but also Kohlberg's conception of

morality, which underlay and gave shape to the studies. What developed from Gilligan's response is the ethics of care.

According to this view, traditional moral philosophy has been one sided and incomplete, stressing reason, impartiality, objectivity, rights, duties, individuality, law, and abstract principles (think "Kant"). Hardly surprising, Gilligan argued, considering that philosophy has been dominated by males. The traditional perspective is typically masculine. But, according to the feminine ethicists, morality requires in addition, if not centrally, a concern for feelings, subjectivity, relationships, nurturing, and community. On this view, ethics is more of a healing, therapeutic activity than a judgmental one, more a matter of the heart than of the mind.

Existentialism

Existentialism can be described as a repudiation of traditional morality. In sharp contrast with the major moral theories that we've examined thus far, existentialism denies that morality has a foundation in reality, either in reason, by way of rational principles, or in God as the source of the right and the good. For this reason, existentialism is commonly, perhaps mistakenly, understood to be the antithesis of morality, a philosophy that denies any sense or substance to the concepts of right and wrong. Indeed, Jean-Paul Sartre (1905–1980), arguably the most articulate spokesperson for existentialism, agrees with Nietzsche (1844–1900) who declares that God is dead, and concludes, as does Dostoyevsky's (1821–1888) Grand Inquisitor, that everything is permissible.

Underlying this view is a metaphysical position. Sartre argues that everything in the universe, with one exception, has a nature, an essence, a certain "fixedness" or form of being. Much of the task of traditional philosophy has been to inquire into the natures or essences of things and in so doing to make reality intellectually accessible to us. Once the nature or essence of something is clear, evident, and manifest, one has understood it, can be said to know the thing, and, in a sense, has exhausted its possibilities. Knowledge of essences is final, complete, and certain. Plato (c. 428–327/8 B.C.) is an excellent example of philosophy at work in this way. (Interestingly, Kant can be seen to have undermined altogether this vision of ancient philosophy by arguing that in principle it is impossible for human beings to know the essences or nature of things, to know "things-in-themselves.")

Given this view of reality and of the function of philosophy, it follows that individuals or particulars are subordinate to something more general and abstract: individuals are regarded as mere instances or representations or examples of a purer, clearer, and higher order of being. The world of particulars is the world of mere existence, where things come into being and then pass away; the world of existence, of particulars, is the temporal world, a world bound in time and space and subject, inevitably, to change and destruction (Heraclitus and Plato agree at this level). The world of essences, in contrast, is eternal and unchanging. Thus, essence, on this view, is prior to existence and is more real and true.

Sartre observes that when a thing, say, a tree, comes into being, it comes with its essence—it is already designed, destined, determined, and fixed. It has no choice whatsoever in the matter; it has no future except what is called for by its nature. Put another way, it must be what its nature dictates. So, too, with a bird, a fish, or a dog. In this way, each is no different from an artifact or a machine—the design and essence guarantee the kind of being, existence, and behavior it has.

The one exception, the being whose existence precedes its essence, the being who comes into being without a nature, is a human being. We have no fixed predetermined essence (God, the Designer, is dead). We make ourselves what we are out of our own freedom, from the consequences of our choices. Unlike all other creatures, we choose to be what we are. As individuals, all we have is a history, a past, and our freedom of choice. We are, as Sartre so graphically puts it, "thrown into the world"; we find ourselves here; we exist, and, through our choices, fashion out a life. So it is that we are "condemned to be free." We have freedom of choice, but, ironically, we are not free to not choose, since that also is a choice. There is no escape (No Exit); we must choose, and we are ultimately responsible for what we become and what we have done.

Without God, says Sartre, we are totally on our own. If we turn to reason for our moral foundation, we'll only discover that there are no universal, absolute principles that will guarantee right action, that will guide our conduct and inform our choices: neither pleasure nor consequences, intuition, rules, or duties. In short, reason can neither determine nor provide a foundation for morality: there is no foundation. We simply choose and live with the consequences of our choices. Of course, we often offer reasons for our choices, as though to justify them, as though these reasons and the principles we appeal to stood outside of us, were independent of our choices. But we are simply kidding ourselves here: In fact, Sartre claims, we even choose our reasons. To demonstrate this, Sartre argues that we can easily conceive of circumstances where principles, rules, or any standard presents us with a dilemma, where the alternatives we face force us to choose one principle and deny another. He offers the example of a student in Nazi-occupied France during World War II. The student faced the choice of joining the Free French Forces in

England and fighting for his country's freedom, or staying home to help his ailing and dependent mother, who was certain to suffer, perhaps die, should he leave. The student was in anguish over this dilemma and sought a resolution. What ought he do? Sartre observes that the student could appeal to any one of a number of familiar maxims or rules (i.e., to any moral theory based on reason), but each of these is either contradicted by another, or can be so interpreted as to support either direction of choice. Nor can the student simply rely on his feelings (intuitionism), since he has feelings pulling him both ways. In the end, he simply must choose, and in choosing, will be choosing those reasons and principles that are consistent with that choice.

So, from the existential point of view, morality is a subjective matter because values, right, and wrong come into being by virtue of the choices we make. We do not discover what is right and then choose it; rather, right (and wrong) comes into being from the choices that we make. In choosing to do X, we are in effect saying, "X is the right thing to do." In choosing, in acting, we are necessarily setting an example of how it is done and thus we are "choosing for all mankind." What begins as an apparent denial of the moral dimension ends as a rather severe moral doctrine: complete, unequivocal, and absolute responsibility for the world. Sartre closes the front door to morality, but lets it enter through the back.

Other Ethical Positions Very Briefly

Stoicism
The Stoics hold that although we should strive to be happy and fulfilled, we should seek this goal by not desiring anything at all so that we will never be disappointed, disillusioned, or unhappy. Stoicism contends that true happiness is best attained by disassociating ourselves from temporal, fleeting pleasures, joys, delights, and values. A detachment from everything in the world and the resulting inner peace is what makes up a life of virtue and happiness.

Epicureanism
Despite its popular reputation, associated as it is with gourmet eating, Epicureanism is not the same as hedonism but focuses, instead, on a higher sort of happiness, associated mainly with the mind in its most cultured state. The reasoning here is somewhat similar to Stoicism: the worldly pleasures are not under our own control, while the joys of the mind are. The view is a version of subjectivism or hedonistic egoism, and urges that everyone should pursue his/her long-range higher satisfactions in life. Contrary to widespread misimpression, Epicureanism does not require the pursuit of sensual thrills or

aesthetic delights. Rather, it counsels that we should attain inner peace and freedom, the basic ingredients of true pleasure.

Asceticism
Like Stoicism, asceticism prescribes self-denial but not for the sake of personal happiness—quite the contrary. At least as far as living in this world is concerned, asceticism requires self-denial and self-discipline so as to achieve various religious, supernatural, or otherworldly goals, for example, eternal salvation or ultimate spiritual unity with the oneness of the universe.

Situationism
We find here an attempt to erect an ethics on a foundation of relativism and subjectivism that seems to the proponents of this view irrefutable. So the only hope for ethics is to admit them and see what can be salvaged. Arising from the convictions of certain existentialists, such as that no human nature can be identified and God does not exist, situationism teaches that if we approach living by way of a feeling of love, of authentic devotion, this will steer us in the only meaningful right course, especially in our relationship with others.

Environmentalism
Environmental ethics is sometimes derived from one or another of the major ethical theories. For example, a utilitarian may argue for conservation or restriction of automobile exhaust emission because this will very likely enhance the general welfare. There are, however, schools of environmental ethics wherein our entire morality is to be derived from certain views about nature, the wilderness, or God (or Gaia) as Nature. Jean-Jacques Rousseau (1712–1778) captures this outlook: "The more we depart from the state of nature, the more we lose our natural tastes. . . . All is good coming from the hand of the Author of all things, all degenerates in the hands of man."[8] This moral position requires frugality, restraint, moderation, and an economy of conservation and sustenance, not growth and abundance. Recycling, setting aside wilderness, restriction of the use of air conditioning, and so on are prescribed as ways of personal conduct and public policy.

Political Systems in Brief

While ethics, politics, public policy, and other normative areas can be kept distinct—meaning one can think of them apart from the others—they are closely intertwined in our lives. Although ethics addresses the issue of how one ought to live and politics deals with how to organize a community of human beings, since so much of our lives is lived in others' company, it is rare that what we do does not involve other people. Between the strictly private and the strictly public, there are all levels of social involvement that we might call "social," as in "social and political philosophy." Most of the matters we look at in examining specific cases in this text belong in the sphere of the social and the political.

This is good reason to look at some of the more general political positions that we find debated throughout the world in our day. These will be very brief characterizations, almost simply definitions, just to familiarize the reader with some of the key ideas and ideals of politics.

Feudalism

Although not so familiar in our hemisphere, the feudal system of social and political life was once extremely popular and some places across the globe are still organized in line with it. In a feudal order, vassals hold land and serfs do the work on it, in return for which they provide overlords with military and other services. The feudal system involves a hierarchical social structure, usually with a monarch or other supreme ruler or family in charge and various layers of nobility in gradually descending order of importance, with the serfs comprising the bottom. It was the predominant type of order of Europe and, indeed, much of the world, and many of the legal features of contemporary societies can be traced to it.[9] This system of government derives largely from historical events and certain prominent ideas advanced in various philosophical and theological systems, including the notion that some people are naturally or by divine edict superior in moral and other respects to the rest and ought, therefore, to have a paternalistic relationship to them. A form of elitism—that is, the entrenched superiority and often rule of the select few—is usually at the bottom of the feudal ideal, including aristocracy (although since this means the rule of the best, there is some ambiguity about whether it can support anything that is entrenched and static, since who the best are can change drastically over time).

In a feudal system, also, major social institutions—such as commerce, religion, property holdings, and professional positions—are usually assigned from above, by the designees of the royal family. Accordingly, the economic system of mercantilism is closely linked to feudalism, as is the institution of a state church. (Although, often the prevailing church authorities can be separated from the state and this can give rise to complex dilemmas of spiritual and political leadership.)

It is fair to say that the idea of a constitution arose, in part, in opposition to feudal rule, so we will consider it next.

Constitutionalism

The term "constitution" derives from "to constitute." This means to be the basic structure for something. Thus, a constitutional system of government usually involves having a written document as the basis for governmental decisions. When one hears the slogan "government by law, not by men," this pertains to the idea that a constitution must guide what those in charge of government will do and they can be held accountable for how they govern— they are not absolute rulers who do what they personally want or deem right.

Constitutionalism could be connected with a monarchy or with a democracy. Although in our time in the bulk of the world it is constitutional democracy that is usually instituted as the system of government, there has been much experimentation with constitutional monarchy. (A parliamentary system is also a form of partly decentralized rule by council via the participation of political representatives from various regions of a country.) Usually, constitutions will list basic principles of decision making and of the limits of power or authority of the governing administration. In the United States, for example, the U.S. Constitution has within it a Bill of Rights that provides a list of limits on government's authority and scope.

Such a system is usually recommended because of the predictability of the rules that govern the lives of people within a given geographical area. Yet, since there is no way to predict for the long range what problems will face people, the constitution usually needs to be interpreted to apply to topics that were not in evidence when it was originally drafted. A great deal of controversy surrounds just how this process should be implemented. The United States has the system of judicial review. If the legislatures or other lawmaking bodies proposed policies that some see to be in conflict with the Constitution, the matter can be brought to the attention, ultimately, of the U.S. Supreme Court and a judgment will be made as to whether this measure accords with or violates the Constitution—that is, whether it is legal.

Another source of controversy about constitutionalism is whether it is ultimately democratic and does justice to the idea that government must be by the people. A constitution stretches the ideas and ideals of the drafters or framers way into the future, past their own lives and citizenship. As such, some have claimed that constitutions are dictatorial and undemocratic. It is also claimed, in criticism of constitutionalism, that it makes permanent or at least unreasonably influential the moral and political misconceptions or narrow-mindedness of the past. Unless some handy way of making moral and political adjustments is part of the constitution itself, this can become a debilitating aspect of constitutional government and a major issue in civil upheaval.

Yet without some basic document by which citizens are governed, government will arguably degenerate into arbitrary rule by the judgments and the passions of either a monarch or the people. This is why it is usually championed by its supporters, such as the U.S. founders (as per their long discussion of the matter in Cato's Letters and The Federalist Papers).

Socialism

In modern political theory, the influence of economic considerations has loomed very large. Among the views that dwell a good deal on the economic features of human communities socialism is foremost. As such, it is most often defined as the political economic order within which the means of production are publicly owned and usually administered by government.

Yet, socialism is actually a system focused on the nature of human life as a whole. Socialists see the human being as part of a large whole, such as a society or even humanity. As Marx (1818–1883) claims, "the human essence is the true collectivity of man,"[10] meaning that a human being is a speciebeing, the kind that is fully aware of belonging to "the organic body"[11] of humanity.

Although not all socialists stress the collective nature of human life, most would agree that human beings are basically part of society and cannot be understood, let alone flourish, apart from others. Not only that, but their mutual flourishing is a precondition of the flourishing of each individually. Thus, the privatization of human life is at best a historical stage, at worst a complete distortion of what human living requires. Private property, for example, or individual rights more generally, conflicts with the proper mode of human living and, thus, in any system that involves the legal affirmation of privacy human beings will be alienated.[12]

The stress in socialism is laid on the health of society or humanity as a whole, although this cannot be separated from the well-being of the constituent parts, namely the individual human beings who comprise the larger wholes. What in particular needs to characterize a good or just human community is cooperation, as opposed to competition or rivalry, in all realms of life—economic, scientific, political, and athletic. In that most important realm, the economic, socialism proposes the collectivization of the administration of all production and distribution of value (although such administration does not preclude subjecting some spheres of economic life to limited competition, a policy that is dubbed "market socialism"). So

while socialists do not necessarily embrace the idea of central microeco-
nomic management and planning, they do favor the supervision of society's
economic affairs from the viewpoint of the public at large with private initiative taking a subservient role. The idea is that only when human beings
collectively manage their economic lives will they experience themselves
as fully emancipated, coming into their own full humanity or realizing their
true human nature. The reason is that by nature human beings are conscious producers. Since production is necessarily a social phenomenon,
only if people participate in the social organization of production can they
experience themselves as they truly are.

Socialism can take several forms. Some claim that at least at the beginning of a socialist society there must be central planning by those who understand the need for socialism, helping thereby to upgrade those who are
lagging behind in their awareness of this need. Some would want a more
democratic socialism whereby members of the community set priorities for
the whole, in a kind of ongoing conversation about the priorities. Some others, as already suggested, see only a limited need for socialization of economic
and other matters, albeit one that is vital (mostly as far as the satisfaction of
basic human needs are concerned).

Just like human language, so human life in general is to be seen as a social
process and the idea that we can make a significant difference to our lives as
individuals is as much of a mistake as the idea that we can invent our own
language. That is perhaps one of the key reasons for claiming that socialism
is the proper form of human social life.

Capitalism

Since we devoted an entire chapter to capitalism, we will say only that it is
the political economic system in which the institution of the right to private
property, that is, to own anything of value (not, of course, other human beings, who are themselves owners), is fully respected. There is dispute about
the label, of course, mostly because its definition is often a precondition of
having either a favorable or unfavorable view of the system. Put a bit differently, "capitalism" is the term used to mean that feature of a human community whereby citizens are understood to have the basic right to make their
own (more or less wise or prudent) decisions concerning what they will do
with their labor and property, and whether they will engage in trade with one
another involving nearly anything they may value. Thus, capitalism includes
freedom of trade and contract, the free movement of labor, protection of
property rights against both criminal and foreign aggression as well as government intervention.

Communitarianism

Communitarianism could be viewed as a sort of halfway house between the collectivist system of socialism and the individualist one of capitalism. The idea is less capable of being sharply defined than these others. Roughly, it comes to the view that human beings are necessarily or essentially parts of distinct human groups or communities, with their diverse values, histories, priorities, practices, laws, cultures, and so on. The organizing principles of these different groups will themselves vary. There is no overriding true social and political order, not even any universal ethics. Rather, it is the particular character of the communities that establish for their parts or members what is the proper way to live, what laws should be enacted, and what aesthetic and religious values need to be embraced.

Some communities can be Spartan, others Stoic, yet others bohemian, and so forth. Each can have its peculiar way of life without implying any objective condemnation of some alternative form. Yet, participation in the community's form of life is not a matter of individual consent. Such an idea derives from a mistake, namely, that there is a transcendent human nature that requires every community to adhere to certain minimal standards of justice. No such transcendent human nature exists, as far as many communitarians see things, so those that, say, grant individuals certain rights are not superior to those that do not—they are simply different.[13]

Actually, there is not much more that can be said about communitarianism because there are simply too many types of community each with its own framework and priorities. The main point is that the rules, laws, ideals, and so forth are all the result of the often slowly evolving consensus or collective practices of the community's membership. Just as socialism sees humanity as the whole to which individuals belong, communitarianism sees different ethnic, national, racial, gender, cultural, professional, or similar distinguishable groups as the whole to which the individual member belongs. One may imagine, for example, that languages have developed, in part, to meet the requirements, imagination, and circumstances of different linguistic communities, with no language superior or completely translatable to any other.

Communitarians often unite in their criticism of bourgeois society or liberal capitalism because of the emphasis in these latter aspects of individuality, privacy, personal freedom, consent, competition, and so on. Communitarians believe that the view of human nature underlying such liberal capitalist views is seriously flawed. They are convinced, also, that the central idea of liberal capitalism is what has come to be known as Homo economicus or "economic man." That idea figures heavily in economic analysis and views individuals as autonomous entities who enter the world fully formed, are ready to make choices in the market, and are self-sufficient. While there are other conceptions of the human individual that might support liberal capitalism, it is this that has occupied the attention of communitarians and it is in contrast to this view that they have advanced their position.

Notes

1. Many critics of moral positions simply assume that some courses of conduct or goals are of prime moral significance and then argue that the theory being examined fails because it doesn't accommodate this assumption. This is highly debatable, however, since it assumes that we "know intuitively" which moral principles are primary. Although we may know that certain principles are morally important, from our ordinary experiences and learning, it is not possible, without further systematic reflection, to determine which of these principles is primary, which secondary, and so on. Moral dilemmas arise from situations that appear to pit our moral principles against one another, so to deal with them these principles need to be properly ordered. And that is where philosophical ethics becomes important.

2. W. G. Maclagan, "Self and Others: A Defense of Altruism," *Philosophical Quarterly* 4 (1954): 109–110.

3. "To explain" can be used narrowly, to mean "to provide external or prior causes for," or more broadly, "to render understandable, meaningful." The former excludes, the latter does not exclude ethics.

4. The religious doctrine of original sin, as well as the more secular one that we are all naturally inclined to be callous toward others, are assumed by most altruists. One good place to find a statement of the former is in Russell Kirk's *The Conservative Mind* (Chicago: Regnery, 1953), while Thomas Hobbes's *Leviathan*, ed. with an introduction by C. P. Macpherson (Baltimore, MD: Penguin, 1968), gives a statement of the latter.

5. Tibor R. Machan and Douglas J. Den Uyl, "Recent Work on the Concept of Happiness," *American Philosophical Quarterly* 21 (1984): 1–31; see also David L. Norton, *Personal Destinies: A Philosophy of Ethical Individualism* (Princeton, NJ: Princeton University Press, 1976).

6. For example, see Nathaniel Branden, *The Psychology of Self-Esteem* (New York: Bantam, 1969).

7. William D. Ross, *The Right and the Good* (New York: Oxford University Press, 1930), 21–22.

8. Quoted in Dixy Lee Ray, *Trashing the Planet: How Science Can Help Us Deal with Acid Rain, Depletion of the Ozone, and Nuclear Waste (Among Other Things)* (Washington, DC: Regnery Gateway, 1990), 80.

9. For example, the police power of states derives from the idea that the head of the feudal order is the "keeper of the realm" and must make sure that the lives of

people within a given jurisdiction are well taken care of materially, spiritually, and morally.

10. Karl Marx, *Selected Writings*, ed. David McLellan (London: Oxford University Press, 1977), 126.

11. Karl Marx, *Grundrisse*, abridged version, trans. David McLellan (New York: Harper Torchbooks, 1971), 33.

12. For extended discussions of these issues, see Tibor R. Machan, ed., *The Main Debate: Communism versus Capitalism* (New York: Random House, 1988).

13. For this line of communitarianism, see Richard Rorty, *Objectivity, Relativism, and Truth* (Cambridge: Cambridge University Press, 1991), especially "Solidarity or Objectivity" and "The Priority of Democracy to Philosophy." A somewhat different, more popular rendition of communitarianism is advanced by Amitai Etzioni, *The Spirit of Community* (New York: Crown, 1994).

~

Case Studies

Case studies are stories in a nutshell. As we know from our own experience going back to early childhood, stories are not only entertaining, they can also be instructive. So, case studies are an excellent way to explore moral principles, theory, and reasoning. A case study usually involves several characters, a setting, some facts, and a conflict. Sometimes, the conflict is left unresolved, a matter to be explored and decided by the student(s) of the study; at other times, a resolution is offered, to be analyzed and evaluated by the student(s). Case study explorations, over time, tend to reveal the following significant insights:

1. All moral conflicts arise in part from the actual facts of the situation
2. Not all the facts are morally relevant
3. A change in a morally relevant fact will likely alter a moral evaluation
4. All moral conflicts arise in part from conflicting moral principles
5. Not all moral principles are equally compelling in all situations
6. Moral reasoning and morally competent conflict resolution depend on the serious consideration of the relevant facts and principles
7. Facts, situations, and principles are often subject to interpretation

It follows from this list that a morally competent analysis and evaluation of a case require critical thinking skills and attitudes, including the ability and willingness to examine a case from more than one point of view. The more interesting and morally challenging a case, the less likely will there be unanimous agreement as to its proper resolution. In any event, a moral analysis, evaluation, and resolution will be as competent and compelling as the reasoning that produces it.

Case Study Strategy

The following method for analyzing a case will be helpful in keeping the study in focus and consistent with the principles of critical thinking. This method does not guarantee fail-safe success—no method can when dealing with problems outside of mathematics and formal logic. Furthermore, the purpose of the method is not so much to yield a specific result as it is to minimize errors, prevent premature judgments, and discourage the opposing but equally pernicious obstacles of dogmatism and subjectivism. Though we may rarely attain complete agreement, those who seriously study ethics do agree that not every position is as good as any other. Some are clearly more reasoned, thoughtful, and well supported than others. The following should be our goal:

1. Identify the facts as given. Which seem to be morally relevant and why?
2. Determine whether there are any questions of interpretation concerning the facts.
3. Can we draw any reasonable and morally relevant inferences from the facts as given?
4. Would any additional facts, if available, be helpful and why?
5. Identify any relevant moral obligations, goods, virtues, rights, and possible conflicts among these.
6. Identify the moral issue that needs to be resolved. If there is more than one, can they be prioritized in terms of moral significance?
7. Identify any relevant moral principles (see the following list). What is deemed "relevant" may depend on a point of view or an interpretation of the facts.
8. Given the facts and relevant moral principles, identify possible resolutions to the moral issue(s).
9. Determine which resolution is best supported by rational argument. This will include (a) a judgment about what is good, obligatory, or virtuous; (b) an appeal to a rule, policy, law, or practice that supports the judgment, and (c) an appeal to a fundamental principle that supports the rule, policy, law, or practice. This last appeal will be the ground principle of a moral theory.

Just as in science, where we understand or explain an event by showing it to be an instance of a general law, in ethics we justify a judgment by connecting it to a general moral principle. So, moral reasoning involves factual premises as well as a premise that states a moral premise connecting the factual premise with the conclusion. For example, given the factual premise that Fred took Jose's car without permission, and the moral premise that one ought not take other people's property without permission, it follows that Fred ought not have taken Jose's car. Of course, there may be other morally relevant facts, such as, Fred needed the car in an emergency to rush someone to the hospital. In this event, one may argue for the moral permissibility of Fred taking the car, but there may be competing arguments, depending on other facts and relevant principles. The point is that moral argument essentially involves factual and morally principled premises. The following are the most commonly appealed to moral principles in moral reasoning.

1. Autonomy: being free to make decisions involving one's own or a family member's health and well-being
2. Beneficence: doing the right thing; providing or promoting well-being and preventing harm
3. Justice: being objective, treating others as they deserve to be treated, and being impartial
4. Nonmalfeasance: doing no harm; acting with no harmful or narrowly selfish motives toward another person or society
5. Veracity: telling the truth
6. Fidelity: keeping all contracts and promises

Writing about Case Studies

A case study analysis is an opportunity to demonstrate your understanding of moral theory, principles, and moral reasoning. There is no single route, formula, or template to follow that will guarantee success. Different cases may inspire different approaches, and individuals will be moved to go in different directions. What's important is not so much the route you take, or the particular moral judgments you make, as how well you support your position and demonstrate good reasoning. That said, the following guideline should be helpful.

1. Begin with a brief summary of the case. Who was involved? What are the undisputed facts? What is the moral issue or problem to be solved?
2. Analysis: What facts, if any, are open to interpretation? What additional facts, if available, would be helpful to know and why? What is

the source of the conflict? Are there conflicting moral duties, principles, laws, or values at issue? What are some possible resolutions? What moral principle(s) supports each resolution? What does each have to offer and what are the drawbacks? Here, you should consider both assumptions and implications of possible resolutions, as well as considering the resolutions from various perspectives.

3. Proposal: Of the competing resolutions, which do you think is morally best and why? This is where you will evaluate the merits of the solutions discussed in your analysis arguing, in effect, that the merits of your proposed solution outweigh those of the alternative solutions. This will be discussed in terms of a basic moral principle that is itself fundamental to a moral theory. Your position should be that, "everything considered," this is the best solution. This implies that you have thought about the assumptions and implications of your proposal and considered it from various points of view; in other words, that you have been thinking critically.

4. Proofread, edit, and rewrite.

Sample Cases Studies

Think of these as opportunities to engage in interesting exploration and dialogue. The value of a case study is directly proportional to the breadth, depth, and significance of the discussion and reflection that it stimulates. Some of these cases are "dated" in that the ethical and legal issues they embody have by now been settled, some of the legal ones at the highest judicial level. However, do not confuse the legal with the moral issue. Regardless of the legal standing of a case, whatever moral issues it illustrates or raises should stand alone. At the most general level, the time and place of a case are not relevant to its proper moral evaluation regardless of the fact that people's beliefs about what is moral have changed over time and varied from place to place. Though our moral reasoning and judgments may (and often ought) to shift depending on the actual facts, the moral principles that guide how we should assess those facts are constant.

Employment

Case 1
Sunny Engineers Co. hired George about ten years ago and he has become a top-notch member of the team, perhaps the main source of income for Sunny. Because the firm is expanding, Sunny is in the market for another en-

gineer and their top candidate is Morton, who is Jewish. George, however, has become not only a top-notch engineer, but also a faithful devotee of the Muslim religion, indeed, its radical sect, Wahhabism, which despises Jews. Sunny is in a small town and the chances of finding a replacement for George or a candidate equal to Morton are slim.

What should the firm do about this?

Case 2

In Sal's company, there are a good many people who believe that it is perfectly okay for someone to use mind altering substances, provided the results do not adversely impact performance on the job. This is not a region of the world where any laws prohibit the consumption of such substances, but there is no doubt that some people engage in substance abuse, not just recreational, moderate use. It would appear to be cost-effective for the company to institute a general rule to the effect that every employee at the firm must be tested for use in order to retain his/her position. But this would also lump together those who merely use and those who abuse the substances in question.

What should the management do in order to keep up high and quality productivity, which require eliminating substance abuse? Would the sweeping rule be the best or is there another approach that might be morally preferable?

Case 3

The level of unemployment in developing countries (which exceeds 40 percent on average) largely accounts for workers in these regions being willing to work under hazardous conditions for very low wages. If the value of life is measured in terms of the risk people are willing to take for money, human life in these countries appears to be worth far less than in the United States.

What is your moral assessment of this?

Case 4

You are the head of the human resources department and in charge of hiring for a large biotech company. The company has advertised for a researcher, and you have narrowed down the search to two people, a white male and a black female. You have received a recent corporate directive, instructing you to hire more women and minorities. You evaluate the remaining candidates and believe that the white male is more qualified and you know he is married, with two children. The black female is single and not as qualified.

As the personnel director, what should you do?

Case 5

(This case was found on the Internet and comes from the Public Administration at the University of Arkansas.)

Johnson, a senior manager, and his newly appointed assistant Ritchie are both newcomers to the state and live close to each other, but commute separately to work. They live in a suburb close to the local airport next to the major highway they take to work. One evening Johnson was unexpectedly detained in an important meeting called by his boss, the director of the agency. As luck would have it, Johnson had promised his wife to pick her up at the airport. Her arrival had been deliberately scheduled to coincide with his normal return home. He is considering requesting Ritchie to pick her up. This should not cause much inconvenience since both live in the same suburban neighborhood.

Should Johnson ask Ritchie for the favor? Are there any other facts that would help you to decide? Which facts and why would they make a difference?

Case 6

Fractious, Inc., is laying off about a third of its employees because of a severe contraction in the market, resulting in a reduction of sales. In short, Fractious is downsizing. Those selected to be laid off are very displeased and blame management for their layoff and consequent hardship. Managers, however, claim they are merely communicating to their employees something that actually comes from consumers, namely, the decision not to do as much business with Fractious as before.

How would you assess this situation? Is management or are the affected employees more likely to be right?

Case 7

A large firm, BigTime Enterprises, needs to reduce its office staff due to a decrease in business. The three executives are not in agreement about the criteria that should be used to select whom to layoff. One proposes the principle "Last hired, first fired." The second executive objects, saying that this approach would guarantee that most of the minority affirmative action employees will be fired, which would be unfair and bad for the company's reputation. A third executive argues that those that need the job most (employees with families, elderly employees, and so on) should be fired last.

Should the firm terminate employees simply on the basis of seniority or should other factors be considered?

Advertising

Case 8

The Happy Cigarette Company is managed by a team of executives who know that tobacco is bad for the health of many people, perhaps nearly all who use their products. Yet, they have come to the conclusion that while health is important, it clearly is not the highest good or most important thing for everyone—this is evident from how many risks people take with their health, even their lives (e.g., race car drivers, mountain climbers, pleasure auto-cruisers, and so on). In promoting their product via advertising, they want to sell to those for whom health isn't such a high priority—ones who find tobacco smoking on balance more important to their overall well-being than being as healthy as they might be. So the executives decide to promote their products to the market in general, via billboards, magazine ads, and whatever means are open to them.

Are they doing the right thing or not and why?

Case 9

Harry saw a television advertisement promoting a car and was attracted to the product right away. It was within his budget, so he purchased it. In time, however, Harry noticed that the car consumed enormous volumes of gasoline and even the most elementary repair was quite expensive, certainly much more than he could afford. Harry began complaining that he was misinformed by the advertisement—it should have made it clear to him that he would incur these costs before he purchased the car.

Is Harry's complaint justified? Who is responsible to establish the burden the car would impose on the buyer/user of it?

Case 10

Washington (Reuters)—The fifty prescription drugs most heavily advertised to consumers accounted for nearly half of the increased spending on medicines last year, a study released on Wednesday said. Drug makers attacked the report, saying it came from a group heavily influenced by health insurers determined only to cut costs and failed to focus on the ads' benefits for patients. The report by the National Institute for Health Care Management Research and Educational Foundation said retail spending on prescription drugs rose by 18.8 percent, or $20.8 billion, from 1999 to 2000. Almost half, or 47.8 percent, of that was due to increased sales of the most-advertised medicines, the group said. The most-advertised drugs in 2000 included Merck and Co.'s arthritis treatment Vioxx,

AstraZeneca Plc.'s heartburn remedy Prilosec, and Schering-Plough Corp.'s allergy medicine Claritin. More prescriptions of those drugs primarily led to the increased spending, not higher prices, the study said.

Isn't advertising just another form of "pushing drugs"? Shouldn't information about drugs come from doctors to their patients rather than from manufacturers to unwitting consumers? Isn't this advertising unfair to insurance companies who have to pay the higher cost of proprietary drugs when doctors begin recommending them because their patients are demanding the relief promised by the ads?

Corporate Social Responsibility

Case 11

Income Generation Manufacturers, Inc., is experiencing a serious market contraction, so until the company can find some alternative line of production that will bring in more business, austerity measures have to be adopted. The management has exhausted all the avenues toward cost containment and now has only one option left, namely, to close the plant in the town where it is the biggest employer. Of course, not only will this mean the loss of jobs to about a hundred and twenty individuals, but nearby businesses that survived and flourished from the presence of IGM will also be adversely affected. Several of the outreach programs IGM has been conducting, such as supporting the local theatre group and ball club, will also be feeling the impact.

Explore the ways the managers of IGM should proceed. Compare the ways that a shareholder versus a stakeholder conception of corporate social responsibility will guide management in reaching its decision.

Case 12

Just outside of São Paulo, Brazil, are scores of petrochemical plants whose emissions have made the area the most polluted in the world. There are more cases of cancer, stillbirths, and deformed babies among workers at these plants than anywhere else in Brazil. The workers have nowhere else to go for employment and the area has a high unemployment rate. Squatters live in shacks that sit precariously above an underground network of aging pipes that carry flammable, dangerous materials. The plants also have a high margin of profit. No laws have been broken and, despite the conditions, countless unemployed continue to seek work at the plants.

What is your assessment of the plants' responsibility for these conditions? What principle(s) should guide corporate policy with respect to its social responsibility?

Case 13

Tris is a flame retardant formerly used on children's pajamas in the United States. It was banned because it is highly carcinogenic. FireStop Chemical, which produces the retardant, has decided to continue to sell the product in Moravia where Tris is still legal. Is this a morally acceptable decision? If not, would a warning label informing Moravian consumers of the cancer risk be sufficient to justify the use of the retardant?

Case 14

It is known that the chief executive officers (CEOs) of U.S. companies earn over a hundred times more than the average U.S. worker, in contrast with Japanese companies, whose executives earn less than twenty times the average Japanese employee. The CEOs of the largest U.S. corporations earn tens of millions of dollars a year. Some critics have argued that these salaries are outrageous and amount to ripping off shareholders, company employees, and consumers. When companies "downsize" during economic slowdown, they typically lay off some or much of the labor force, but the CEOs remain in their palatial offices, continuing to receive their extraordinary incomes. Narrowing the gap between worker wage and corporate management wage would be just and overall more beneficial to society, the critics conclude.

Do you agree with this perspective? What could be said in defense of the extreme disproportion between executive pay and worker pay?

Case 15

NoSpill Chemical Co. has been operating a plant on the outskirts of a town on the East Coast. It has for years buried production waste on the property, in compliance with existing regulations. The company has decided to relocate. Given that the property has underground chemical waste, disposal of which would be extremely costly, the owners decide to donate the property to the local school district. They inform the school administrators of the dumped materials and strongly advise them not to put buildings there that would house people. Years later the school district does construct buildings to house administrative staff. Several years after that some employees develop health problems. Investigation links the health problems to waste seepage from the underground dump. The district decides to sue NoSpill.

Did NoSpill act responsibly in donating the property knowing that in the future someone might ignore its warning and use the property in a way hazardous to people? Would it not have been more responsible of NoSpill to pay for the cleanup and then sell the property at market value, thereby guaranteeing that the site was safe?

Insider Trading

Case 16
Harry was in the lavatory, in one of the stalls, both answering to nature and reading a magazine. Two men entered to wash their hands at the sink and were exchanging information, including that the firm Good Luck Today, Inc., is probably going to be bought out by a major competitor that sees a great future for it. Harry finished his business and went to a public phone downstairs and requested that his stockbroker immediately buy several hundred shares of Good Luck Today. What he heard was true and Harry made a huge return from his investment.

Did Harry do anything wrong? Should what he did be prohibited by law? What other profession might make use of information obtained this way that's highly rewarded and honored?

Environmentalism

Case 17
CowDrops, Inc., a U.S. fertilizer plant in a developing nation, produces sulfur dioxide pollution far in excess of U.S. standards. The factory is operating nearly around the clock to assist in increasing food production for a hungry population. Imposing the higher standards would drastically curtail production. Some argue that this practice harms the environment as well as the very people that it purports to help and that this double standard is bound to tarnish the reputation of the company.

Do you agree? Should the same environmental, health, and safety standards be adhered to in all locations where a company has plants? Why or why not?

Case 18
This case comes from *Applying Moral Theories* by C. E. Harris Jr., page 201. "During the 1960s, a controversy erupted over the proper use for the Mineral King Valley, a wilderness area adjacent to Sequoia National Park in California. On the one hand, Walt Disney Enterprises wanted to develop the valley as a ski resort that would bring an estimated 14,000 visitors to the valley each day. The development would involve building ski slopes, hotels, restaurants, parking lots, and other facilities. The Sierra Club argued for keeping the area in an undeveloped state and allowing only hiking, camping, hunting, and fishing. Making its decision in favor of Walt Disney Enterprises, the U.S. Forest Service argued that the Disney proposal would serve more people and that the higher prices people were willing to pay for skiing showed that peo-

ple wanted to ski more than they wanted to camp, hunt, and fish. The Sierra Club argued that this economic approach failed to give due consideration to the aesthetic and ecological factors, as well as the animals, plants, rivers, and mountains.

Which side was right in this debate?"

Case 19

GoodWrite Paper, Inc., has several plants in Arkansas where it has been competing successfully for years with a number of other paper mills. The state does not require scrubbers on their smokestacks, which has allowed the mills to continue operating without the additional burden of expensive scrubbers. The CEO of the company, deeply concerned about the pollution caused by his industry, is considering installing scrubbers at his plants. This would certainly reduce shareholders' dividends and would likely put the company at a market disadvantage, given the cost of the scrubbers.

What should the CEO do? Does he have a responsibility to protect the environment and the health of the public? If so, how is this responsibility to be weighed against his obligation to the company and its shareholders?

Case 20

According to a recent press release by the Greenpeace Toxic Patrol, Louisiana's vinyl industry is one of the world's toxic hot spots. It has been targeted by Greenpeace for international attention and protests. The companies making vinyl located along the Mississippi River and inland Lake Charles (or Cancer Alley, as Greenpeace calls it) produce many persistent organic pollutants (POPs) as the result of vinyl production. Among the most toxic of the POPs is dioxin, a carcinogen that has been linked to male and female reproductive disorders, immune suppression, and birth defects. Dioxin and the other toxic chemicals resulting from vinyl production can travel thousands of miles on air currents to contaminate people and the environment around the earth. According to Damu Smith of Greenpeace USA, "the citizens of Louisiana have suffered profound health and environmental damages at the hands of the vinyl industry." At a recent demonstration by sixty Greenpeace activists from twenty-two nations, Smith asked Louisiana governor Mike Foster to clean up Cancer Alley by enforcing existing environmental protection laws, stopping pollution, and supporting clean production and safe jobs.

Do you agree with the Greenpeace position on Louisiana's vinyl industry? Why or why not? (For more information on Louisiana's vinyl industry, see the Greenpeace Web site at <http://www.greenpeaceusa.org>.)

Case 21

Automobiles using fossil fuel gasoline pollute the atmosphere; this is particularly obvious in large cities like Los Angeles and Denver. An increasingly popular proposal is that the auto industry start producing and selling vehicles that use alternate fuels such as methanol, which are cleaner burning. They could start with, say a few hundred thousand cars a year, and then gradually increase the number. If the automobile companies did not do this voluntarily, Congress could mandate them to do so.

What is your opinion of this proposal?

Bribery and Kickbacks

Case 22

Bill is employed by HiRise Industries, a U.S. corporation producing modular homes and buildings in Torbunia, a rapidly developing but politically and socially unstable country with considerable corruption. Bill has recently been promoted and transferred from his position in Seattle. He is the manager in charge of procurement of raw materials in Torbunia. Bill learns from the supplier that he cannot get the materials delivered on time unless he pays $2,000 a month to the local chief of police, who will then see to the "safe and speedy" delivery. Bill considers moving his office to another location, but has reason to believe that he will likely face the same situation there.

Given that bribes are a common practice in Torbunia, is it *morally* permissible for Bill to pay the money? Isn't it just another cost of doing business or is there more than that involved? If you believe that bribery is an inherently wrong business practice, are there any conditions under which you would find it excusable? Would it make any difference if the bribe went to, say, an employee of the supplier, rather than a public official? Why or why not?

Case 23

Pipe and Tub is the largest wholesale distributor of plumbing supplies in Fortunado County, serving numerous customers. Jack Steel, the owner of the company, is approached by the general manager of ABC Rooter and Plumbing, one of Pipe and Tub's biggest clients. The ABC manager proposes to Jack that Pipe and Tub cut prices to ABC by 15 percent, 5 percent of which will be returned in cash to Jack. In addition, ABC will buy exclusively from Pipe and Tub, thereby increasing overall sales. This will give ABC an edge over competitors. Jack will get income on which he can avoid taxes as well as the additional sales to Pipe and Tub.

What moral considerations come to mind here? Suppose Jack reasons that since it is his business, it is his right to charge whatever he likes to whomever and for whatever reason. As for taxes, he is already paying more than his fair share, which he resents, especially since he receives such poor service from public agencies. This would be a way to level things out a bit. What do you think of this reasoning?

Case 24

Managers of an international firm find that corrupt officials in one country where their products are likely to sell very well are demanding payments under the counter, so to speak, before they will issue permits for the firm to do business there. The payments are not very large and there is no one to complain to since it seems most officials are themselves involved—they all want to take bribes.

Should the firm pay the bribe? Who is ethically responsible for the corruption? Should the firm's home country prohibit such bribes?

Globalization

Case 25

Julio, one of Mary's supervisees in a Mexican plant, complains about being paid $4 an hour, after learning that his counterpart in a U.S. factory, employed by the same company, is paid $11 an hour for the same work. It happens that $4 an hour is higher than the going wage for the same work in Mexico.

This is a moral question in the area of distributive justice (which is to say about how resources ought to be acquired and held): Is Julio's complaint morally legitimate? Is it just that two employees of the same company be paid different wages for doing the same work? Is their being in two different countries a morally relevant difference? Is this an unfair employment practice? Isn't it discriminatory for employees of the same company, performing the same work, to be paid differently? What difference, if any, does location make?

Case 26

Deep Oil Corp., Inc., has branches around the globe, including one in Saudi Arabia, where the CEO has just retired and a replacement is urgently needed. The Saudi branch is one of the most active ones, with the CEO paid the highest of income (including stock options and other benefits) at Deep Oil. Among the up and coming executives at Deep Oil, Susan has made the best showing of the kind of managerial talent Deep Oil needs at a branch such as the one in Saudi Arabia. However, it is very likely that sending a woman to head up Deep Oil's Saudi branch would pose certain problems in a country the cultural and religions traditions of which do not tolerate women in high-business executive positions.

Should Deep Oil's top managers send Susan to Saudi Arabia, where she would be able to confront business challenges commensurate with her background and previous accomplishments? Or should they send a man, less qualified than Susan, because that may be less controversial and avoid confrontations with Saudi traditions? Why?

Case 27
It has been argued that starving workers in Third World countries such as Bangladesh, who accept work at barely subsistence wages, cannot reasonably be said to do so "voluntarily." On this view, companies who locate in such areas to take advantage of cheap labor are actually engaging in exploitation. What moral principle(s) should guide our thinking in these cases?

Case 28
A U.S. member of congress, after visiting North Korea, asked, "Should the world allow North Koreans to starve because their Stalinist government denies them freedom?" Many people argue against trade relations with countries whose governments are oppressive, dictatorial, undemocratic, or otherwise in serious violation of human rights. They believe that trade amounts to support for the oppressive regime. Others argue that such trade restrictions only contribute to the suffering of the people, without significantly affecting the government. Increased trade, they argue, would improve the condition of the people and incline them more to seek political reform.

Which position do you believe is morally better grounded and why?

Case 29
One of Jim's supervisees in a plant in India points out that the standards for in-plant asbestos pollution are lower than U.S. standards. The standards fall within Indian government guidelines and, indeed, are stricter than those maintained by other Indian asbestos manufacturers.

Is it ethical for a company to put its employees of one country at greater risk than its employees in the United States? Isn't this a discriminatory practice? Would it make any difference if the company employed only workers in India?

Case 30

Italian tax law essentially involves negotiating with corporations rather than engaging in formal transactions. It is typical for companies to expect to negotiate a tax settlement with the state, and so considerable "creativity" is involved in corporate accounting and tax forms. Jonathan Smith, a recently transferred accountant sent to manage tax matters for the Italian branch of his U.S. firm, is adamant in "going by the book," refusing to abide by Italian convention and arguing that such compliance only encourages bad business practice. He insists that the tax returns are correct, despite the Italian court's insistence that the matter be "negotiated," which from Smith's point of view amounts to legal extortion. He argues that, in the United States, "negotiating" a settlement comes only after some impropriety has been determined. In this case, he says, the books are impeccable. Corporate headquarters back in Dallas have instructed him to "do as the Romans do," but he refuses on the grounds of professional integrity. As a result, Smith involves his company in a legal tangle that brings the issue to light and sparks public debate about the merits of the system. Before the matter is settled (at considerable cost to Smith's company), Dallas has dismissed Smith for insubordination. Smith protests on the grounds that he acted according to the highest professional standards. He threatens to sue the company unless they reinstate him.

Did Smith act professionally? Was he right in disobeying the company directive?

Price Fixing

Case 31

Sotheby's and Christies, the two auction houses, have been involved in a price-fixing incident. The allegation is that the owners of the two companies met after finding competitive bargaining with customers a source of revenue loss and decided they would no longer bargain but simply tell the client what price they charge, which will be the same for both companies. They then instructed their respective CEOs to implement the policy, which went on until one wanted to fire his CEO who asked for a big payoff to keep silent. The attorneys got wind of the situation and advised Christies to go to the authorities and get a deal before things got worse.

Now aside from the fact that this is illegal in the United States, is there anything ethically wrong with price fixing and why or why not? What legal remedies might exist even without prosecution for price fixing? (Notice that not all countries have antitrust laws, nor even laws prohibiting price fixing.

For example, in the case just sketched, Christies, which is an English firm, is shielded by the fact that English law is not like U.S. law on this score and England will not extradite the owner and staff of Christies.)

Case 32
The Informant by Kurt Eichenwald: a nonfiction account of the Archer Daniels Midland price-fixing scandal. The most interesting criminals in the world live in the real world.

"The FBI was ready to take down America's most politically powerful corporation. But there was one thing they didn't count on." So reads the cover of this high-powered true crime story, an accurate teaser to a bizarre financial scandal with more plot twists than a John Grisham novel. In 1992, the Federal Bureau of Investigation (FBI) stumbled on Mark Whitacre, a top executive at the Archer Daniels Midland (ADM) corporation, who was willing to act as a government witness to a vast international price-fixing conspiracy. ADM, which advertises itself as "The Supermarket to the World," processes grains and other farm staples into oils, flours, and fibers for products that fill the United States' shelves, from Jell-O pudding to StarKist tuna. Dwayne Andreas, the company's chairman and CEO, was so influential that he introduced Ronald Reagan to Mikhail Gorbachev, and it was his maneuvering that ensured that high fructose corn syrup would replace sugar in most foods (ever wondered why Coke and Pepsi don't taste quite like they used to?). There were two mottoes at ADM: "The competitors are our friends, and the customers are our enemies" and "We know when we're lying." And lie they did. With the help of Whitacre, the FBI made hundreds of tapes and videos of ADM executives making price-fixing deals with their corivals from Japan, Korea, and Canada, all while drinking coffee and laughing about their crimes. The tapes should have cinched the case, but there was one problem: Their star witness was manipulative, deceitful, and unstable. Nothing was as it seemed, and the investigation into one of the most astounding white-collar crime cases in history had only just begun.

Kurt Eichenwald, an investigative reporter, covered the story for the *New York Times* and interviewed more than one hundred participants in the case. He methodically recorded the six-year investigation, leaving no plot twist or tape transcript unexplored. While his primary focus was on deconstructing the disturbed Whitacre and revealing the malleability of truth, the portrait of ADM (and even the Justice Department) is damning enough to make anyone a cynic.—Lesley Reed

Comment on this and show some of the moral issues that emerge from the case.

Consumer Conduct

Case 33
A shopper who harbors ill feelings for people of Arab origin (as he sees it for legitimate reasons for he thinks most of them hate the people of his own country), notices that some of the stores in the mall where he is doing some shopping employ clerks who look like ethnic Arabs. He refuses to shop in those establishments.

What is going on here? What ethical problems, if any, do you see with what the consumer is doing? What if the owners of shops learn that this is a widespread sentiment and begin to discriminate as they do their hiring, in favor of those who do not appear to be from Arabic countries? Are they making prudent economic decisions or are they committing some sort of vice?

Black Markets

Case 34
In a border town, between a country where it is not forbidden to sell a risky but also effective medication against a serious, often fatal disease, and one in which such sales are prohibited, a pharmacist is able to smuggle in the contraband and thus provide the medicine to buyers who want it and are willing to take the risk the medicine poses.

Is there anything ethically wrong with breaking the law that prohibits the sale of this medicine?

Cost-Benefit Analysis

Case 35
Certain policies, such as reduced safety procedures or the use of certain pesticides, may decrease the life expectancy of field-workers, but increase the life expectancy of countless more city dwellers who benefit from the increased productivity, availability, and lower cost of products because of the policies. From a social cost-benefit analysis perspective, such policies would be justified. Is this perspective morally sound or does it demonstrate the limitations of cost-benefit analysis?

Professional Ethics

Case 36
Insurance companies claim to lose a good deal of money each year from physicians "misreporting" procedures, a practice called "upcoding," when a minor procedure is reported as more serious than it actually is, or when

a procedure such as a single surgery is reported as several smaller surgeries so that each can be charged. In many of these cases, the physician knows that the actual procedure is not covered by the patient's insurance and the patient cannot afford it, so the report is "upcoded." At other times, the physician performs the procedure or authorizes expensive lab work or diagnostic scans, knowing that they are unnecessary, but believing that doing so will relieve the patient of anxiety and worry.

Are these practices morally justified or always a case of insurance fraud?

Case 37
It's possible for a large company to achieve its business goals, say, getting a larger share of the market, by using lawsuits to eliminate small competitors who cannot afford litigation. This is a very effective practice.

Ethically evaluate such a practice.

Case 38
Suppose a company has a chance to benefit from government subsidies, from bringing or urging an antitrust measure against a competitor, or from supporting protectionist legislation. Even if managers were opposed to these on principle, they may become liable to shareholder lawsuits for failing to take advantage of them to increase shareholder value.

What ought a manager who is on principle opposed to such practices do?

Employer Liability

Case 39
Martha, a nonsmoker, worked as a secretary in an office building with several accountants, three of whom were heavy smokers and who smoked in their offices, which was permitted by company policy until just two years ago. Martha occasionally complained to management about the smoke and brought the matter up a number of times at staff meetings, but her complaints were ignored and she was even reminded that she was free to look for other work. Martha left the firm after six years of employment. Three years after that, she was diagnosed with lung cancer. After talking to her attorney, she initiated a lawsuit against the firm for $5 million, alleging that her employers failed to provide her with a safe working environment.

Do you think that Martha has a good argument? To what extent are employers responsible for the safety of their employees?

Whistle-Blowing

Case 40

Advertising often involves degrees of misrepresentation, stretching of the truth, and so on, which is usually not intended to mislead. But suppose someone in a company discovers something bad about a product and is told to cover up the evidence so as not to threaten sales. The management tells the employee that the problem is not as serious as he/she thinks, and certainly not serious enough to run the risk of bad press for the company's product. The employee believes his/her job may be at stake.

Is the employee morally obliged to disclose this evidence? What ought he/she do? What other facts here would be relevant to helping you make a decision?

Bibliography

Anderson, Terry L., and Donald. R. Lea. *Enviro-Capitalists: Doing Good While Doing Well*. Lanham, MD: Rowman & Littlefield, 1998.

———. "Nature's Entrepreneurs." *The Freeman* 48 (November 1998): 647.

Aristotle. *Nicomachean Ethics*. Bk. 6. Trans. W. D. Ross, in *A New Aristotle Reader*, ed. J. L. Ackrill. Princeton, NJ: Princeton University Press, 1987.

Arrow, Kenneth J. "Two Cheers for Government Regulation." *Harper's* (March 1981).

Barry, Norman. *Business Ethics*. West Lafayette, IN: Purdue University Press, 1999.

Barry, Vincent. *Moral Issues in Business*. Belmont, CA: Wadsworth, 1983.

Bastiat, Frédéric. *The Law*. 2d ed. Trans. Dean Russell. Irvington-on-Hudson, NY : Foundation for Economic Education, 1998.

Beauchamp, Tom L., and Norman E. Bowie, eds. *Ethical Theory and Business*. Englewood Cliffs, NJ: Prentice Hall, 1983.

Becker, Gary. *The Economic Approach to Human Behavior*. Chicago: University of Choice Press, 1976.

Bellah, Robert, et al. *Habits of the Heart: Individualism and Commitment in American Life*. New York: Harper and Row, 1984.

Bennet, J. T. *Does a Higher Wage Really Mean You Are Better Off?* Springfield, VA: National Institute for Labor Relations Research, 1985.

Black's Law Dictionary. St. Paul, MN: West, 1991.

Bowie, Norman E., and Ronald F. Duska. *Business Ethics*. Englewood Cliffs, NJ: Prentice Hall, 1990.

Branden, Nathaniel. *The Psychology of Self-Esteem*. New York: Bantam, 1969.

Buono, Anthony F., and Lawrence T. Nichols. "Stockholder and Stakeholder Interpretations of Business Social Role." In *Business Ethics*, ed. W. Michael Hoffman and Jennifer Mills Moore. New York: McGraw-Hill, 1990.

Burtless, Gary, Robert Z. Lawrence, Robert E. Litan, and Robert J. Shapiro. *Globaphobia: Confronting Fears about Open Trade.* Washington, DC: Brookings Institution, 1998.

Carson, Thomas. "Friedman's Theory of Corporate Social Responsibility." *Business and Professional Ethics Journal* 12 (spring 1993): 3–32.

Chamberlain, John. *The Roots of Capitalism.* Princeton, NJ: Van Nostrand, 1968.

Chesher, James E. "Business: Myth and Morality." In *Business Ethics and Common Sense,* ed. Robert W. McGee. Westport, CT: Quorum, 1992.

———. "The Ethics of Employment." In *Commerce and Morality,* ed. Tibor R. Machan. Lanham, MD: Rowman & Littlefield, 1988.

Chesher, James E., and Tibor R. Machan. *The Business of Commerce: Examining an Honorable Profession.* Stanford, CA: Hoover Institution Press, 1999.

Chiarella v. United States. No. 78–1202. Argued November 5, 1979. Decided March 18, 1980. 445 U.S. 222.

Coase, Ronald. "The Problem of Social Cost." *Journal of Law and Economics* 3 (1960).

Cunningham, Robert L. *Liberty and the Rule of Law: Essays in Honor of F. A. Hayek.* College Station, TX: Texas A&M University Press, 1979.

Danielson, Peter A. "Making a Moral Corporation: Artificial Morality Applied." Centre for Applied Ethics at the University of British Columbia, http://www.ethics.ubc.ca/pad/amcorp/amcorp.html.

Dawkins, Richard. *The Selfish Gene.* London: Oxford University Press, 1976.

De George, Richard T. *Business Ethics.* New York: Macmillan, 1982.

Den Uyl, Douglas J. *American Philosophical Quarterly* (April 1987): 107–124.

———. "Corporations at Stake." *The Freeman* (July 1992).

———. "Teleology and Agent-Centeredness." *The Monist* 75 (January 1992): 14–33.

Den Uyl, Douglas J., and Tibor R. Machan. "Recent Work in Business Ethics: A Survey and Critique." *American Philosophical Quarterly* 24 (April 1987): 107–124.

Derrett, J. D. M. "A Camel through the Eye of a Needle." *New Testament Studies* 32 (July 1986).

Donaldson, Thomas. *Corporations and Morality.* Englewood-Cliffs, NJ: Prentice Hall, 1982.

Eagleson, John, ed. *Christians and Socialism.* Maryknoll, NY: Orbis, 1975.

Estes, Ralph. *Tyranny of the Bottom Line.* San Francisco, CA: Berrett-Koehler, 1996.

Etzioni, Amitai. "Money, Power and Fame." *Newsweek,* 18 September 1989.

———. *The Moral Dimension.* New York: Free Press, 1988.

———. *The Spirit of Community.* New York: Crown, 1994.

Ezorsky, Gertrude, ed. *Moral Rights in the Workplace.* Albany: SUNY Press, 1987.

Falk, Richard. *Predatory Globalization.* Oxford: Polity, 2000.

Farr, Richard. "The Political Economy of Community." *Journal of Social Philosophy* 23 (winter 1992).

Friedman, Milton. *Capitalism and Freedom.* Chicago: University of Chicago Press, 1961.

———. "The Line We Dare Not Cross." *Encounter* 47, no. 5 (November 1976).

———. "The Social Responsibility of Business Is to Increase Its Profits." *New York Times Magazine*, 13 September 1970.

Galbraith, John Kenneth. *The Affluent Society*. Boston: Houghton Mifflin, 1958.

———. "The Dependence Effect." In *Ethical Theory and Business*, ed. Tom L. Beauchamp and Norman E. Bowie. Englewood Cliffs, NJ: Prentice Hall, 1983.

Garrett, Garet. "Business." In *Civilization in the United States: An Inquiry by Thirty Americans*, ed. Harold E. Stearns. New York: Harcourt, Brace, 1922.

Gewirth, Alan. "Replies to My Critics." In *Gewirth's Ethical Rationalism*, ed. Edward Regis Jr. Chicago: University of Chicago Press, 1984.

Gilpin, Robert. *The Challenge of Global Capitalism: The World Economy in the 21st Century*. Princeton, NJ: Princeton University Press, 2000.

———. *Global Political Economy: Understanding the International Economic Order*. Princeton, NJ: Princeton University Press, 2001.

Govier, Trudy. "The Right to Eat and the Duty to Work." *Philosophy of the Social Sciences* 5 (1975).

Grant, James. *Money of the Mind: Borrowing and Lending in America from the Civil War to Michael Milken*. New York: Farrar, Strauss and Giroux, 1992.

Hamburger, H. *Money, Coins, the Interpreters Dictionary of the Bible*. Vol. 3. Nashville, TN: Abingdon, 1962.

Hardin, Garrett. "The Tragedy of the Commons." *Science*, no. 162 (December 13, 1968).

Harris Jr., C. E. *Applying Moral Theories*. 4th ed. Belmont, CA: Wadsworth, 2002.

Hasnas, John. "Social Responsibility of Corporations and How to Make It Work for You." *The Freeman* (July 1994).

Hayek, F. A. von, ed. *Capitalism and the Historians*. Chicago: University of Chicago Press, 1954.

———. *The Constitution of Liberty*. Chicago: University of Chicago Press, 1960.

———. "The Non Sequitur of the Dependence Effect." In *Ethical Theory and Business*, ed. Tom L. Beauchamp and Norman E. Bowie. Englewood Cliffs, NJ: Prentice Hall, 1983.

———. *The Road to Serfdom*. Chicago: University of Chicago Press, 1944.

Hessen, Robert. *In Defense of the Corporation*. Stanford, CA: Hoover Institution Press, 1979.

Hetherington, John A. C. "Corporate Social Responsibility, Stockholders, and the Law." *Journal of Contemporary Business* (winter 1993).

Hinman, Lawrence M., ed. *Contemporary Moral Issues*. Upper Saddle River, NJ: Prentice Hall, 1996.

Hobbes, Thomas. *Leviathan*. Ed. with an introduction by C. P. Macpherson. Baltimore, MD: Penguin, 1968.

Hoffman, Nicholas von. *Capitalist Fools: Tales of American Business, from Carnegie to Forbes to the Milken Gang*. Garden City, NY: Doubleday, 1992.

Hoffman, W. Michael, and Jennifer Mills Moore, eds. *Business Ethics*. New York: McGraw-Hill, 1990.

Holmes, Stephen, and Cass R. Sunstein. *The Cost of Rights: Why Liberty Depends on Taxes*. New York: Norton, 1999.

Hospers, John. *Libertarianism*. Los Angeles: Nash, 1970.

Hughes, Jonathan R. T. *The Governmental Habit*. 2d ed. Princeton, NJ: Princeton University Press, 1991.

Hume, David. *The History of England*. Vol. 2. Indianapolis, IN: Liberty Fund, 1983.

Hunt, Lester H. "An Argument against a Legal Duty to Rescue." *Journal of Social Philosophy* 36 (1994).

Hutt, William. *The Strike Threat System: The Economic Consequences of Collective Bargaining*. Indianapolis: Liberty, 1975.

Johnson, M. Bruce, and Tibor R. Machan, eds. *Rights and Regulation*. Cambridge, MA: Ballinger, 1983.

Jones, Donald G., and Patricia Bennet, eds. *A Bibliography of Business Ethics 1981–1985*. Lewiston, NY: Mellen, 1986.

Kane, Robert. *The Significance of Free Will*. London: Oxford University Press, 1998.

Kelley, David, Jeff Scott, and Gekko Echo. "A Closer Look at the Decade of Greed." *Reason* (March 1993).

Kelman, Steven. "Regulation and Paternalism." In *Rights and Regulation*, ed. M. Bruce Johnson and Tibor R. Machan. Cambridge, MA: Ballinger, 1983.

Kelso, Louis O., and Mortimer J. Adler. *The Capitalist Manifesto*. New York: Random House, 1958.

Kennedy, Allan A. *The End of Shareholder Value*. Cambridge, MA: Perseus, 2000.

Keynes, John Maynard. *The End of Laissez-Faire*. London: L. and Virginia Woolf, 1926.

Kirk, Russell. *The Conservative Mind*. Chicago: Regnery, 1953.

Kirzner, Israel. "Producer, Entrepreneur, and the Right to Property." *Reason Papers*, no. 1 (fall 1974).

Kornai, Janos. *The Road to the Free Economy*. New York: Norton, 1990.

Kristol, Irving. *Two Cheers for Capitalism*. New York: Basic, 1978.

Kuttner, Robert. *The End of Laissez-Faire*. New York: Knopf, 1991.

Leiser, Burton. "Deceptive Practices in Advertising." In *Ethical Theory and Business*, ed. Tom L. Beauchamp and Norman E. Bowie. Englewood Cliffs, NJ: Prentice Hall, 1979.

Lester, J. C. *Escape from Leviathan: Liberty, Welfare and Anarchy Reconciled*. New York: St. Martin's, 2000.

Letwin, William. "Economic Due Process in the American Constitution and the Rule of Law." In *Liberty and the Rule of Law: Essays in Honor of F. A. Hayek*, ed. R. L. Cunningham. College Station, TX: Texas A&M University Press, 1979.

Lewis, Michael. "Lend the Money and Run." *The New Republic*, 7 December 1992.

Lux, Kenneth. *Adam Smith's Mistake*. Boston: Shambhala, 1990.

Machan, Tibor R. "Applied Ethics and Free Will." *Journal of Applied Philosophy* 10 (1993): 59–72.

———. "Between Parents and Children." *Journal of Social Philosophy* 23 (winter 1992): 16–22.

———. "Bhopal, Mexican Disasters: What a Difference Capitalism Can Make." In *Liberty and Culture: Essays on the Idea of a Free Society*, by Tibor R. Machan. Buffalo, NY: Prometheus, 1989.

———, ed. *Business Ethics in the Global Market*. Stanford, CA: Hoover Institution Press, 1999.

———. *Capitalism and Individualism: Reframing the Argument for the Free Society*. New York: St. Martin's, 1990.

———. *Classical Individualism: The Supreme Importance of Each Human Being*. London: Routledge, 1998.

———, ed. *Commerce and Morality*. Lanham, MD: Rowman & Littlefield, 1988.

———. "Corporate Commerce vs. Government Regulation: The State and Occupational Safety and Health." *Notre Dame Journal of Law, Ethics and Public Policy* 2 (1987): 791–823.

———. "Do Animals Have Rights?" *Public Affairs Quarterly* 5 (April 1991): 163–173.

———. "Environmentalism Humanized." *Public Affairs Quarterly* 7 (April 1993): 131–147.

———. "Ethics and Its Uses." In *Commerce and Morality*, ed. Tibor R. Machan. Lanham, MD: Rowman & Littlefield, 1988.

———. *Generosity: Virtue in Civil Society*. Washington, DC: Cato Institute, 1998.

———. "How to Understand Eastern European Developments." *Public Affairs Quarterly* 6 (1992).

———. *Individuals and Their Rights*. La Salle, IL: Open Court, 1989.

———. *Initiative—Human Agency and Society*. Stanford, CA: Hoover Institution Press, 2000.

———, ed. *The Main Debate: Communism versus Capitalism*. New York: Random House, 1988.

———, ed. *Morality and Work*. Stanford, CA: Hoover Institution Press, 2000.

———. "A New Individualist Basis for the Free Market." *International Review of Economics and Ethics* 2 (1987): 27–39.

———. "The Nonexistence of Basic Welfare Rights." In *Contemporary Moral Issues*, ed. Lawrence M. Hinman. Upper Saddle River, NJ: Prentice Hall, 1996.

———. "The Non-existence of Basic Welfare Rights." In *Moral Controversies*, ed. Steven Jay Gold. Belmont, CA: Wadsworth, 1993.

———. "Pollution, Collectivism and Capitalism." *Journal des Economists et des Estudes Humaines* 2 (March 1991): 83–102.

———. "Pollution and Political Theory." In *Earthbound: New Introductory Essays in Environmental Ethics*, ed. Tom Regan. New York: Random House, 1984.

———. *A Primer on Ethics*. Norman: University of Oklahoma Press, 1996.

———. *Private Rights and Public Illusions*. New Brunswick, NJ: Transaction, 1995.

———. "Professional Responsibilities of Corporate Managers." *Business and Professional Ethics Journal* 13 (fall 1994).

———. *The Pseudo-Science of B. F. Skinner*. New Rochelle, NY: Arlington House, 1974.

———. "Reason in Economics versus Ethics." *International Journal of Social Economics* 22 (1995).

———. "Recent Work in Ethical Egoism." In *Recent Work in Philosophy*, ed. Kenneth G. Lucey and Tibor. R. Machan. Totowa, NJ: Rowman and Allanheld, 1983.

———. "The Right to Private Property." *Critical Review* 6 (1992).

———. "Should Business Be Regulated?" In *Just Business: New Introductory Essays in Business Ethics*, ed. Tom Regan. New York: Random House, 1983.

———. "Some Reflections on Richard Rorty's Philosophy." *Metaphilosophy* 24 (January–April 1993): 123–135.

Machan, Tibor R., and Douglas J. Den Uyl. "Recent Work in Business Ethics." *American Philosophical Quarterly* 24 (April 1987): 107–124.

———. "Recent Work on the Concept of Happiness." *American Philosophical Quarterly* 21 (1984): 1–31.

Mack, Eric. "Bad Samaritarianism and the Causation of Harm." *Philosophy and Public Affairs* 9 (summer 1980).

MacKinnon, Catherine. *Only Words*. Cambridge, MA: Harvard University Press, 1994.

Maclagan, W. G. "Self and Others: A Defense of Altruism." *Philosophical Quarterly* 4 (1954): 109–110.

Macpherson, C. B. *The Political Theory of Possessive Individualism: Hobbes and Locke*. Oxford: Clarendon, 1962.

Mandeville, Bernard. *The Fable of the Bees*. Indianapolis, IN: Liberty Classics, 1988.

Manne, Henry G. *Insider Trading and the Stock Market*. New York: Free Press, 1966.

———. "What Kind of Controls on Insider Trading Do We Need?" In *The Attack on Corporate America*, ed. M. Bruce Johnson. New York: McGraw-Hill, 1978.

Marx, Karl. *Das Kapital*. New York: International, 1967.

———. *Grundrisse*. Trans. David McLellan. New York: Harper Torchbooks, 1971.

———. *Selected Writings*. Ed. David McLellan. London: Oxford University Press, 1977.

Mavrodes, George. "Property." In *Property in a Humane Economy*, ed. Samuel I. Blumenfeld. LaSalle, IL: Open Court, 1974.

McGee, Robert, ed. *Business Ethics and Common Sense*. Westport, CT: Quorum, 1992.

McKenzie, Richard. *The Limits of Economic Science*. Boston: Kluwer-Nijhoff, 1983.

Midgley, Mary. *The Ethical Primate*. London: Routledge, 1994.

Mill, John Stuart. *Principles of Political Economy*. Rev. ed. Vol. 5. New York: Colonial, 1899.

Miller, Fred D., Jr., and John Ahrens. "The Social Responsibility of Corporations." In *Commerce and Morality*, ed. Tibor R. Machan. Lanham, MD: Rowman & Littlefield, 1988.

Mises, Ludwig von. *The Anti-capitalist Mentality*. Princeton, NJ: Van Nostrand, 1956.

———. *Human Action*. New Haven, CT: Yale University Press, 1949.

Moorehouse, John C. "The Mechanistic Foundations of Economic Analysis." *Reason Papers*, no. 4 (1978).

Murchland, Bernard. *Humanism and Capitalism: A Survey of Thought and Morality.* Washington, DC: American Enterprise Institute for Public Policy Research, 1984.

Nader, Ralph, Mark Green, and Joel Seligman. *Taming the Giant Corporations.* New York: Norton, 1976.

Nederman, Cary J. "Political Theory and Subjective Rights in Fourteenth-Century England." *The Review of Politics* 58 (spring 1996): 323–344.

Norton, David L. *Personal Destinies: A Philosophy of Ethical Individualism.* Princeton, NJ: Princeton University Press, 1976.

Novak, Michael. *The Spirit of Democratic Capitalism.* New York: Simon and Schuster, 1982.

Nozick, Robert. *Anarchy, State, and Utopia.* New York: Basic, 1974.

———. *Invariances.* Cambridge, MA: Harvard University Press, 2001.

Pols, Edward. *Mind Regained.* Ithaca, NY: Cornell University Press, 1998.

Posner, Eric A. *Law and Social Norms.* Cambridge, MA: Harvard University Press, 2000.

Pub. L. 100-704, Sec. 7, Nov. 19, 1988, 102 Stat. 4682.

Rand, Ayn. *Capitalism: The Unknown Ideal.* New York: New American Library, 1966.

———. *The Virtue of Selfishness: A New Concept of Egoism.* New York: New American Library, 1964.

Rawls, John. *A Theory of Justice.* Cambridge, MA: Harvard University Press, 1971.

Ray, Dixy Lee. *Trashing the Planet: How Science Can Help Us Deal with Acid Rain, Depletion of the Ozone, and Nuclear Waste (Among Other Things).* Washington, DC: Regnery Gateway, 1990.

Regan, Tom, ed. *Just Business: New Introductory Essays in Business Ethics.* New York: Random House, 1983.

Roberts, Edward B., and Ian C. Yates. "Large Company Efforts to Invest Successfully in Small Firms." *Journal of Private Enterprise* 10, no. 2 (spring 1995).

Rorty, Richard. *Objectivity, Relativism, and Truth.* Cambridge: Cambridge University Press, 1991.

Ross, William D. *The Right and the Good.* New York: Oxford University Press, 1930.

Sadowsky, James. "Private Property and Collective Ownership." In *The Libertarian Alternative: Essays in Social and Political Philosophy,* ed. Tibor R. Machan. Chicago: Nelson-Hall, 1974.

Saka, Paul. "Ought Does Not Imply Can." *American Philosophical Quarterly* 37, no. 2 (April 2000): 93–105.

Schmookler, Andrew Bard. *The Illusion of Choice.* Albany: SUNY Press, 1993.

Searle, John. *Rationality in Action.* Boston: MIT Press, 2001.

SEC v. Texas Gulf Sulpher. 2nd Circuit (1968).

Securities Exchange Act of 1934, at www.sec.gov/divisions/corpfin/forms/exchange.shtml.

Sen, Amartya. "Human Rights and Asian Values." In *Business Ethics in the Global Market,* ed. Tibor R. Machan. Stanford, CA: Hoover Institution Press, 1999.

Shaw, William H. *Business Ethics.* Belmont, CA: Wadsworth, 1991.

Shorris, Earl. *A Nation of Salesmen: The Tyranny of the Market and the Subversion of Culture.* New York: Norton, 1994.

Shue, Henry. *Basic Rights.* Princeton, NJ: Princeton University Press, 1980.

Smith, Adam. *Inquiry into the Nature and Causes of the Wealth of Nations.* New York: Modern Library Edition, 1927.

Smith, J. C. "The Processes of Adjudication and Regulation: A Comparison." In *Rights and Regulation*, ed. M. Bruce Johnson and Tibor R. Machan. San Francisco: Pacific Institute for Public Policy Research, 1983.

Sorell, Tom. *Scientism.* London: Routledge, 1991.

Sowell, Thomas. "Middleman Minorities: Why the Resentment?" *The American Enterprise* (May–June 1993).

Sperry, Roger W. "Changing Concepts of Consciousness and Free Will." *Perspectives in Biology and Medicine* 9 (autumn 1976): 9–19.

———. *Science and Moral Priority.* New York: Columbia University Press, 1983.

Stepelevich, Lawrence S., ed. *The Capitalist Reader.* New Rochelle, NY: Arlington House, 1977.

Stigler, George. *The Economist As Preacher and Other Essays.* Chicago: University of Chicago Press, 1982.

Stone, Christopher. *Should Trees Have Standing.* Palo Alto, CA: William Kaufmann, 1975.

Toulmin, Stephen. *Return to Reason.* Boston: MIT Press, 2001.

———. *The Uses of Argument.* London: Cambridge University Press, 1964.

United States v. Newman. 2nd Circuit (1981). 664 F.2d 12, 18.

Veblen, Thorsten. *The Nature of Peace.* New Brunswick, NJ: Transaction, 1998.

Werhane, Patricia H. *Persons, Rights and Corporations.* Englewood Cliffs, NJ: Prentice Hall, 1985.

Index

244

regulation, 16; and hostile takeovers, 9; human rights, 27; and nepotism, 3; philosophical effects, xii; scope of, xiii–xvi; standards, xiv

capitalism: Adam Smith, xii; combined with socialism, 32n3; and crass egoism, 59; as creative destroyer, 163; criticisms of, xiii, 6, 49–51, 213; definition, 47–49; economists, 55–56; and human nature, 50; as immoral, 176; individualism, 55; labor conflicts, 2; "private vice, public benefit," xii–xiii, 49; property rights, 47, 50; public good, xi–xiv; selfishness, 63; summary of, 212; wealth creation, 49; vs. welfare, 50
Carson, Thomas, 126n1, 128n17
Compte, August, 191
corporate raiders, 10, 45, 71
corporations: as arm of state, 12, 19; criticism of, 119; as individual beings, 7; limited liability, 12; origin, 11; raiding of, 7; responsibilities, 9–12; and social engagement, 14

Dallas (television show), xi;
Danielson, Peter A., xii
Dawkins, Richard, xxiiin15;
Den Uyl, Douglas J., 72n12, 127n12–13;
distributive justice, 88, 188;

eminent domain law, xviii
ethics: ancient vs. modern, 174–76; basic issues, 38; definition, xiii; and employment, 79–80; and entrepreneurship, 43; happiness, 39; human nature, 158; and law, 38; and the professions, 124, 138, 175; public policy, 139n5; rationalistic,

44; relativism, 208; social science, 38; systems of, 38–40
Etzioni, Amitai, 57n16, 215n13

Farley, William F., 42
freedom: and globalization, 165; negative, 48; political, 143; positive, 51; of trade, 108; of will, xiii, 38–42, 127n8, 142–43
Friedman, Milton, 13–15, 29, 32n6, 33n9, 59–60, 119–25

Galbraith, John Kenneth, 18, 19–20, 34n19, 103, 105–6
Gewirth, Alan, 18, 20
Gilligan, Carol, 204–5
Gilpin, Robert, 170n2
Govier, Trudy, 99n11
Green, Mark, 33n10

von Hayek, F. A., 49, 103
health and safety, 93–95
hedonism, xiii, 181–85
Hegel, Georg, 32n5
Hessen, Robert, 126n2
Hetherington, John, 134–35
Hobbes, Thomas, xii, 64, 83, 121, 143, 176, 201–3
hostile takeovers, 7–11
Hughes, Jonathan R. T., 56
human nature: ancient roots, 32n5; basic ethical principles, 158; creature of the state idea, 15; criticism of, 192–93; denial of, 208; and environmentalism, 142–47; the good life, xv; guidelines, 120; Hobbes's view of, 176; individualistic feature, 55, 163; lack of inherent conflict, 69; natural law, 202–3; response to criticisms, 196–97; and socialism, 211; stability, 50; transcendent, 213; virtues arising from, 45

About the Authors

Tibor R. Machan is professor emeritus of philosophy at Auburn University and currently Distinguished Fellow and Freedom Communications Professor of Business Ethics and Free Enterprise at Chapman University.

James E. Chesher is assistant professor of philosophy at Santa Barbara City College.